TURKEY

AUTHOR

Gilbert Horobin is a playwright and poet who lived for a number of years in Turkey before moving to Greece. Horobin has travelled extensively throughout the Middle East, Egypt and the Sudan, North Africa, East and Southern Africa, the Indian Ocean islands, India and Nepal, and the Far East. He has co-edited travel hand-books on Africa, the Middle East and the Far East. Horobin's published work includes *African Notes and Other Poems*, and plays *Tangent, Man With A Guitar* and *The High Stool*.

PHOTOGRAPHER

Adam Woolfitt was a freelancer for 26 years with National Geographic Magazine, and has worked for prestigious clients such as Fortune, Newsweek Books and the New York Times. He now specializes in digital photography, founding the Digital Imaging Group of the Association of Photographers as well as running a specialist company.

(previous page) İşak Paşa Palace, built to guard the mountain passes, looks down over Doğubayazıt

TURKEY

GILBERT HOROBIN

PHOTOGRAPHY
BY
ADAM WOOLFITT

© 1999, 1994, 1991 Odyssey Publications Ltd
Maps © 1999, 1994, 1991 Odyssey Publications Ltd

Odyssey Publications Ltd, 1004 Kowloon Centre, 29–43 Ashley Road,
Tsim Sha Tsui, Kowloon, Hong Kong
Tel. (852) 2856 3896; Fax. (852) 2565 8004; E-mail: odyssey@asiaonline.net

Distribution in the United Kingdom, Ireland and Europe by
Hi Marketing Ltd, 38 Carver Road, London SE24 9LT, UK

Distribution in the United States of America by
W.W. Norton & Company, Inc., New York
Library of Congress Catalog Card Number has been requested.

ISBN: 962-217-535-X

Although the publisher and author(s) of this book have made every effort to ensure that all
information was correct at the time of going to press, the publisher and author(s) do not
assume and hereby disclaim any liability to any party for any loss or damage caused by
errors, omissions or misleading information.

Grateful acknowledgment is made to the following authors and publishers:
Pantheon Books for *Anatolian Tales* by Yashar Kemal; Collins Harvill Publishers for *The Birds
Have Also Gone* © 1978 Yashar Kemal; John Murray (Publishers) Ltd for *The Lycian Shore* by
Freya Stark; Eland Books for *Portrait of a Turkish Family* © 1988 Ates D'Arcy Orga

Editor: Julie Gaw
Series Co-ordinator: Jane Finden-Crofts
Design: Kevin Bishop
Maps: Bai Yiliang
Cover Concept: Margaret Lee
Index: Françoise Parkin

Photography by Adam Woolfitt

Production by Twin Age Ltd, Hong Kong
Printed in Hong Kong

Hosap Castle, situated 35 miles from Van. This imposing castle was built in 1643 by the chief of the Mahudis as a base from which to prey on passing trade caravans. The outer walls were made of mud brick and are heavily weathered

CONTENTS

Introduction

For the traveller in Turkey, there could be a sense of romance at this close brush with oriental mystery, even if tempered by an awareness of historical facts and events. Whether sauntering through the streets of İstanbul, one of the oldest cities of our era, or any other of Turkey's major centres, the visitor finds the past everywhere to be savoured. Homer is believed to have lived near İzmir, Midas was king at Gordium (near Ankara) and Croesus ruled at Sardis (inland from İzmir). Modern Bodrum was Halicarnassus for Herodotus, the first great European historian. The cynic philosopher Diogenes kept to his tub at Sinop, St Paul was born in Tarsus and St Nicholas, or Santa Claus, was a bishop at Demre. The appellation 'Christian' may have been used for the first time at Antioch, today's Hatay.

Asia Minor's history is apocalyptic with invasions, migrations, devastation and the displacement of one culture by another. When Alp Arslan led his Seljuks into Western Anatolia after his defeat of the Byzantine emperor Romanus IV at Manzikert

in 1071, he rode under the banner of Islam, but not every subsequent Seljuk sultan was absolutely opposed to Christianity, and Mongol khans even toyed with the idea of conversion. Early Ottoman sultans did not refuse to accept Christian Slavs and Byzantine princes as allies or as vassals, nor were Byzantine emperors averse to employing Turkish contingents against Christian monarchs.

Venice, Genoa, Pisa and Ragusa, the Italian maritime republics, all enjoyed trading agreements with the sultans, and 17th-century France was the first Western kingdom to sign reciprocal military agreements with the Ottoman Sublime Porte.

Archaeological discoveries of the 1960s established human habitation back beyond the Palaeolithic, while in southwestern Turkey evidence of very early artistic and technological accomplishments came to light at Çatal Hüyük, Haçılar

(above) Cotton harvesters, Miletus   *(opposite) Yalis (or villas) line the European shore of the Bosphorus in Arnavutköy, İstanbul*

and Yümüktepe (see Ankara Archaeological Museum, page 223). For Turkey is also a history of peoples: Hittites, Urartians, Phrygians, Mysians, Carians, Ionians, Aeolians, Assyrians, Galatians, Cimmerians, Paphlagonians, Pamphylians, Armenians, Greeks, Persians, Romans, Slavs, Arabs, Kurds, Jews, Lazes, Georgians, Circassians, Seljuks, Mongols, Osmanlis. Today over 57 million Turkish-speaking people, among whom there are minorities who retain their ethnic identities within the state, occupy a land of 780,000 square kilometres (301,000 square miles).

From the western frontiers with Greece and Bulgaria to the eastern ones with Georgia, Armenia, Nakhechetan and Iran, Turkey's length is 1,760 kilometres (1,100 miles). Its average depth between the Black Sea to its north and the Mediterranean Sea and the Syrian and Iraqi frontiers to its south is 400 kilometres (250 miles). The Bosphorus is a narrow waterway between the Black Sea and the Sea of Marmara, which is connected to the Aegean and Mediterranean seas by another narrow waterway, the Dardanelles. Until 1973 these waterways physically separated Asia from Europe, but in that year the opening of the first Bosphorus suspension bridge ended that historic dichotomy. East of the Bosphorus, Turkey's land area is known as Anatolia.

Because of its maritime connection with three seas, Turkey offers countless beaches for private or public pleasure, along with beachside hotels, motels, camping sites and yacht marinas, as well as the gamut of aquatic pastimes. East of the Bosphorus, however, the interior of the country is almost wholly mountainous, having a high central plateau with, along the Black Sea coast, peaks rising to an average height of 3,300 metres (10,800 feet), and on the eastern extremity Noah's Mount Ararat, 5,165 metres (16,950 feet) in height. In the extreme southeastern region the wild Hakkâri mountains spread into Iran and Iraq. The Taurus Mountains run impressively along Anatolia's Mediterranean edge, while inland on Turkey's border with Syria the Amanus Mountains form a congenial backdrop to desert and plain. Facilities for mountaineering, skiing and hunting are therefore legion.

Throughout western Anatolia, a European cultural way of life, blended with inherited Turkish mores, predominates. In the eastern regions of Anatolia, with the exception of the major cities, a pastoral or semi-nomadic culture is prevalent. Although the Turkish Republic has no established religion, Turks are in the main Muslim, and the principal Islamic feasts, festivals and fasts are observed. Ethnic minorities maintain their places of worship.

Because of its long history and as a cradle of European cultures, Turkey offers unlimited opportunities for archaeological, scholarly or simply enjoyable exploration. For the time being special permission from the military authorities may be needed to travel in the frontier region of southeastern Turkey: check with your travel agent, or with the Turkish embassy or consulate in your country.

Facts for the Traveller

Getting There

BY AIR

İstanbul's international Atatürk airport, at Yesilköy, west of the city, has separate terminals for international and domestic flights. Large and modern, it has banking and other facilities, and its international terminal has a duty-free section for incoming and outgoing passengers, though purchases have to be made in foreign currency. This duty-free service is available in the international airports of Turkey—Ankara, İzmir, Dalaman, Antalya, Trabzon and Adana—and has been extended to the cities where tax-free shops are established. Turkish Airlines (Türk Havayollari or THY) is the national carrier.

From the United Kingdom, British Airways and Turkish Airlines have two direct flights daily to İstanbul from Heathrow; flying time is approximately 3 hours 45 minutes. Charter flights operate regularly in high season from Gatwick and UK regional airports to İzmir, Dalaman and Antalya airports for holiday packages on the Aegean and western Mediterranean coasts. Less well known are charter flights from Stansted Airport with İstanbul Airlines that operate year-round on Mondays and Thursdays in both directions, and summer flights from Stansted to İzmir on Tuesdays and Thursdays.

From Athens, Olympic Airways and Turkish Airlines each have daily flights to İstanbul, İzmir and Trabzon. There are flights as well to Denizli (three weekly), Gaziantep (four weekly) and Kayseri (twice weekly).

From New York's Kennedy Airport, both Turkish Airlines and Delta fly direct to İstanbul on Mondays. There may be extra flights added during the summer. Lufthansa, BA, Alitalia, Air France, KLM, Swissair, Sabena and SAS all have European stopover connecting flights to İstanbul or Ankara. Lot, Jat, Balkan and Turkish Airlines have services to İstanbul from most major European cities. From Hong Kong, Cathay Pacific has a twice-weekly service.

There is a 30-minute passenger service from Atatürk airport to the Turkish Airlines terminal at Sishane in the new city (Beyoğlu). The airport bus stops at Aksaray for those intending to stay in the old city of Sultanahmet, the area of the mosque of Sultanahmet and St Sophia. It continues to Sishane, the city terminal, and on to Taksim Square for those intending to stay in Beyoğlu. All taxis are metered; you pay only what is on the meter, except after midnight when there is a 50 per cent surcharge.

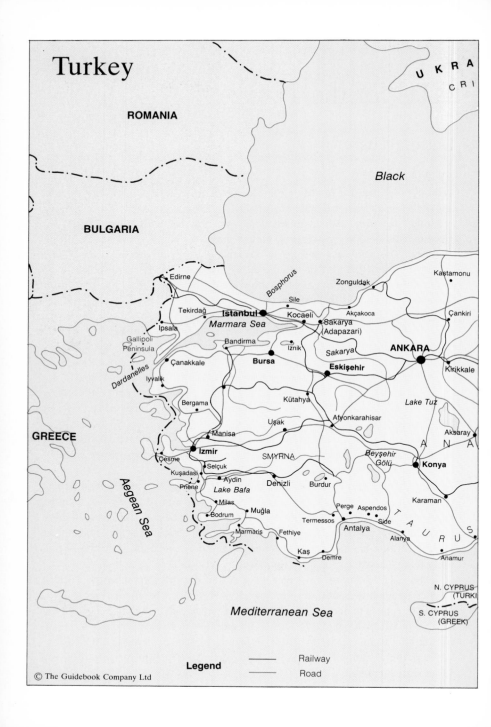

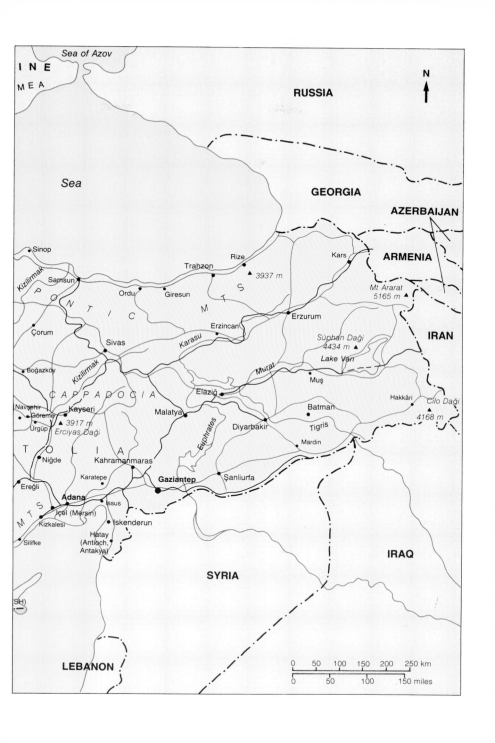

There are internal flights by Turkish Airlines daily to Antalya, Bodrum, Dalaman, Denizli, Diyarbakır, Elazig, Malatya, Mus, Samsun, Şanliurfa, Trabzon and Van; twice daily to Erzurum, Gaziantep, Ağri, Kahramanmaraş, Kars, Erzincan and Sivas. THY flies to Sinop on Mondays only, to Tokat on Tuesdays, and to Siirt and Konya daily except Friday. There are 14 flights daily to Ankara, nine to İzmir, and daily flights to Lefkosia in Cyprus. From Ankara there are three or four flights daily to Adana, and daily flights to Batman, Turkey's oil centre.

BY CAR

From London the distance to İstanbul is approximately 3,000 kilometres (1,870 miles). There are any number of routes through Austria, Slovenia, Croatia, Yugoslavia, the Republic of Macedonia and Bulgaria to the Turkish frontier at Edirne. Alternatively, there is the route via Belgrade to Thessaloniki in Greece, then by way of Macedonia-Thrayka to Alexandroupolis and the Turkish frontier crossing at Ipsala. As an alternative to the route through Maribor, Zagreb, Belgrade and Nis, the motorist could aim for Sofia in Bulgaria by way of Munich, Prague, Budapest and Bucharest, and after Sofia to Plovdiv in Bulgaria and then to the Turkish frontier city of Edirne. On this route visas would be needed for Romania and Bulgaria, but not for the Czech Republic or for Hungary.

Formerly the Byzantine city of Adrianopolis, Edirne also served as an Ottoman capital prior to the fall of Constantinople and has several fine mosques, including the architect Sinan's Selimiye. At an annual festival in the vicinity of Edirne, a national oil-wrestling championship is held. The distance from Edirne to İstanbul is 250 kilometres (155 miles). Taken at average speed, and allowing for overnight and other stops, a road journey from London to İstanbul by this route should take about five days.

Citizens of Britain and the United States may need transit visas for Bulgaria, valid for only 48 hours. Visas should be obtained beforehand, but can be obtained at the frontier. The distance from Sofia to Edirne is 300 kilometres (188 miles).

By shipping from Ancona in Italy, to Igoumenitsa in Greece, a road journey could continue through the northern parts of Greece to Thessaloniki, from where the road runs east through northern Greece (Macedonia and Thrace) via Kavala to Alexandroupolis and so on to the Turkish frontier at Ipsala. The distance from Ipsala to İstanbul is approximately the same as from Edirne to İstanbul. Turkey's main border crossings have duty-free shops for ingoing and outgoing travellers, for payment in currency other than Turkish lira.

Car insurance is required, and if your insurance or Green Card is not endorsed for Turkey, temporary third-party cover can be bought at the frontier. A personal driving licence is acceptable so far as your own car is concerned, but possession of an international driving licence could make for ease of communication in an out-of-the-way place, particularly if you are considering hiring a car.

BY FERRY

Turkish Maritime Lines operates services from Venice to İzmir weekly from April to November, and fortnightly from December to March. It has a fortnightly service to Antalya from June to October, and fortnightly to İstanbul and Marmaris in August, September and October. There is a sailing from Brindisi to Çeşme (port of İzmir) each Wednesday and Saturday from mid-June to mid-September. For information contact TML directly at the World Trade Centre, St Katherine's Way, London E1 9UN, or Sunquest Holiday Ltd, 23 Princess Street, London W14 7RG (tel 0171 499 9991; fax 0171 499 9995). Discounts are available for students, journalists and groups.

Greek and Turkish companies have cruise-line services to Piraeus and İstanbul. Italian ships and those of other countries touch on Turkish ports. Potential voyagers who find themselves in Piraeus can inquire at the offices of shipping lines on Akti Miaouli, the main avenue on the waterfront at Piraeus, as there are frequent sailings.

The Aegean Islands of Mytilini, Chios, Samos, Kos, Symi and Rhodes all have passenger or passenger-car ferry sailings to towns on the Turkish coast, as indicated in sections of the text concerned with the Aegean and Mediterranean seas.

BY COACH

Turkish companies Ulusoy-Bosfor Turizm and Varan run twice-daily coach services (7am and 5pm) from Athens to İstanbul in conjunction with the Greek National Railways Company (OSE). Coaches leave from the Athens Peloponessus Railway Station, and the journey takes about 22 hours, with stops for eating and conveniences. Travellers can board these coaches at Thessaloniki Railway Station. In İstanbul, Turkish coaches continue to their offices at Taksim in the new city, whereas Greek buses on the route terminate at the less convenient Topkapi Gate.

From Western Europe the Turkish companies named above have a twice-weekly service in high season (weekly otherwise) from The Hague, Cologne, Berlin, Frankfurt, Munich, Vienna, Paris and Milan, and there are services from Salzburg, Strasbourg and Zurich.

From London, International Express has a summer service to İstanbul (Coach Travel Centre, 13 Regent Street, SW1Y 4LR), but as several coach companies co-operate on this service, bus changes are likely to occur at one or other scheduled stop. Eurolines has a daily service from Victoria Coach Station to Munich, from where it operates in tandem with Ulusoy-Bosfor Turizm. Ulusoy-Bosfor Turizm's office in Munich is Deutsche Touring GmbH Stadburo, München Arnulfstr,

31 Stamberger Bahnhof (tel 089 591824; fax 089 596133); in Vienna at Argentiner-strasse 67 1040 (tel 650644). In İstanbul it is at Ceval Açkalim Caddesi, 18 Çirpici Mekvii Merter (tel 504 8039; fax 584 6100).

BY TRAIN

From London, the İstanbul or Orient Express runs daily via Paris to Dijon, Lausanne, Milan and Venice, from where it continues to Zagreb, Belgrade and Nis, Sofia and Plovdiv in Bulgaria, and so via Edirne in Turkey. Total journey time is about 72 hours, with sleeping cars as far as Venice.

From Munich the İstanbul Express runs daily through Salzburg, Ljubljana, Zagreb, Nis, Sofia and Plovdiv to Edirne and İstanbul. The Balkan Express to İstanbul starts daily from Vienna, through Maribor to Zagreb and on through to Bulgaria and Edirne. The journey by either train takes about 40 hours. Reductions are available for minors and students.

In general, rail travel beyond Vienna or Venice is recommended only for the more hardy traveller. A train can comfortably be taken to Munich, or Salzburg, or Vienna, from where a transfer can be made to one of the coach services or, at Venice or Ancona, to one of the ferry services to İzmir or Kuşadası. From Venice there is a rail service to İstanbul with second-class couchette supplement available. The *Thomas Cook Continental Timetable* is an invaluable publication when planning extensive rail travel.

TRAIN AND FERRY CONNECTIONS

As well as from Venice, there are ferry crossings to Patras in Greece from Ancona and Brindisi in southern Italy. Once in Greece, Greek National Railways has a daily rail service from Athens through Thessaloniki to İstanbul, the track passing through that section of Thrace where the three frontiers of Greece, Bulgaria and Turkey conjoin. This journey could in fact begin at Patras by taking the train from there to Athens. Again, once in Greece, by taking one of the daily sailings from Piraeus to one of the Greek Aegean Islands mentioned in the section on ferries, you could then cross by ferry to the Turkish coast. There are also local flights by Olympic Airways, the Greek national carrier, to each of these islands.

The İstanbul railway terminus for trains coming from the west is at Sirkeci, near the waterfront at Eminönü on the western side of the Golden Horn. For continuing a rail journey through Anatolia, east of the Bosphorus, the railway terminus is at Haydarpaşa, which is reached by ferry boat from the quays of Eminönü. The İstanbul Metro, now under construction, will carry two lines of its planned six under the Bosphorus, one of which will connect with Haydarpaşa, the main railway station for travel on the Anatolian side of the Bosphorus.

Sirkeci Harbour, İstanbul

Visas

A valid passport or equivalent
international document is
required. Nationals of the
United Kingdom, United States,
Ireland, Spain, Portugal and
Australia need a visa, which is valid for three months, and can be obtained at point
of entry. A visa for citizens of Russia, Hungary, Poland, Czech Republic, Slovakia,
Lithuania, Latvia, Estonia, Georgia, Federal Republic of Yugoslavia, Jordan and
Taiwan is valid for one month. Albanians and Guatemalans may have visas for 15
days only. All European Union citizens, and Swiss and Maltese nationals may enter
on identity cards in lieu of passports.

Visa-free entry for a stay of up to two months is available to citizens of Croatia,
Slovenia, Bosnia, Romania, Republic of Macedonia and Indonesia; for one month to
citizens of Bolivia, Kazakhstan, Kyrgyzstan, the Republic of South Africa and
Bulgaria. For citizens of countries not mentioned herein, no visa for a stay of three
months need be applied for.

For permission to extend your stay, apply at the offices of the Aliens Bureau
(Yabançilar Sube Müdürlügü), situated in the main police stations of towns. The
Aliens Bureau in İstanbul is at Cagaloğlu, Sultanahmet, north of Divan Yolu (tel 528
5173). Or apply through the *vali* (governor of a province) or his representative, the
kaymakam in cities or larger towns.

Customs Regulations

A visitor may take the following items into Turkey duty free: 200 cigarettes, 50 cigars or 200 grams of tobacco; 5 litres of wines or spirits; 1 kilogram of chocolate; 5 phials of perfume. In addition, on entry, 400 cigarettes, 100 cigars and 500 grams of tobacco may be purchased from the duty-free facility.

Personal effects can include sports and camping equipment, guns and ammunition for hunting, still and cine cameras, five rolls of film, spares for a car, a portable typewriter, a portable radio and a musical instrument. Items of value, however, such as cameras, a radio or typewriter, should be entered in the passport to facilitate export on leaving the country.

Although there is no limit to the amount of any foreign currency that can be imported and exported, no more than US$5,000 worth of Turkish currency may be imported or exported. Receipts for the exchange of foreign currency should be kept, particularly with respect to items of jewellery and carpets. Refund of VAT (value-added tax) on purchases can be obtained from authorized dealers, identified by the appropriate sticker attached to the entrance door or window. Three copies of the invoice should be issued, two of which the customs officials will keep.

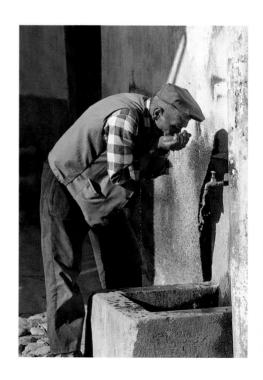

Climate and Clothing

A Mediterranean climate dominates on Turkey's Aegean and southern coasts. In general, hot, rainless summers offset spring and autumn showers, followed by mild winters with the rare excitement of snowfall. Along the coast of the Black Sea the summer weather is akin to that of eastern Europe—plus a degree or two. The sea here is less tranquil at times than at the other two coasts, and rain showers or sudden storms can occur.

With sea or waterways seldom out of sight on three of its sides, İstanbul can still be hot and dusty on summer days, and somewhat close with humidity on others, but some rain should be anticipated. In winter, rain, sleet and snow are not exceptional.

Inland on the central plateau of western Anatolia, summers are hot and dry, winters cold and crisp. Ankara experiences heavy frosts and snowfalls, lightened frequently by meridian blue skies and untroubled sunshine. The inland summer of eastern Anatolia resembles that of the western plateau, but in winter it is a colder place altogether, with some mitigation along the southern region that borders Syria and Iraq and between the two great rivers, the Euphrates and the Tigris.

Winter sports can be enjoyed in several locations without the anxiety of a sudden or premature thaw. Innumerable mountain ranges are seldom without snow on their upper slopes and peaks, in particular, on Mount Olympus in Mysia in the Bursa region and on Mount Ararat, the mother and father of mountains in far-eastern Turkey.

For clothing along the Mediterranean and Aegean coasts, beachwear is quite clearly the order of the day, with something a bit more substantial than a G-string perhaps on the Black Sea. Windcheaters should be at hand for those who aspire to yachtsmanship. Evening dress can be light and casual, with a pullover or cardigan available against a cooler breeze or an appreciable drop in temperature between sunset and moonrise.

Casual travellers going by bus and minibus throughout this extensive country should pack items such as shirts and underwear that can be dipped in a hotel or pension bathroom and dried overnight on the balcony. Slightly heavier woollies than those for the coast will be appreciated when eating at open-air restaurants in mountainous regions or beside lakes.

Women are advised to dress conservatively once among the less-Westernized inhabitants of the inland regions of eastern Turkey, and when visiting a mosque anywhere long skirts and covered heads are expected. Sometimes the sacristan is able to provide a length of cloth for wrap-around use. Everyone goes shoeless, but at many of the larger mosques overshoes are available at the entrance.

Sandals help keep the feet cool and protected from blisters on burning sands. But for those who intend to visit at least some of Asia Minor's countless ancient and historic sights, a stout pair of walking shoes and frequent changes of socks are recommended.

Turkey is a thirst-inducing place throughout the summer, but bottled water, mineral and otherwise, abounds, and in general tap water is safe. On long-distance buses bottled water is available free of charge to the passenger, and all you have to do is to ask the conductor for *su* (water) *lütfen* (please).

Health

In any personal medical crisis, go into an *eczane* (chemist) and ask for a *doktor* (doctor). Repeat the request until the chemist understands that you are in need of one. For first aid treatment there is a First Aid Hospital (Taksim Ilkyardim Hastanesi) on Sıraselviler Caddesi, Taksim, down on the right-hand side of the street (tel 243 1040). Another recommended emergency hospital is the state-run Tip Fakultesi Hastanesi, Koca Mustafa Paşa Caddesi, Cerrah Paşa (tel 585 2100), or the private American Admiral Bristol Hospital, Guzelbahçe Sokak, Nisantasi (tel 231 4050). In place of a red cross, Turkey's medical symbol is a *kızılay* (red crescent moon on a white background). In an emergency, dial 77 for an ambulance or mobile medical assistance.

Other hospitals in İstanbul are: the French Lape at Sisli (tel 246 1020); the Italian, Tophane Defterdar Yokusu 37 (tel 249 9751); the German, Sıraselviler Caddesi 119, Taksim (tel 246 2150); the International, İstanbul Caddesi 82, Yesilköy (tel 663 3000); the Balat Jewish at Fatih (tel 524 1156); the Austrian, St George, Bereketzade Sok 5/7, Beyoğlu (tel 243 2590).

Money

The unit of currency is the Turkish lira (TL). Banknotes are issued in denominations of 20,000TL, 50,000TL, 100,000TL, 250,000TL, 500,000TL, 1,000,000TL and 5,000,000TL. Coins are 1,000TL, 2,500TL, 5,000TL, 10,000TL and 25,000TL. Because of the rate of inflation it is impossible to give a reliable exchange rate.

In general coins are good for bus, trolley and *dolmuş* (shared taxi) travel, with bank notes used for most other transactions. A price quoted as *yüz* means 'a hundred'; for example, *yüz bin* (literally, one hundred one thousands) is 100,000TL.

There are over 60 major banks in Turkey. The largest ones have branches throughout most major cities and in the towns or centres where visitors in general find themselves. Some of the better publicized with exchange facilities are Akbank, Koç-Amerikan Bankası (American Express), Citibank, Egebank, Garanti Bankası, Osmanli Bankası, Ziraat Bankası and Yapı ve Kredi Bankası.

Banking hours are from 8.30am to midday and from 1.30pm to 5pm, Monday to Friday. Banks close on Saturdays, Sundays and public holidays. Most approved hotels are permitted to exchange currency, and this facility is also applicable to post offices (PTT). *Doviz*, or foreign exchange offices, are established in many places on

Cağoloğu Hamamı, İstanbul's oldest Turkish bath, is still in use

main thoroughfares of each city. These deal mainly in currencies, and the rates posted are frequently higher than in the banks. Traveller's cheques may also be accepted, but in general for these a bank is likely to offer a more favourable rate. Unlicensed dealers should be ignored.

Garanti Bank and branches of Yapı ve Kredi have reliable automated teller machines with instructions in English, German and French, among other languages. Facilities are open day and night.

Eurocheques are accepted on production of a Eurocard; traveller's cheques require that a passport or other universally accepted identification card or document be presented. MasterCard, Diners Club, Eurocard and Visa are accepted credit cards, though there might be difficulty making use of these outside the cities and major towns.

Transportation

BY AIR

Flights from İstanbul leave from the domestic terminal at Atatürk airport. There are daily flights to Ankara (45 minutes), Adana (80 minutes), Antalya (45 minutes), Dalaman (75 minutes), Diyarbakır (95 minutes), Elazig, stopover Ankara (3 hours 35 minutes), Erzurum, stopover Ankara (2 hours 35 minutes), İzmir (40 minutes), Kayseri (75 minutes), Malatya, stopover Ankara (3 hours 45 minutes), Samsun, stopover Ankara (2 hours 45 minutes), Trabzon, stopover Ankara (3 hours 10 minutes) and Van, stopover Ankara (3 hours 25 minutes). These flights are operated by the national carrier THY and popular schedules are increased during the summer season.

Family discounts are available for a husband, wife and their children under 23 years of age. There is a discount for children aged two to five. Other airline discounts are available for those between the ages of 12 and 24, for sports groups of five or more, for journalists and other professionals, as well as for persons over the age of sixty. Such concessions may change without prior notice.

Students who hold a card issued by TMGT (The Turkish National Youth Organization), with offices at İstiklâl Caddesi 471/2, Tünel, İstanbul, or TOGTO (Turkish Tourism Organization for Students and Youth), Samanyolu Sokak 62/8, Sisli, İstanbul, can claim discounts of 20 per cent on Turkish Railways, ten per cent on domestic air flights, 60 per cent on international flights out of Turkey and 15–50 per cent on Turkish Maritime Lines.

Private air companies operate scheduled flights to Bursa and other destinations. Flights can also be arranged for sightseeing or aerial photography, although the latter requires a military permit. Helicopter flights can be arranged for up to six passengers, and for charter flights or air-taxi services. Information is available at İstanbul's international airport, or in advance from the Turkish Private Air Carriers Association (Türkiye Özel Sektor Havaçilik Isletmeleri Dernegi; TOSHID), Firusköy Yolu, Avçilar, İstanbul (tel 593 6543; fax 593 8742).

The skyline of the old city dominated by St Sophia and the Blue Mosque

BY CAR

To hire a car in Turkey, you must present a valid national driving licence and be 19 years of age or over.

Outside the main cities and holiday centres, unleaded petrol may not be so easily available as it is in Western European countries. Motorists are advised to obtain information from the offices of the Türkiye Turing ve Otomobil Kurumu (TTOK), 1, Oto Sanayi Sitesi Yani 4, Levent (tel 282 8140; fax 282 8042). This organization has also undertaken tourist development projects such as the rehabilitation of old buildings in the Sultanahmet area of İstanbul and the reconstruction of tourist accommodation, restaurants and the Artisan Centre there.

TTOK has branches at Ipsala and Edirne (Kapikule), the Turkish frontier with Greece; Dereköy, the frontier with Bulgaria; Cilvegozu, the Turkish-Syrian frontier post; Habur on the Turkey-Iraq border; Gorbulak, the Turkish-Iranian frontier post near Dogubayazıt; Tasucu, the ferry station for Cyprus, Abdi Ipekçi Caddesi. Locations in Turkey include İzmir, Atatürk Bulvarı 370, Alsançak; Mersin, Muçahitler Caddesi, Karadag Ishani; Trabzon, Devlet Caddesi, Tünel Çikisi 2/2; İskenderun, Cumhuriyet Meydani, Besim Yücel Ishani, 2; Ankara, Maresal Fevzi Çakmak Caddesi, 31/8 Besevler; and Gaziantep, Ali Fuat Cebesoy Bulvarı 5D.

BY YACHT

İstanbul has a large yacht marina at Ataköy on the European Marmara shore between the airport and the city, and another at Kalmis (the Amiral Fahri Korütürk) on the Asian shore, both of which offer a 24-hour service. There are manifold marinas on the South Aegean and Mediterranean coasts on the southwestern corner of Anatolia, at the principal resorts of İzmir, Çeşme, Kuşadası, Bodrum, Datça, Bozbürünü, Marmaris, Goçek, Fethiye, Kemer, Kalkan, Kaş and Antalya, with the accompanying expansion of tourist residential accommodation, beach facilities, restaurants and entertainment.

Bare-boat charter is available as a form of yacht hire. Information can be obtained from the Yacht Enterprises Association (Yat Isletmecileri Dernegi), Eski Çeşme Mah, Firkateyu Sokak 19, 48400 Bodrum (tel 252 316 2398; fax 252 316 1601).

The Ministry of Tourism has issued important regulations concerning the use of foreign yachts in its publication *Blue Voyage*, obtainable at Information Offices of the Ministry in the country and abroad. The brochure also lists yacht berthing facilities under the control of the regional municipalities.

Communications

The main post office in İstanbul, Büyük Postane, is in Sehinsah Caddesi 22, Sirkeci, in the old city, behind the buildings opposite the main railway station there. Another main post office is at Kadiköy, Damga Sokak 1, on the Asiatic side of the Bosphorus. Both are open from 8am to 12am, Monday to Saturday, and from 9am to 7pm on Sundays. All post offices are distinguished by a yellow sign with PPT in black.

Branch post offices are less numerous than in western European countries. Beyoğlu, the new city, has offices at İstiklâl Caddesi 190, Galatasaray; at the start of Cumhuriyet Caddesi from Taksim Square; and in Osmanbey on Halaskargazi Caddesi, the extension of Cumhuriyet Caddesi; all are open from 8am to 8pm. After 8pm there is an office at Yenicarsisi Caddesi 3, Galatasaray, or at Büyükdere Caddesi 8, Sisli.

Minor branches close at 6pm. Some post office services such as stamp sales and posting can be handled, of course, by reception staff at major hotels or, as at the Hilton, by a sub-post office on the premises. Fax messages can be sent by residents from major hotels, and there are fax facilities at the post offices at Sirkeci, Beyoğlu and Kadiköy.

A *jeton* (token) is needed for use in public call boxes. They can be bought at post offices, from concessionaires at public call boxes, or at ferry stations as *jetons* are also used on some ferries. When making an international call from a public call box, make sure it has the second slot for this purpose and have an ample supply of *jetons*. They come in small-sized *kuçuk* for local calls, *orta* for trunk calls and *büyük* for international calls. Should you need to make a local call and there is no unoccupied call box in sight, ask at an *eczane* (chemist)—there are countless chemist shops, and using the telephone in one is common practice.

The dialling code for intended trunk calls to another part of Turkey is 03, and for international calls dial 528 2303. Operators on international lines speak at least one language other than Turkish, mainly English. When placing international calls, the country code is 99 44 for the United Kingdom and 99 1 for the United States and Canada. The *Turkey Travel Guide*, published by the Ministry of Tourism and issued free, has a list of local code prefixes. Calls can be booked for a normal connection, but for a rush call, place your request with the word *acele* (pronounced 'ajela') or, if extremely urgent, *yildirim* (lightning). The cost of *acele* is three times that of a normal call; *yildirim* is five times that of *acele*. Reduced rates are applicable for international calls made on Sundays or between 8pm and 8am daily.

Most familiar foreign-language newspapers from European countries and the United States are on sale a day after publication. The Sunday papers are available around the middle of the week. The English-language *Turkish Daily News* is published in Ankara but circulates in İstanbul and elsewhere. It has extensive international and local news coverage. *Apoyevmatini* is a Greek-language newspaper, as is *ISO*.

Haset at İstiklâl Caddesi 469, Tünel, is the largest of the multinational booksellers and also stocks international newspapers and magazines. Among its branches in İstanbul, Haset has outlets at both the Hilton and Intercontinental hotels, while in Ankara there is branch at Ziya Gokalp 14, off Kızılay. Back in İstanbul on Halaskargazi Caddesi—a continuation of Cumhuriyet Caddesi—at Harbiye, Hitit has a selection of paperbacks and perhaps even an out-of-print edition of a book you want. Sander, also on Halaskargazi Caddesi, 275, is a larger, enterprising bookseller

with a good range of English books, including Penguin and Pelican, and some French and German offerings. The International Bookstore is on Valikonagi Caddesi 85, at Nisantasi (at the north end of Cumhuriyet Caddesi). Net has a shop opposite the Yerebatan Cistern at Sultanahmet; Redhouse has one on Riza Paşa Yokusu 50, at Sultanhamam—call for its location as the shop is not in one of the more

familiar districts of the city (tel 527 8100). Tas Yayincilik is on Mesrutiyet Caddesi, Asi Han 13, not far from the British and American consulates. Bilimsel Eserler is at Sıraselviler Caddesi, Ayla Is Hani 66, off Taksim. For secondhand books, the Sahaflar Çarsisi at Beyazıt Square, down below the Grand Bazaar, is one of the oldest and most fascinating of bibliophile establishments. Türk-Aman (Deutsche Buchhandlung) at İstiklâl Caddesi 481, near Tünel, has been open since the 1950s.

The Voice of Turkey (VOT-TR) reports news in English, French and German from 8.30am to 10.30am and 12.30pm to 4.30pm. TM Radio has bulletins at 9am, 12pm, 2pm, 5pm, 7pm and 8pm. Programmes in English, French and German can be heard on tourist radio from 8.30am to 12.30pm, and 6.30pm to 9.30pm.

A few television channels now carry English news and feature programming, with television sets almost standard in three-star hotels and upward. Ask about programme information at your hotel.

Time and Measurements

Turkey is two hours ahead of Greenwich Mean Time and observes the extra hour of daylight saving between 30 March and 25 October. Government office hours are Monday to Friday, 9am–1.30pm and 2pm–5.30pm. Shopping hours are 9am–1pm and 2pm–7pm daily except Sundays and national holidays. Some shops close all day or for a half day on Saturday throughout the summer months—1 June to 31 August.

Many shops in the Covered Bazaar area stay open all the time. Note that hours listed are subject to frequent change. Most major banks now offer automated teller machines which are accessible 24 hours a day.

Electricity is generally 220 volts AC, although in some older parts of İstanbul it is 110 volts. Weights and measures are metric.

Public Conveniences

These are few and far between in Turkey, and where they exist often leave much to be desired in the way of hygiene. Cubicle or closet installations tend to be of the seat-less kind. In general, other than in hotels in the approved categories, the cleanest conveniences are in mosques, which are open to all.

Tourist Information

The head office of the Turkish Ministry of Culture and Information is in Ankara, but it has centres throughout the country, in almost every place in which a visitor might feel in need of help or advice. Brochures and regional maps are readily available at all Ministry of Tourism Centres.

A comprehensive listing of international offices for the Turkish Ministry of Culture and Information may be found at the end of this book.

Language

Turkish, considered to be among the Uralo-Altaic group of languages, has some affinities with Hungarian and Finnish. As the languages of this group of the Indo-Aryan tongue do not differ appreciably, the language can be understood and spoken throughout Turkic populations from the borders of China to southeastern Europe. Until 1928 Turkish was written in Arabic script, but Kemal Atatürk changed this by introducing the Latin script and reforming the language, clarifying it and eliminating its accumulation of alien words and expressions.

Atatürk himself travelled the country, introducing the new script and teaching it to villagers. As well as reforming the language, he reformed the clothing by introducing European styles and abolishing the fez, replaced by the cloth cap.

Turkish has only one anomalous verb and one irregular noun. It is an agglutinizing language with an unchanging root to which suffixes are added for tense, number and case. In general, in spoken Turkish the accent comes on the first syllable of a word, with a tendency to raise the pitch of the voice on the last syllable.

The Turkish alphabet has 29 letters, eight vowels and 21 consonants. Some of these letters do not occur in English, namely, İ,ç, ğ, ş, â, ı, ö, ü. For near rather than exact pronunciation: 'c' occurs but is pronounced like the English 'j' followed by a vowel, as in the word 'jug'; 'j' occurs but is pronounced with a soft sound as in French 'gendarme' or 'jour'; 'g' occurs but is hard as in 'ghost'; while 'ğ' is not pronounced but lengthens the preceding vowel.

Turkish 'ç' is as in 'change'; 'e' is as in 'bed', not as in 'her'; 'h' is always pronounced and never elided, except with the name 'Mehmet', in which the first syllable is lengthened; 'ö' is as French 'eau', while 'ü' is the umlauted German 'löwen' or French 'ü' in 'tu'; and, finally, the undotted 'ı' is exclusively Turkish and has a shortened, slightly guttural sound as the 'u' in 'mum'. İ is pronounced 'ee' as in 'feet', and ş has an 'sh' sound.

EVERYDAY LANGUAGE:

TIME

sabah	morning	Pazar	Sunday
gün	day	Pazartesi	Monday
akşam	evening	Salı	Tuesday
gece	night	Çarşamba	Wednesday
dün	yesterday	Perşembe	Thursday
bugün	today	Cuma	Friday
yarın	tomorrow	Cumartesi	Saturday
hafta	week		
ay	month		

GENERAL EXPRESSIONS

günaydın	good morning	kaç para?	how much?
iyi akşamlar	good evening	bu	this
iyi geceler	good night	şu	that
güle güle	goodbye	evet	yes
saat	time	hayır	no
saat kaç?	what time?	yok	none
erken	early	sıfır	zero
tabak	late	pek	very
sonra	later	çok peki	very much
lütfen	please	biraz	a little

güzel	good	*arkadas*	friend
fena	bad	*is*	work
büyük	big	*kitap*	book
kücük	small	*para*	money
sicak	hot	*mektup*	letter
soguk	cold	*pul*	postage stamp
kapalı	closed	*deniz*	sea
açik	open	*Akdeniz*	Mediterranean
usak	far	*kara*	black
yakin	near	*beyaz*	white
yeni	new		

VERBS

anlamak	to understand	*gelmek*	to come
almak	to buy	*gitmek*	to go
bakmak	to look	*etmek*	to do
görmek	to see	*birakmak*	to leave
gordum	I saw	*bulmak*	to find
çalismak	to work	*satmak*	to sell

NUMBERS

bir	a, an	*yirmi*	twenty
bir	one	*otuz*	thirty
iki	two	*kirk*	forty
üç	three	*elli*	fifty
dört	four	*altmış*	sixty
beş	five	*yetmiş*	seventy
altı	six	*seksen*	eighty
yedi	seven	*doksan*	ninety
sekiz	eight	*yüz*	one hundred
dokuz	nine	*bin*	one thousand
on	ten		

TRAVEL, HOTELS AND HOSPITALS

iskele	quay	*oda*	room
vapuri	steamer	*yatak*	bed
otogar	bus station	*anahtar*	key
bilet	ticket	*hasta*	ill
istasyon	railway station	*hastanesi*	hospital
tren	train		

EATING

lokanta	restaurant	*yumurta*	egg
hesap	bill	*tereyag*	butter
yemek	food	*çatal*	fork
kahvalti	breakfast	*biçak*	knife
kahve	coffee	*kasik*	spoon
çay	tea	*bardak*	glass
su	water	*sise*	bottle
süt	milk	*seker*	sugar
ekmek	bread		

Food

Turkish cuisine has been classified with that of France and China as among the innovative delights of the culinary world. Opinions on eating, however, and the comparative excellence of dishes can be very personal to a diner, whose health, weight and susceptibility to ulcers might well influence his or her assessment of quality. Others, enflamed by environmental or ecological convictions, might consider a bowl of porridge a banquet compared to a veal cutlet cooked rare on a French grill, bird's-nest soup or braised dog—whatever the Chinese call this domestic animal—or the raw liver served in an Arab restaurant (which is not a Turkish way of presentation, since a Turkish chef will spice his liver and fry it with onions, or he will dice it and serve it well-seasoned as a salad with olive oil).

Since Turkish cooking originated in the Central Asian plains and the mountainous Altai, in a pastoral and nomadic setting, lamb is preferred to beef as a staple of meat dishes. Lamb is spitted, stewed, grilled in kebabs or minced as *köfte* (meatballs or rissoles); mutton is roasted or casseroled. Beef is served as steak, less often roasted, or as *döner* kebab, spiced and compacted into a huge inverted cone and turned on a vertical rotating grill, from which fine slices are carved. There are regional variations in the way in which *döner* and other kebabs are prepared and served. Stuffed vegetables, including tomatoes, peppers, vine leaves, aubergine (eggplant), marrow, pumpkin and courgettes (zucchini); stuffed mussels, and shelled mussels dipped in batter, deep fried and served with a garlic sauce; chicken boned and spiced (chicken Kiev) and chicken cooked in a Circassian way with walnut sauce; a variety of *pilav* dishes—all very simple to explain, and nothing out of the ordinary, many might say. But it is far from simple to describe the taste that expert hands and the professional mind of a dedicated chef can concoct. Those who have travelled in Greece might brush off any special claim made on behalf of such dishes, assessing them as mediocre on the palate and low in satisfaction, which could be true of Greece but is an error where its neighbour's kitchen is concerned. The difference is not so much one of temperament as of obeisance to culinary art and care in preparation and presentation, as well as a willingness to please the diner.

As an alternative to meat kebabs, try pieces of swordfish grilled on a skewer interspersed with peppers and onions. There are fish of all varieties, particularly from the Black Sea, perhaps seeking their escape to an illusory freedom by way of the Bosphorus. Fish, large or small, for grilling, frying or baking on a brick or tile, can be chosen alive from the restaurant's tank in an inland city such as Ankara, to where sea bass are flown in and trout are caught in nearby mountain streams.

The danger is for the weight-watcher, the traveller on a diet who cannot avoid the overpowering temptation of honeyed sweetmeats; the *baklava*, a tiny roll of leaf pastry enriched with crushed nuts and soaked in honey, *bülbül yuvasi* (nightingale's nest, a variety of *baklava*), *tel kadayif* (shredded wheat subjected to a similar process of preparation), *kabak tatlisi* (baked pumpkin served with pounded walnuts) and walnuts in strained yoghurt and served with honey; these are some of the available honeydew amongst the wealth of paradise. Not to ignore Turkish Delight—most visitors probably will have tasted this sweet, or 'pudding' as it is sometimes translated, prior to their arrival but now will discover in what variety it can be enjoyed.

It has to be confessed, though, that with the development of international tourism the variety of dishes in tourist centres has become minimal.

GUIDE TO A TURKISH MENU

SOUP (*ÇORBA*)

Düğün çorbası	Lamb soup with egg and lemon sauce
Iskembe çorbası	Tripe soup with egg and lemon sauce
Mercimek çorbası	Lentil soup
Sehriye çorbası	Chicken soup with noodles
Yayla çorbası	Rice soup

EGGS (*YUMURTA*)

Çilbir	Poached
Menemen	Scrambled
Pastirmali yumurta	Fried with bacon (pastirma)
Sahanda yumurta	Fried

MEAT (*ET*)

Düğün eti	Chopped leg of lamb or mutton roasted in spicy tomato sauce
Haslama	Chopped leg of lamb or mutton cooked with celery and carrots
Kuzu dolması	Roast leg of lamb with rice, raisins and pine nuts
Kuzu guveçi	Casseroled lamb with potatoes and tomatoes
Kuzu incik patlicanli	Lamb stew with aubergine
Kuzu karamaşi	Grilled lamb with salad
Papaz yahnisi	Diced beef with onions, spices and cinnamon

KEBABS (*KEBABI*)

Bahçivan kebabi	Diced lamb or beef with carrots, potatoes and peas
Çomlek kebabi	Lamb with green beans, aubergine, potatoes, carrots, okra and green beans
Çop kebabi	Diced (small) beef on a stick grilled on charcoal
Döner kebabi	Sliced mutton off vertical spit
Islim kebabi	Lamb in pastry with tomatoes, peppers, etc
Kağit kebabi	Lamb cooked in foil with carrots, potatoes and peas
Orman kebabi	Roast lamb with tomatoes, carrots and peas
Şiş kebabi	Lamb on a skewer grilled on charcoal
Tas kebabi	Sliced beef in sauce
Adana kebabi	Heavily spiced and peppered minced meat

MINCED MEAT (KÖFTE)

Çizbiz	Grilled meatballs
Icçi köfte	Mince with crushed walnuts, spices and parsley
Terbiyeli köfte	Meatballs with egg and lemon sauce
Kadin budu köfte	Meatballs with rice dipped in egg yolk and fried

FRIED AND GRILLED MEAT

Arnavut cigeri	Diced fried liver
Beyin tava	Sautéed lamb's brains
Böbrek izgara	Grilled kidneys
Ciger izgara	Fried liver
Dil	Tongue
Koç yumurtasi	Lamb's sweetbreads grilled with herbs

POULTRY

Bagendili tavuk	Chicken with aubergine and cheese
Çerkez tavugu	Circassian chicken
Hindi dolması	Turkey with spiced rice
Bildirçin pilavli	Quail with rice

COOKED VEGETABLES

Biber dolması	Stuffed green peppers
Domates dolması	Stuffed tomatoes
Kabak dolması	Stuffed marrow
Patlican dolması	Stuffed aubergine
Yaprak dolması	Stuffed vine leaves
Bamya etli	Okra with slices of mutton or beef
Enginar dolması	Stuffed artichokes
Etli fasulye	Green beans with mutton or beef
Havuç kizartmasi	Fried carrots with yoghurt
Işpanak kavurtmasi	Sautéed spinach and minced meat with yoghurt
Kabak kizartmasi	Fried squash
Kapuska	Cabbage with minced meat
Karnabahar kizartmasi	Fried cauliflower dipped in egg yolk and flour
Kiş türlüsü	Potatoes, celery, carrots, leeks with pieces of lamb
Patlican begendi	Aubergine with cream and cheese
Patlican tava	Fried aubergine
Pirasa	Leeks with lamb
Yaz türlüsü	Green beans, aubergine, tomatoes, green peppers, potatoes, squash with lamb

FISH (*BALİK*)

Barbunya kagitta	Red mullet baked in foil
Hamsa tava	Fried anchovies
Kiliç sis	Swordfish portions on a skewer
Levrek kagitta	Sea bass grilled in foil
Mersin sis	Sturgeon grilled on a skewer
Üskümrü dolması	Fried mackerel
Sardalya asma yapranda	Sardines in vine leaves
Midye plakisi	Mussels in olive oil
Midye tava	Deep-fried mussels in batter

SALADS IN OIL AND HORS D'OEUVRES (*MEZE*)

Ayse fasulye	Green beans
Bakla zeytiynagli	Broad beans
Barbunya plakisi	Red beans
Imam bayildi	Aubergine stuffed with sliced onions and garlic
Kereviz zeytinyagli	Celery
Lahana dolması	Cabbage leaves stuffed with spiced rice
Midye dolması	Mussels stuffed with spiced rice
Beyin salatası	Sheep's brains in olive oil and lemon juice
Cacık	Chopped cucumber and garlic in strained yoghurt
Ciroz salatası	Dried mackerel and dressing
Patlıcan salatası	Mashed aubergine salad
Tarama salatası	Fish roe salad
Tarator salatası	Sesame seed ground with walnuts and garlic

RICE DISHES AND SAVOURY PASTRIES

Buhara pilavi	Rice with carrots, almonds and mutton
Cigeri pilav	Rice with liver
Bulgur pilavi	Cracked wheat with onions and tomatoes
Firinda makarna	Baked macaroni
İç pilav	Rice with chopped liver, raisins and pine nuts
Manti	Turkish-style ravioli
Bohça böregi	Meat and cottage-cheese pie
Ispanakli borek	Spinach pie
Muska böregi	Small triangular shaped meat and cheese pies
Peynirli börek	Cheese pie
Sigara böregi	Meat and cheese in roll of flaked pastry
Talaş böregi	Diced beef in flaked-pastry pie

A shopper's paradise, the Kapalı Çarşı (covered market) or Grand Bazaar

PUDDINGS

Firin sütlaç	Baked rice pudding
Keskülu fükara	Cream pudding with pounded almonds
Sütlaç	Creamed rice
Tavuk gögsü	Pounded chicken's breast in cream

SELECTION OF FISH

Hamsi	Anchovy
Levrek	Bass
Palamut	Bonito
Pisi	Brill
Mezgit	Whiting
Yengeç	Crab
Yilan balığı	Eel
Çipura	Bream
Istakoz	Lobster
Üskümrü	Mackerel
Kefal	Mullet
Barbunya	Red mullet
Midye	Mussel
Ahtapot	Octopus
Kerevit	Prawn
Karides	Shrimp
Kalamar	Squid
Dil	Sole
Kalkan	Turbot
Bakalyaro	Cod
Kılıçbalığı	Swordfish
Mersin balığı	Sturgeon

Drink

Turkey has a large wine-producing industry, based on domestic strains of vine and on recognized imported ones from France. Currently on offer are over 52 varieties of red wine, 50 varieties of white, 16 rosé and eight sparkling wines. Of the red, the wines of Atatürk Orman Çiftligi can be recommended: Ankara, Ankara Altini, Boga Kani and Kilis. Other reds include those from Doluca Bagcilik ve Sarapcilik such as Villa Doluca, Doluca Antik, Doluca; those of Tekel Buzbag, Buzbag (Madalyali), Güzel Marmara, Hosbag, Trakya; those of Kavaklidere Saraplari Yakat, Kavaklidere

Eski, Dikmen. In light wines Ankara and Ankara Altini have white versions; Tekel has Barbaros and a white Güzel Marmara, Narbag and Trakya; Doluca has white versions of Villa Doluca, Doluca Antik and Doluca; Kavaklidere has its Çankaya and Kavak. Among the rosé are Aral (Aral Sarap Ltd), Bortaçina (Yigitler Sarap Istl), Dona (Villa) (Mütük Sarap San Ltd) and Truva (Talay Saraplari); the other companies mentioned above all have their rosé wines. Among the sparkling wines, Altin Köpük is a Kavaklidere champagne. This is only a selected list, and other labels you might come across in major cities and towns, or outside of them, are not to be excluded from palatability.

Not all Turkish restaurants serve wine or alcoholic drinks, and those that do add an extra 15 per cent to the bill. Therefore, if you like to drink with your meal, make sure the service is offered before taking a table. *Ayran* is a sour-milk drink, generally available in non-alcoholic restaurants.

Bottled drinking water is a Turkish industry almost as major as wine production. Citizens who have acquired a palate for the water of a particular spring will travel long distances to obtain a magnum of it, and itinerant vendors with their carts or motorized transport circulate with giant jars of water from one natural spring or another. Many Turks are as expert in their connoisseurship of water as a taster of vintage wines. Claims are made for the medicinal effectiveness of some bottled waters—for stomach or kidney disorders—such as Circir from Sariyer on the Bosphorus, which is also a location of other springs. There is recommended water from Alemdag, Beykoz and Büyükdere, Maden Suyu is a palatable bottled mineral water that is stocked by most restaurants, and there is a Maden Sodasi, too, which is good as a mixer. Of many labelled products Kızılay, from Afyon Karahisar, is highly recommended.

Raki is the national alcoholic beverage. It is distilled from raisins, and anise is added, making it a similar product to Greek *ouzo*, Arabic *arak* or French *pastis*. The principal brands are made by Tekel, Yeni Raki or Altinbas. Drunk as an aperitif, a *meze* (or hors d'oeuvres) is generally served with it. Tekel also manufactures *kanyak* (cognac), *votka* (vodka), *cin* (gin) and whisky, and there is a variety of liqueurs from Tekel and other manufacturers. The import of noted international brands of alcoholic liquor is considerably increased.

Sira is a delicious non-alcoholic grape drink, often available in non-alcoholic restaurants. Another drink for a cold day is *salep*, made from hot milk and orchis root, sprinkled with cinnamon. On a warm day *ayran*, the sour-milk drink, can be a first-class thirst quencher, often made in local neighbourhoods and sold out of large porcelain or metal tubs, in the way ice cream is sold elsewhere. Best made locally, it is also available in bottles from grocery shops.

Turkish coffee is served black, *sade* without sugar, *az sekerli* with little sugar, *orta sekerli* medium sweet or *sekerli* sweet. Tea-drinking is a national habit. The tea is prepared in a samovar, or metal urn, and served in a small glass brought on a saucer. The tea is served without milk, but sugar lumps are placed on the saucer, alongside the spoon.

Tuborg Gold, Tuborg Pilsner and a rarer Draught Pilsner are beers produced in conjunction with Danish Tuborg; a dark beer, Ozel, is also on sale. There is Efes Pilsen, Pilsen on draught, and a Löwenbrau. Tekel manufactures a light and dark beer, and a *fici bira* (draught beer).

Tekel was the state monopoly organization for cigarettes, liquor and other commodities, but Turkey has extended its state corporation economy to production and marketing responsibilities in the country's private sector.

Tobacco

Turkey has a large tobacco industry; its cultivation is centred principally on the Black Sea coast. Turks are heavy smokers and according to one Turkish commentator cigarette consumption is growing, not diminishing as in Western European countries. The presence of multinational manufacturers has made imported brands of cigarettes, tobacco and cigars widely available. Among local brands claiming lower tar and nicotine content, and the filter-tipped varieties, king-sized Maltepe or the stronger flavoured well-established Samsun brand are recommended. Cigarettes for export, in particular a brand called Best, are also being produced. For prestige smoking, Tekel introduced the packing of cigarettes in individual wrappers printed with a person's initials, company name, submitted emblem or idiosyncratic motto. There is a parliamentary attempt to ban smoking in public places.

For cigars, Ankara in boxes of 20 and İstanbul in packages of five are well regarded. For the cigarillo and panatella type, Marmara in packets of five and ten and Pazar in packets of five are considered favourites.

Industry

Turkey's economy is predominantly a heavy industrialized one. More than 30 per cent of the country's industrial activity occurs in İstanbul and vicinity. Among the largest enterprises are shipbuilding, pharmaceuticals, automobiles, machine assembly plants, building materials, household appliances, machine and automobile spares, food, textiles, leather, tobacco, glassware, cement, sugar, iron and carpets. Other than the appropriate government department, the Yapı-Endustri Merkezi

(The Building and Industry Centre) has an information service for those interested in setting up a cooperative industrial or contracting enterprise in the country. The office is on Cumhuriyet Caddesi 329, Harbiye. Tüsiad, also on Cumhuriyet Caddesi 233/4, Harbiye, is the Turkish Industrial and Businessmen's Association, and therefore a repository of the kind of information needed by an overseas businessman or industrialist who is contemplating activity in Turkey. Yased, the Association for Foreign Capital Coordination, offers information and assistance on capital investment in the country. Contact can be made at Ihlamur Sergi Sarayi, Besiktas.

Museums, Galleries, Sound and Light

Museums throughout Turkey are open from 9am to 5pm but do close at least one day a week, usually Monday. There are some variations in closing days, for example Topkapi Palace closes on Tuesdays, and a check should be made locally on others. The entrance fee to most museums varies from 50,000TL to 250,000TL.

Where a museum has been established on an archaeological site, there is usually a charge for visiting the museum in addition to the site charge.

A museum of particular interest in İstanbul is the Sehir, which has a collection of exhibits from the conquest of the city to the present day. Entrance is by way of the Yildiz Palace Garden at Besiktas. The museum closes on Thursdays. At the Military Museum (Askeri Muze) on Valikonagi Caddesi, the Ottoman Military Band, the Mehter Takimi, gives performances between 3pm and 4pm daily. The museum closes on Mondays and Tuesdays. The Sadberk Hanim Museum at Büyükdere, closed on Wednesdays, has a collection of Turkish arts and handicrafts, including an archaeological section.

The new Museum of Modern Art is at Ayvansaray. It has been established in a former textile factory, the first ever to be built in the city in the 19th century. Not too far away, at Fener, a Byzantine building has been established as a Women's Library, certainly the first ever in this part of Europe.

In İstanbul and Ankara there are a number of private galleries where special exhibitions of Turkish art and artists, rather than international ones, are held from time to time. Opening hours are usually from 10am to 7pm daily except on Sundays. A few selected galleries are Berk at Cumhuriyet Caddesi 69, El-madag; Atatürk Kultur Merkezi (Atatürk Cultural Centre), Taksim Square; Galeri Baraz, Kurtulus Caddesi, Kurtulus; Bestek Art Gallery, Abdi Ipekci Caddesi

Lion's head in bronze, eighth century BC,
in the Museum of Anatolian Civilization, Ankara

Tugra (monogram) of Suleiman the Magnificent, Topkapi Palace, İstanbul

75, Maçka; Illhami Atalay Art Gallery, Alemdag Caddesi 28/2, Sultanahmet; Kobi Art Gallery, Valikonagi Caddesi Pasaj 85, Nisantasi; Imaj, Rumeli Caddesi, Villa Is Hani 4–6, Nisantasi; and Koleksiyon, Intercontinental Hotel, Cumhuriyet Caddesi.

Moda Kultur Merkezi at Bahariye Caddesi 53, Kadiköy, is an art centre where international art films are screened, plays performed and art exhibited. Ortaköy Kultur Merkezi at Dereboyu Caddesi, Barbaros Pasaj 110/1, Ortaköy, on the Bosphorus, and Bilsak, Sıraselviler Caddesi, Soganci Sokak 7, Cihangir, are similar centres. Bilsak also runs a restaurant and bar.

Sound and light performances are held at the Sultan Ahmet Cami (The Blue Mosque) from May until September and are given in English, German, French and Turkish. Evening performances start at about 8.30pm each evening. In Ankara similar performances are given at the Anit Kabir (Atatürk's Mausoleum) from 19 May to 30 September. For details of programmes, call at Türk Anit, Ceyvre ve Turizm Degerlerini Koruma, Vakfi (Foundation for the Preservation of Monuments, Environment and Tourist Attractions), Mesrutiyet Caddesi 57/3, Tepebasi. The performances are free of charge.

National Holidays, Festivals and Folklore

The two principal religious feasts of the Turkish year are the four-day Kurban Bayrami and the three-and-a-half-day Seker Bayrami. The first commemorates Abraham's willingness to obey God's command to sacrifice his son Isaac (for whom the ram in the thicket was then substituted). The second, the Sugar Festival, follows the month-long fast of Ramadan, the anniversary of the Hegira (Mohammed's flight from Mecca to Medina). The timing of these feasts varies each year in accordance with the Muslim calendar, which is 11 days shorter than the Western one. One-day holidays are:

1 January	New Year's Day
23 April	National Sovereignty and Children's Day
19 May	Youth Day (anniversary of resistance that ultimately led to the foundation of the republic)
30 August	Victory Day
29 October	Republic Day

There are annual international and/or local festivals in over 30 cities and towns throughout Turkey. Complete details can be obtained from the Ministry of Tourism and Information at its information centres at airports, harbours and in major cities, towns and tourist centres. The following is a selection of those most publicized:

January	Selçuk Camel Wrestling Festival
April	İstanbul International Film Festival
April/May	Ankara International Film Festival
May	Ephesus Festival
June	Marmara Folk Dancing Festival
June	Bergama Festival
June	Çeşme Sea and Music Festival
June	Rize Tea Festival
June/July	İstanbul International Arts and Culture Festival
	Kirkpinar Oil Wrestling, Edirne
July	Bursa Culture and Arts Festival
20 August–20 September	İzmir International Trade Fair
September	Ürgüp Wine Harvest
September	Kemer Carnival
December	Mevlana Anniversary Ceremonies

Turkish music, making use of quarter tones, betrays no polyphony, or harmony in an accepted Western sense, but is nevertheless pervasive, with a modal line that has some resemblance to monastic plainsong. Some dances have no musical accompaniment; the dancers perform to the rhythmic hand-clapping of those watching. Often an instrument when used is simply a reed pipe or a form of bagpipe. The Zeybek is a dance of the Aegean region; a similar dance is performed in Greece and the Balkans. There are Bar dances from the eastern regions, a Halay dance from central Anatolia and a Horon dance from the Black Sea. The Karsilamalar is from the Marmara region, and a sword and spoon dance, the Kiliç Kasik, is from Bursa. There are also spoon dances, Kasik, from the south. Men predominate in the dance, which can be acrobatic at times, but there are professional troupes now of men and women dancers who perform at dance festivals throughout the country, wearing traditional and regional costumes.

Nasreddin Hoca is a figure out of Turkish folklore and legend. He was a humble teacher but wily, practical and earthly wise in his dealings with fellow villagers. His concerns were the intricacies of marital and domestic life, town manners and mores, bazaar intrigues and gossip, and the cupidity of government officials. Stories of the Hoca's contemporary adventures are a matter of continuous invention in *çay ev* (tea house) and *kulup* (club), as with invented folk heroes of other countries. The shadow theatre of Hacivat goes back into a remote central Asian beginning, migrating through Persia into Anatolia and further west into Greece. The repertoire is traditional, as evergreen for children and enthusiasts as Punch and Judy or the tales of the Arabian Nights. Scripts often have a bearing on contemporary foibles.

Crafts and Souvenirs

At Sultanahmet, an 18th-century *medrese* (theological school) has been restored as the Artisan Centre (İstanbul Sanatlari Çarsisi). It is a court surrounded by a portico, and the cells of the former students have been restored as workshops. Artisans work on embroidery, lacework, calligraphy, bookbinding, doll-making, gilding and *ebru* (*papier-marbre*, the art of decorating paper for use on the inside covers and flyleaves of fine books). The artisans are happy to be observed at work, and orders are welcome.

CARPETS

Modern carpets in traditional patterns come mainly from Kayseri. Valuable antique carpets have either been sold or grace a museum or a private collection. Unless you happen to be an expert, you simply have to trust in the honesty of the merchant or employ a reputable agent to advise or buy for you. *Kilims* are rugs that may be referred to elsewhere as 'peasant rugs'. Colourful and in bold patterns, they are suitable for floors, bed covers or for wall decoration. Traditional *kilim* weaving is encouraged, among other crafts, by the Association for Promoting Turkish Handicrafts (Türk El Sanatlari Dernegi) at Yenisehir in Ankara; their showroom is located at 30/32 Selanik Caddesi. If you are footweary, would like a rest, and are interested in carpets and *kilims*, drop in for a coffee courtesy of Pegasus, whose display is of products from Kayseri. You will be under no obligation to buy. The showroom is at Ates Pasaji, a little beyond the entrance to the Yerebatan Cistern, opposite St Sophia. A prayer rug from Kula in northwestern Anatolia or from Gordes in the İzmir area can be a good buy, if found.

JEWELLERY

Genuine antique heirlooms are as hard to find as valuable carpets. If a reputable dealer has an item that interests you, he will weigh the gold or silver item and charge according to the current market price of the precious metal. There are many acceptable reproductions and imitations. Mehmet Kabas, of Urart, has the reputation of being the best jeweller in İstanbul. Some of his designs are based on originals belonging to ancient Anatolian civilizations. His workshop is on the Bosphorus at Baglarmevkii, Yunus Sokak 2, Yeniköy, with a showroom at the Maçka Hotel, Maçka, near Nisantasi.

COPPER

Traditional ware is handmade, but what is on view in souvenir shops is mostly machine-made. If the products of a master craftsman, Alaeddin Yanik, can be found, the additional cost over a machine-made product will be amply justified.

CERAMICS

This traditional craft was brought by potters transplanted by Sultan Selim I from Tabriz. After İznik, Kutahya became the most important centre of pottery, along with İstanbul, but today the products of Kutahya, based on traditional patterns, are pre-eminent. The best designers are said to be teenage girls, who follow a two-year course of training after selection.

BRASS

This is another, though deteriorating, Turkish craft. There are still some traditional craftsmen who are not mass-producing for the tourist trade. Look at the work at Bronze Is (Riza Paşa Yokusu, Uzuncarsi, Beyazıt).

MARBLE AND ONYX

Onyx (colour-layered quartz) objects proliferate in stores and souvenir shops throughout the country. The acquisition of onyx and marble items is very much a matter of personal taste.

MUSICAL INSTRUMENTS

One of the most traditional and unusual of Turkish instruments is the *saz*, which might be

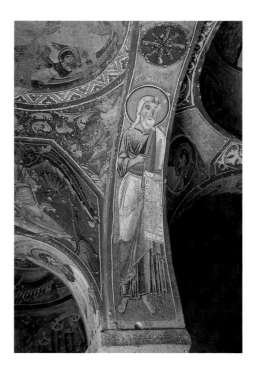

Frescoed rock cut church, Göreme, Cappadocia

described as an elongated mandolin but with a very long fingerboard and a much smaller sounding base. There are three sizes of this instrument: *cura*, the smallest, medium-sized *baglama* and *divan sazi*, the largest.

SILK

Bursa is today's centre of the *ipek* (silk) industry, which flourished in Byzantine times but declined in later Ottoman days. Bursa, too, produces excellent cotton-towelling items.

LEATHER GOODS

Turkey, justifiably, is noted for the high standard of its leather and suede. By all accounts (though this could deter a sensitive buyer) the use of the skins of young animals rather than the tougher hides of older ones explains the quality. The range throughout countless shops in the Grand Bazaar and elsewhere is enormous. Items of clothing are tailored in a matter of hours for the customer in a hurry.

MEERSCHAUM

This absorbent clay is quarried near Eskişehir, southeast of Bursa. Smokers' pipes, some in fanciful shapes, cigarette holders and many other assorted decorative items, both large and small, are also manufactured from it.

Hunting and Sport

HUNTING

A favoured hunting ground for animals and birds is in Trakya, the section of the country between İstanbul and the Greek and Bulgarian frontiers. The season, with quail the favourite quarry, starts in mid-September and runs through to March. The season for the wild boar, also a hunter's favourite throughout Turkey, begins in late autumn. In İstanbul there is a Hunters and Shooters Club (İstanbul Avçilar ve Aticilar Ihtisas Kulubu) at Sıraselviler Caddesi 58/1, off Taksim Square. The brown bear can be hunted in the Hakkâri Mountains of southeastern Turkey, in the Taurus Mountains and in some Pontic Black Sea Mountain areas. The hunting of jackal, hyena, lynx and wolf is permitted at all times, while there is a total prohibition on the fox, gazelle, chamois, otter, deer of all kinds and wild sheep. If birds interest you, note that total prohibition is extended to the crane, bustard, flamingo, francolin, pheasant and swan, while seasonal permits are given for partridge, quail, wild duck and wild goose. Foreigners may hunt only in parties organized by a bona fide member of Tursab (Travel Agencies Association), whose address is Esentepe, Gazeteçiler Sitesi, Haberler Sokak, İstanbul (tel 275 1361; fax 275 0066).

BIRD-WATCHING

The favoured viewing area for bird-watching is on the hills of Camlica behind

Üsküdar on the eastern shore of the Bosphorus. Tours to other favourable sighting areas can be arranged through, or advised by, the Bird-watchers Associations throughout Europe and America. In İstanbul a good season for watching is between 15 September and 10 October when birds are migrating south, and an estimated 40,000 storks cross İstanbul each day. Not far from Bandirma in Balikeşir province near the Sea of Marmara's southern shore, the Kuscenneti (Bird Paradise) is an ornithological reserve where some 200 species have been identified. Contact National Wildlife Protection Association, Dogan Hayati Koruma Dernegi, PK 18, Bebek, İstanbul (tel 221 0934; fax 222 5140).

FISHING

In İstanbul many Turks obtain a meal by fishing from the bridges, or at Rumeli Hisar, Tarabya, on the Bosphorus and from the long esplanade at Üsküdar. Boats can be hired, or fishing trips can be arranged with individuals at harbours along the coasts of the various seas. Trout-fishing is bountiful in the mountain streams of Anatolia, particularly in the Pontic Mountains of the northeastern area and in the hinterland of Trabzon and Rize. There is lake fishing in Lake Abant (southeast of Sakarya (Adapazari), mentioned in the Black Sea Coast section), İznik Golu (the lake at İznik), Bafa Golu (Lake Bafa, south of İzmir) and elsewhere. However, the water in some lakes, such as the large Lake Van in eastern Turkey, is too sodium-slaked to harbour fish. No permit is needed for fishing. The Balik Muzesi (fish museum), which has a collection of more than 4,000 species of fish, is on Kennedy Caddesi 11, Kumkapi, in İstanbul. The sea products wholesale market—Balikhane or Su Urunleri Hali—is in this area, too. For more information, contact Orman Bakaligi, Kurumu ve Kontrol, Gen Müdürlügü, Akay Caddesi, 3 Bakanliklar, Ankara (tel 312 417 4176; fax 418 8005).

MOUNTAINEERING

Mountain ranges occupy the largest area of Anatolia, providing unlimited and challenging—hazardous even, in the case of Ararat, Erciyes and other peaks—mountaineering opportunities. In Ankara at Ulus Ishani, Ulus Meydani, there is a Federation of Mountaineering and Skiing that can put visitors in touch with local alpine clubs in Ankara, Ağri (Ararat), Erzurum, Adana, Elazig, Van, Kayseri, Içel (Mersin) and Hakkâri. Contact the Ministry of Foreign Affairs in Ankara (tel 312 212 5125; fax 212 5966).

THERMAL SPAS

Thermal spas exist at Bursa, Pamukkale, İzmir, Yalova, Afyon, Sivas, Ankara, Konya and elsewhere. Contact the Ministry of Tourism and Information for further details.

OIL WRESTLING

Oil wrestling is a sport indigenous to Turkey, and an annual championship (over 600 years old), in which more than 500 wrestlers participate, is held in June each year at Kirkpinar, near Edirne. With their arms and bodies covered in oil and wearing only leather breeches, competitors wrestle for a fall. The İstanbul Gures Ihtisas Kulubu at Cingirarkli Bostan Sokak, 39/41, Aksaray, is a club for freestyle and Graeco-Roman wrestlers and can offer a special arrangement for non-members.

Participants in the annual oil wrestling championship held in Kirkpinar, near Edirne

CAMEL FIGHTING

Camel fighting, which sounds terrifying, is in fact a bloodless and harmless sport in which the camels push and shove rather than wrestle and tear each other. Matches are arranged during rutting periods, and an annual competition is held at Selçuk, İzmir.

FOOTBALL

Association football (soccer) has become a spectator sport as popular as in every other country in the world. The performances of Turkish players have improved appreciably in recent years, and Turkish clubs now regularly reach the advanced rounds of European competitions, and its national team the European and World Cups. Players and managers of both countries are now contracted by the indigenous clubs. This holds true for basketball as well.

GOLF

Golf can be played on a number of 18-hole courses in the İstanbul area, at Silivri, Kemburgaz, at Sincan near Ankara and at Belek near Antalya. For information contact Classis Country and Golf Club, Silivri, İstanbul (tel 727 4049; fax 266 9450). Non-members are permitted for an arranged membership fee and a course fee.

TENNIS

Tennis players may like to visit Dalyan Spor Tesisleri (at Adlihan Sokak, Dalyan, Fenerbahce, on the Golden Horn), which runs an instruction course from June to September. İstanbul Tennis Kulubu has courts at Bayildim Yokusu, Taslik, while Tennis Eskrim Dagçilik Kulubu is at Askerocaği Caddesi, Taksim. To play on the above courts, which are for members only, a visitor would have to pay the annual fee or sign up for Dalyan Sport's instruction course. Tacspor, however, accepts non-members, and their courts are at Yenigelin Sokak, Suadiye (tel 358 4125).

MARATHON

The Eurasia Marathon is an annual event, started in 1983, which attracts runners to the tune of 10,000 and more. On the shorter ten-kilometre (six-mile) course, more than one waiter carrying a serving napkin and tray, and perhaps a fully rigged, newly wedded couple can be seen participating for the sheer fun of it. The start is from Beylerbeyı on the eastern Bosphorus shore, then across the first of the two bridges to bring the runners through the new city and across the Golden Horn into the old, to end the course at Sultanahmet. The longer course also starts on the eastern shore, crosses the Bosphorus, goes up to Büyükdere and returns to the new city to end the run at the Dolmabahçe Palace on the Kabatas waterfront.

Interested athletes can obtain full information from the Intercontinental Eurasia Marathon, Cumhuriyet Caddesi 187/4, Elmadag.

YACHTING
Yacht-chartering is covered in the Transportation section; see page 24.

SCUBA DIVING
With proper equipment and training, scuba diving is permissible in non-restricted areas. Divers should present official documents concerning specifics of their training certification, and must be accompanied by an accredited Turkish guide. Maximum depth limit is 30 metres, which can be extended for educational purposes under proper supervision. The exportation of antiquities and natural specimens is illegal. Checks should be made in advance on possible regulation changes.

There are diving schools *in situ* at many major resorts, including one at Kemer under the direction of Don Frey, the American underwater archaeologist. For detailed information contact Gençlik Ve Spor Müdürlüğü, Ulus Ishani, A Blok Kat 3, 303/4 Ulus, Ankara. Instruction can be arranged through Satt-Sub Aquatic Tourism and Travel Corporation, Gazi Caddesi 39/1, Sinop.

For information on these other international sporting activities:

RAFTING
Nature Seyahat Ascentasi, Aydere Caddesi 13/8, Taksim, İstanbul (tel 254 7275; fax 254 4526)

WIND SURFING
New Neptune Holiday Village, Büyük Akkum 5, Sigaçik-Serehisar, İzmir (tel 232 745 7455; fax 745 7038)

AIR SPORTS
Turkish Air Defence General Directorate, Atatürk Bulvarı 33, Opera, Ankara (tel 312 287 3430; fax 310 0413)

CAVING
Maden Tetlik Arama (MTA), Genel Müdürlüğü Jioloji, Etidiler Dairesi, 06520 Ankara (tel 312 287 3430; fax 285 4271)

WINTER SPORTS
Youth and Sports General Directorate, Ulus Ishani, 4 Kat, Ulus, Ankara (tel 312 311 0764; fax 311 0766)

THE DOGS OF CONSTANTINOPLE

I am half willing to believe that the celebrated dogs of Constantinople
have been misrepresented—slandered. I have always been led to
suppose that they were so thick in the streets that they blocked the way;
that they moved about in organized companies, platoons and regiments,
and took what they wanted by determined and ferocious assault; and that
at night they drowned all other sounds with their terrible howlings. The
dogs I see here cannot be those I have read of.

I find them everywhere, but not in strong force. The most I have found
together has been about ten or twenty. And night or day a fair proportion
of them were sound asleep. Those that were not asleep always looked as
if they wanted to be. I never saw such utterly wretched, starving, sad-
visaged, broken-hearted looking curs in my life. It seemed a grim satire
to accuse such brutes as these of taking things by force of arms. They
hardly seemed to have strength enough or ambition enough to walk across
the street—I do not know that I have seen one walk that far yet. They are
mangy and bruised and mutilated, and often you see one with the hair
singed off him in such wide and well defined tracts that he looks like a
map of the New Territories. They are the sorriest beasts that breathe—
the most abject—the most pitiful. In their faces is a settled expression of
melancholy, an air of hopeless despondency. The hairless patches on a
scalded dog are preferred by the fleas of Constantinople to a wider range
on a healthier dog; and the exposed places suit the fleas exactly. I saw a
dog of this kind start to nibble at a flea—a fly attracted his attention, and
he made a snatch at him; the flea called for him once more, and that
forever unsettled him; he looked sadly at his flea-pasture, then sadly
looked at his bald spot. Then he heaved a sigh and dropped his head
resignedly upon his paws. He was not equal to the situation.

The dogs sleep in the streets, all over the city. From one end of the
street to the other, I suppose they will average about eight or ten to
a block. Sometimes, of course, there are fifteen or twenty to a block.

They do not belong to anybody, and they seem to have no close personal friendships among each other. But they district the city themselves, and the dogs of each district, whether it be half a block in extent, or ten blocks, have to remain within its bounds. Woe to a dog if he crosses the line! His neighbors would snatch the balance of his hair off in a second. So it is said. But they don't look it.

They sleep in the streets these days. They are my compass—my guide. When I see the dogs sleep placidly on, while men, sheep, geese, and all moving things turn out and go around them, I know I am not in the great street where the hotel is, and must go further. In the Grand Rue the dogs have a sort of air of being on the lookout—an air born of being obliged to get out of the way of many carriages every day—and that expression one recognizes in a moment. It does not exist upon the face of any dog without the confines of that street. All others sleep placidly and keep no watch. They would not move, though the Sultan himself passed by.

In one narrow street (but none of them are wide) I saw three dogs lying coiled up, about a foot or two apart. End to end they lay, and so they just bridged the street neatly, from gutter to gutter. A drove of a hundred sheep came along. They stepped right over the dogs, the rear crowding the front, impatient to get on. The dogs looked lazily up, flinched a little when the impatient feet of the sheep touched their raw backs—sighed, and lay peacefully down again. No talk could be plainer than that. So some of the sheep jumped over them and others scrambled between, occasionally chipping a leg with their sharp hoofs, and when the whole flock had made the trip, the dogs sneezed a little, in the cloud of dust, but never budged their bodies an inch. I thought I was lazy, but I am a steam-engine compared to a Constantinople dog. But was not that a singular scene for a city of a million inhabitants?

Mark Twain, Innocents Abroad, 1869

İstanbul

Its beauty etched in floodlit dome and minaret at dusk, İstanbul announces its unabashed longevity. Divided by waterways, the city mounts and descends on seven hills, pulsating as a living entity should. For the vitality of this city owes as much to its citizens of today as it does to past Byzantine emperors and Ottoman sultans.

İstanbul is undergoing re-embellishment under the guidance of a city administration that, while maintaining an awareness of history and tradition, is giving essential and considerate attention to the interests and well being of the present inhabitants, and its future ones in a city whose population, for Greater İstanbul, now stands at some 12 million, a figure that is increasing relentlessly.

Much debris has been cleared to be replaced by parks and gardens, most noticeably in the vicinity of the city's ancient walls. Pedestrian complexes have been established, as at Ortaköy on the European shore of the Bosphorus, below the stanchions of the lower Bosphorus bridge. The 19th-century floodlit baroque mosque of the village has been disencumbered of what were unsightly irrelevancies, as has its accompanying park, to become the showpiece of a pedestrian-dominated quayside as lively with restaurants, cafés, antique shops, bric-a-brac stalls and a book enthusiast's quarter as any you would find on a Parisian riverside. Here the city's youth gathers each evening to eat, drink, walk and talk.

There is Kumkapi, too, down below those few remains of the greater Byzantine Palace, at a sea gate, always noted for its fish restaurants. It too has been turned into a pedestrian complex, with a burgeoning of small, unpretentious restaurants offering seafood.

Along the Bosphorus shores many of the lovely old timbered houses and mansions have been restored to pristine elegance, an architect's delight. Elsewhere, blatant and unsightly hoardings have been discouraged, and traffic has been disciplined by roadway reconstructions and routings. One of the new city's principal thoroughfares has been totally allocated to pedestrians, except for a newly re-installed, ancient tramway that runs all the way from Taksim Square to Tünel. Almost three-quarters of Taksim Square itself is now reserved for strollers and *flâneurs*. New buses run on redesigned routes, and steel trams run in the old city.

The area of the Kariye Cami, the Church of St Saviour in Chora, with its beautiful 14th-century frescoes and mosaics near the walls in Edirne Gate, has also been converted to a peaceful complex, with many of the area's old houses restored, and a gracious hotel added.

A new and wider Galata Bridge now spans the Golden Horn between Karaköy and Eminönü, and a second suspension bridge graces the middle reaches of the Bosphorus. A Byzantine building has been converted into the International Press Club on the waterside a little beyond the ferryboat quays at Eminönü, along with a terrace restaurant for non-members. A modern Art Museum now occupies a former textile factory at Ayvansaray, and yet another Byzantine building has become a Women's Library at Fener, in the patriarchate quarter.

Building and reconstruction in the city is taking place at such an intensive rate that areas are changing almost daily, and a mention could be out of date almost as soon as uttered. Roadways, buildings, industrial complexes, condominiums and hotels are extending İstanbul along very nearly the entire European side of the Bosphorus, and to some extent on the Asiatic side. A motorway along the western Bosphorus shore, constructed like a causeway at ground level, has essentially pushed villages like Bebek and Arnavutköy back from the water's edge. This sharply diminishes their waterside attraction, as evidenced by the dropping of a former Bosphorus ferry service which zig-zagged customers from shore to shore.

Getting Around

The main airport bus runs along Florya Highway and eventually turns left into Atatürk Bulvarı to go through Aksaray to Unkapani, where it passes under the Aqueduct of Valens. If you intend to stay near the district of Sultanahmet, where the principal monuments of the old city are, dismount from the airport bus at Aksaray. Recent road construction now carries incoming traffic from Unkapani along the Golden Horn to Galata Bridge where a revamped road system leads either to the THY air terminal station at Sishane or by way of Tarlabaşı Caddesi to Taksim Square. Another route from Galata Bridge takes traffic past the main quay at Karaköy and along the Bosphorus waterfront through Kabatas to Beşiktas.

An alternative form of transport in İstanbul and elsewhere in Turkey is the *dolmuş*, or shared taxi. These services run between fixed destinations and stop on a single charge, as with buses. Though *dolmuş* were once in the style of small, private taxis, the minibus with its expanded seating capacity has superseded the traditional taxi-style *dolmuş*—not without some regret to travel purists.

To cross to İstanbul's eastern shore of the Bosphorus, take one of the main ferries from Eminönü on the old city side of the Golden Horn to Üsküdar, Kadiköy and the main railway station for Anatolia, Haydarpaşa. Closer to the new city of Beyoğlu, a smaller passenger ferry runs to Üsküdar from Kabatas, the ferry station near the Dolmabahçe Palace. Though taxis do cross the bridges, this ferry affords a fine view of the city's hills, domes and minarets. Wherever you choose to stay, be sure to visit the monuments of the old city—Topkapi Palace, St Sophia, the Blue Mosque, the Archaeological Museum and the Grand Bazaar. All lie within easy walking distance of Sultanahmet, near the first walled city of Byzantium.

Historical Background

When Mehmet II breached the walls of Constantinople in May 1453, the Byzantine Empire had been reduced in size to little more than the area of the city. For the last emperor, who died in the breach, the battle had been fought courageously with few defenders, a lack of arms and money and almost no Western support—a Genoese naval contingent arrived too late to participate. On entering the city, Mehmet went at once to St Sophia and, prostrating himself at the altar, re-dedicated the building to Allah, after which he rode to what was left of the Great Palace where he reflected philosophically on triumph, time and mortality. His troops were then allowed to indulge in three days of looting and licensed mayhem—the customary privilege of a conquering army, whatever its creed. However, Mehmet II allowed only one day of licence, after which rehabilitation of the city as an Ottoman possession began.

It would be a mistake to believe that the Ottoman Turks (or Osmanlis) were a savage horde, destroying and invading the Byzantine Empire on impulse. The Osmanlis entered Anatolia as a small tribe under their leader Ertogrul in the early thirteenth century. In 1230, having given service to the Seljuk sultan at Konya, they settled in the area of Sogut in the north-western corner of Asia Minor near the Gulf of İznik, little more than a day's journey from the Bosphorus and Constantinople. The Seljuk Turks entered Anatolia after they defeated the Roman Emperor at Manzikert in 1071 and occupied large areas of Byzantine territory, setting up their Sultanate at Konya. The Seljuks had formerly occupied Persia and adopted much of Persian civilization. Mongols overthrew the Seljuks in the mid-13th century, dividing their territories among some 40 independent rulers or emirs, of which the Ottoman was one. The title Osmanli is derived from the name of the great leader Osman, Ertogul's son.

At the time of the fall of Constantinople, the Ottomans therefore had been established near the Byzantine capital for some 200 years and were far from being newcomers to that culture. Their first major conquest had been the taking in 1329 of the city of Bursa to the west of them by Orkhan, Osman's son. He shortly afterwards took Nikaia, which had been the capital of the Byzantine emperors in exile after the Latins, under the Doge of Venice, sacked Constantinople and then ruled a Latin Empire from there for 60 years; Nikaia had also been the location of the first Ecumenical Council of the Church, convened by Constantine, at which bishops first drafted and approved the Nicene Creed. Orkhan then took Nicomedia, which had been Diocletian's capital in the East after he set up administration of the Roman Empire under two Emperors and two Caesars.

After Orkhan, Murat I extended Osmanli power in Europe by occupying Gallipoli and much of Thrace and Macedonia. He defeated the Serbians at the battle of Kosovo in 1389, having made Adrianople (Edirne) his capital, but was assassinated on the battlefield by a captured Serbian prince. His son Beyazıt wreaked a dire revenge on the Serbs, and afterwards overran what remained to the Byzantines in the Balkans. Beyazıt made a half-hearted attack on Constantinople, and his army might well have taken the city by a second attempt, but he was defeated by Timur in a battle near Ankara while campaigning in Asia Minor. He was captured and kept in a cage by his conqueror until he died.

The Tartars did not settle in territories they conquered, and after Timur's retirement the four sons of Beyazıt fought a civil war over the succession. Mehmet I, the eventual victor, then made Bursa his capital. Mehmet's son, Murat I, continued the expansion of Ottoman power in the Balkans and held the whole of Thrace up to the very defences of Constantinople; he recaptured too all those parts of Anatolia Timur had taken. The majority of the independent Emirates were subsequently conquered by Beyazıt II, Mehmet II, the Conqueror, capturing Constantinople, and Selim I and Suleiman the Magnificent later completed the expansion of Ottoman power, then at its zenith, into the Middle East, Egypt and Africa.

Mehmet repopulated the city with Turks, but he also encouraged people of other nationalities, Greeks and Jews in particular, to set up businesses to help restore the city's commercial prosperity that throughout the later years of the Byzantine Empire had seriously declined.

Gennadius, a Byzantine scholar, was installed as Patriarch of the Greek Orthodox Church. Mehmet allocated the Church of the Holy Apostles as the seat of the patriarchate and, as with other ethnic communities, established the Greeks as a *millet* (self-administrating unit) under the patriarch, which included judicial control, though not for criminals who were subject to trial in the Turkish courts. The authority of these *millets* would decrease with time. The patriarchate was later moved to the Pammakaristos Church and Monastery on the fifth hill overlooking the Golden Horn, while the Fatih Cami (Mosque of the Conqueror) was built on the site of Holy Apostles, on the fourth hill of the city, to the northwest of the Aqueduct of Valens. The church had been the burial place of emperors, and later Mehmet himself would be buried on the same hill. Murat III took over the Pammakaristos in order to build the Fethiye Cami, and the patriarchate was then established at St George's Church in Phanar (now Fener) on the Golden Horn, where it is today.

L'AFFAIRE DU SOFA

*T*he French Ambassador, the Marquis de Nointel, is summoned to the court of Mehmet IV in 1677...

On arriving at the Porte on the appointed day (Sunday, April 22nd), Nointel had to wait three whole hours in the room of the Kehaya—a surly Turk—without conversation or any other entertainment; and when at last he was called in, he found the narrow corridor that led to the Audience Chamber crowded with chaoushes who jostled him most rudely. Truth to tell, this rudeness, at all events, was not premeditated. The poor chaoushes had come in the turbans of ceremony worn on such occasions, but had been ordered by the Vizir to go and exchange them for their ordinary headgear: hence their hurry to get back to their places before the Ambassador made his entry. Nointel, however, whose nerves were already on edge with the long waiting, saw in their behaviour a fresh insult, and he elbowed his way down the passage fiercely flinging the chaoushes to right and left against the walls. In this temper he entered the Audience Chamber, and there he observed something at which his resentment reached the height of exasperation: the stool destined for him was not upon the Soffah, but on the floor below! He ordered his Dragoman to set it where it should be; one of the Vizir's pages brought it down again. Then the Ambassador, in a towering rage, seized the stool with his own hand, carried it to the Soffah, and sat upon it.

When this act was reported to the Vizir, who was in an adjoining apartment, he sent for the Ambassador's Dragoman and commanded him to tell his master that he must move his seat back where he had found it. The trembling Dragoman delivered the message and was bidden by the angry Ambassador to hold his tongue. Next the Vizir sent his own Dragoman, Dr Mavrocordato, with whom Nointel maintained the closest friendship. In vain did the Greek try to soothe the enraged Frenchman, imploring him to moderate his temper and yield gracefully to the inevitable. Nothing could prevail over M de Nointel's obstinacy: the pride *of the wig was pitted against the pride of the turban, and it must be remembered that both wigs and turbans were then at their zenith. In the end, Mavrocordato, finding argument useless, changed his tone and said, in Italian: 'The Grand Vizir commands the chair to be placed below.' Nointel replied: 'The Grand Vizir can command his chair: he cannot command me.' At that moment the Chaoush-bashi burst into the room, roaring, 'Calder, Calder—Take it away, take it away!'—and before he knew what was happening, Nointel found the stool snatched from under him. In an access of fury, his Excellency dashed out of the room, sword on shoulder, pushed his way through the throng, and, ordering the presents which he had brought to follow him, mounted his horse and departed, exciting, as he boasted by his firmness, 'the astonishment of the Turks and the joy of the French'. Kara Mustafa alone remained calm. His comment, when he heard that the Ambassador was gone, was one word: 'Gehennem' (Let him go to Hell).*

Such was the beginning of the celebrated 'Affaire du Sofa'—a quarrel which drew the attention of all Europe and nearly led to a rupture between France and Turkey.

G F Abbott, Under the Turk in Constantinople, *1920*

FRAGILE BEAUTY

*T*here are no roads here; so by a lane that would shame the roughest in Ireland, came the Sultan's married daughter, married to Aali Ghalib Pasha, the son of Reschid Pasha. Edmund helped Lady Robinson into some brambles on the steep bank; I was already safely wedged in the roots of an old fig-tree; and thus we quietly awaited the passing of the Asiatic beauties....We could not see much of the lady (who is said to be very lovely), the Negroes keeping close to the windows, as they splashed up the mud all over their uniforms; besides which, her yashmak was thickly folded. I could only see plainly her beautiful fan of snow-white feathers, the handle glittering with emeralds.

The lady on the opposite seat (there were three in the carriage) was more thinly veiled, very young, and very pretty. I saw her face plainly, and her feridjee being a little off her shoulders, I threw an envious glance on a violet-coloured velvet jacket embroidered with gold, and fastened at the throat with a large jewelled clasp, which gleamed through the gauzy veil. As to beauty of mere dress and ease of attitude, nothing that I have seen in life or in pictures can give the slightest idea of the wonderful grace, the extreme delicacy, and bird-of-paradise-like uselessness of the Turkish belle. Women of rank look like hothouse flowers, and are really cultivated to the highest perfection of physical beauty, having no other employment but to make their skins as snow-white and their eyebrows as jet-black as possible. When young, their skin is literally as white as their veils, with the faintest tinge of pink on the cheek, like that in the side of a shell, which blends exquisitely with the tender apple-leaf green, and soft violet colours, of which they are so fond.

The reverse of the picture is, that after the first bloom of youth is past, the skin becomes yellow and sickly-looking, and you long to give the yashmak a pull and admit a fresh breeze to brighten up the fine features.

Lady Hornby, Constantinople During The Crimean War, *1863*

In the initial period of occupation the Ottomans converted many existing churches, but later built mosque complexes that often included a *medrese* (theological school), a *hastanesi* (hospital) and an *imaret* (soup kitchen). As well as Turkish architects, craftsmen of other nationalities were employed, and many high officers of state were selected from among foreigners who had converted to Islam.

With the first four sultans, up to the reign of Suleiman the Magnificent, the Ottoman Empire achieved its apogee of influence and expansion. Imperial control lasted until this century, but in the aftermath of the country's defeat in World War I and the repulse of the Greek invasion of 1920–2, the empire ended with the declaration of a republic. Kemal Atatürk, its first president and great reformer, established the capital at Ankara. Besides Parliament and the embassies, the head offices of banks and large commercial and industrial enterprises are located there. İstanbul, though, retains much of its principal city aura, and its acquired authority as a former imperialistic masterpiece.

THE EARLY HISTORY

About the middle of the seventh century BC the Megarans, neighbours of the Athenians, are believed to have built the first city on the site. Its name of Byzantium is said to derive from their leader Byzas, but authentic records of this early time are scant. In 506 BC, it was occupied by the Medes, but seems not to have been all that important to the Persian Xerxes who, when launching his invasion of Greece, built a bridge of boats across the Hellespont, at the lower end of the Dardanelles. The Spartan general Pausanias captured it in 478 BC, and due to its strategic and political importance in the long power struggle between Sparta and Athens the city changed hands on several occasions. Byzantium repulsed Philip of Macedon when he besieged it in 340 BC, and Alexander a year or two later chose to ignore it, making his crossing into Asia Minor by way of the Gallipoli Peninsula. In the early days of the city of Byzantium, coinage bore the stamp of the crescent moon and star, a symbol that in a much later age was to spread panic among those in the path of Ottoman expansion.

In the second century BC the city elders signed a treaty of alliance with Rome and agreed to pay tribute, but Vespasian annexed it for the empire in AD 73. A civil war followed on the death of Commodus (AD 192), and the Byzantines made the mistake of supporting the rival of Septimius Severus who after a three-year siege avenged himself on the citizens by thoroughly sacking the city. Then, in recognition of its unique strategic value, he rebuilt it; his new city of Antoninia occupied the snout of high land above the Marmara Sea. Temples to Artemis, Aphrodite and Apollo are associated with Antoninia, with Apollo's temple located between those to Artemis (where St Sophia now stands) and Aphrodite (on the St Irene site). Of

Antoninia, only some sections of the city's walls now remain.

In AD 330, after defeating Licinius, his last remaining rival from the civil war that followed the death of Diocletian, Constantine chose Antoninia as the site for his capital of New Rome, which on completion was designated Constantinople. Constantine extended the boundaries of Antoninia, building his walls further to the west. With Constantine's declaration in favour of Christianity—his mother Helena was a convert who had been on pilgrimage to the Holy Places of Jerusalem and had returned with Christian relics—the city became the capital of the Eastern Roman Empire, though Constantine himself is thought not to have been baptized until upon his deathbed. For a brief spell under Julian (361–63), there was a reversion to paganism, but Julian died in battle in the Middle East. The future of Christianity was assured when Theodosius I (378–95) declared the empire Christian and ordered the destruction of all remaining pagan shrines. Rome fell to the Goths in 476, and Constantinople became the sole political capital of a developing Christian world.

In Justinian's time (527–65) much of the city was destroyed in the Nika Riot, but Justinian, one of the greatest of East Roman rulers and, as Hadrian had been, a prolific builder, reconstructed the city on a magnificent scale. His brilliant generals Belisarius and Narses regained most of Italy, Spain and the North African provinces for the empire, though the cost of doing so was irrevocably to damage the economic resilience of the state.

Some historians base the switch in nomenclature from Roman Empire to Byzantine Empire during the reign of Justinian. He codified the laws that until that time had existed only in decrees. He recognized the predominance of Greek-speakers among the empire's citizens by making Greek an official language of state along with Latin. Greek later became the empire's sole official language.

Throughout the ensuing centuries, citizens of Constantinople successfully repulsed assaults from Goths, Alans, Serbs, Bulgarians, Russians and seventh-century Arabs. Its defences held, reinforced by new walls built in the fifth century under Theodosias II. These fifth-century walls, still standing today, are situated to the west of the walls that Constantine had built surrounding the city.

In 1204, the knights and soldiers of the Fourth Crusade under Dandolo, the Doge of Venice, successfully attacked the city. The Latin Empire they established survived until 1261, when the Byzantines re-occupied the city. The city remained impregnable to attack, warding off serious assaults by the Ottoman Beyazıt I and Mehmet II until finally succumbing to attack by the latter in 1453.

In general the Crusades were hardly of benefit at all to the Byzantine Empire, or Christianity in the Middle East. During his reign the Emperor Alexis I Comnenos (1081-1118) might have been glad of the support of the Christian West in helping him reconquer Byzantine territory in Anatolia lost to the Seljuk and other Turks, but he was by no means an advocate of a Holy War against Islam, being not without mutual accommodations with the occupiers. The Seljuk Sultanate at Konya may have been in decline, its territory becoming fragmented by the independent declarations of Emirs, but Alexis had no desire to strike until he had an army that could ensure his success.

Nor was the West interested in the restoration of Byzantine property, being in any case in schism with the Orthodox Church; what the West wanted was Jerusalem and other Christian cities that had been in Arab Islamic control since 638.

The Arabs, in recognition of Jerusalem as a Holy City for Christians, allowed pilgrims to visit the holy places; but stories were current of pilgrims subjected to abuse, robbery and general harassment; this may have been an excuse for action.

Pope Urban II launched the First Crusade in 1096, calling on princes and noblemen to take the Cross. Not only nobles responded, but French and German peasants did too, and a first contingent set off under the leadership of Peter the Hermit, a wandering monk with, among the intending warriors, a very large number of women and children. Much havoc was caused by these crusaders long before they even reached Constantinople; many hundreds of Hungarians were murdered on the army's way through that country, and the city of Belgrade was set on fire. When, after a good deal of trouble, Alexis succeeded in getting this rabble over into Anatolia, the Seljuk Turks defeated them close to annihilation in a battle near the city of Nicomedia.

Other, better organized contingents of this Crusade reached Constantinople within the ensuing months, led by their kings and princes, from each of whom Alexander demanded an oath of fealty, which they were reluctant to swear, particularly Godfrey of Bouillion and Baldwin of Boulogne, who were concerned more with carving out for themselves kingdoms in the East than freeing Jerusalem from Arab control. There was as well Bohemund of Taranto, the eldest son of Robert Guiscard, Duke of Apulia, who had already given the Byzantine Emperor trouble by his aggressive incursions into mainland Greece and the islands, and had laid a claim to the emperor's seat in Constantinople itself. Another of the Crusaders was Robert, Duke of Normandy, a son of William the Conqueror, victor in England.

These Crusaders gave Alexis as much trouble as had Peter the Hermit's, but when they did eventually cross the waterways into Anatolia they defeated a Seljuk army and captured Nicaea, and then went on to take Dorylaeum (Eskisehir), and in June 1098 captured Antioch (Antakya-Hatay) after a long and trying siege.

In July 1099 they defeated the defenders of Jerusalem and reclaimed it for Christianity, then carried out a wholesale slaughter of Muslims and Jews.

Baldwin was not among the victors at Jerusalem, nor was Bohemund; the first had captured Edessa (Şanliurfa) to the east, on a frontier with Syria, while

Bohemund had made himself Prince of Antioch, both now claiming territory the Emperor considered rightfully to belong to him.

Jerusalem, Antioch and Edessa and the areas occupied by the Crusaders now became known in the West as Outremer. Yet another contingent of this Crusade, led by Raymond of Toulouse, captured Ancyra (Ankara), but his army was afterwards ambushed by Danishmend Turks, losing more than three-quarters of its strength including women and children. Raymond himself escaped back to Constantinople.

The Danishmend Turks were distinct from the Seljuk Turks and the Osmanlis; they were a Turcoman people who had established themselves in Cappadocia in central Anatolia, and at Melitane and Sivas to the northwest of there; to be overrun eventually by the Seljuks in 1178.

In 1100 Bohemund of Antioch was captured by Danishmend Turks and kept captive for three years, until ransomed. Later on, in 1104, he was defeated by a Muslim force at Harran, near Edessa, though he himself escaped capture this time, and returned to the West to raise a new army. Tancred his nephew then became Prince of Antioch. Baldwin of Edessa was captured at Harran, and subsequently ransomed. Later he became Baldwin I King of Jerusalem after he had lost Edessa to an Arab prince in 1145, after a siege that lasted 25 days.

Pope Eugenius III raised a Second Crusade in 1147. This was led by King Louis VII of France and Bernard, Abbot of Clairvaux. There was a second contingent of Germans under the command of Conrad, King of the Romans, a friend of the then Byzantine Emperor, Manuel I Comnenus. The intention of this Crusade was to recapture the territory lost on Outremer to the Muslim prince Nur-ed-Din and to increase the population of Christians. On his way Conrad was defeated by a Seljuk army at Dorylaeum again. Other contingents caused as much trouble to the countries they passed through on their way to Constantinople as the earlier crusade, including a sacking of Thessaloniki, and Manuel was obliged to ask the Venetians for help in controlling them. Later in the Crusade King Louis, having reached Jerusalem, launched an ill-conceived attack on Damascus, an inglorious failure, whereupon the Crusade was abandoned.

A Third Crusade was launched in October 1187, following the recapture of Jerusalem by the Saracen Saladin, who, like Nur-ed-Din, may have been of Kurdish origin. Pope Gregory VIII was the inspirer of this Crusade, with one leader the German Emperor, Frederick Barbarossa. King William of Sicily was another, as were King Richard Lionheart of England, and King Philip Augustus of France. On his way to Outremer by sea, Richard captured Cyprus from the Byzantines, in 1191, then passed it to the Knights Templar for safekeeping, and afterwards to Guy of Lusignan, the King of Jerusalem in exile. Frederick Barbarossa on his landward

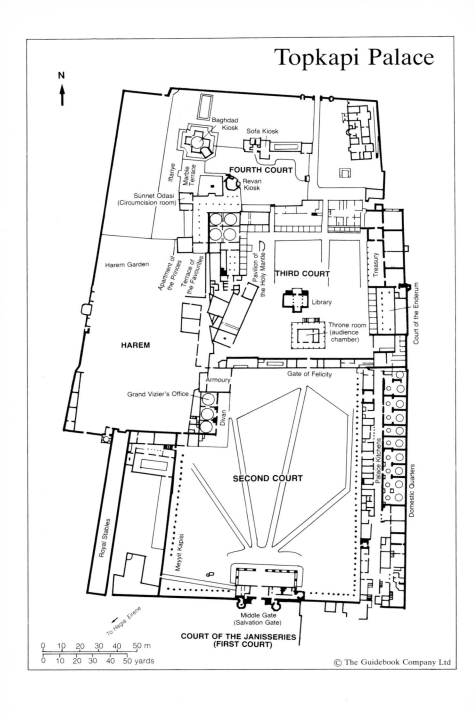

Topkapi Palace

N

Baghdad Kiosk

Sofa Kiosk

İftariye

Marble Terrace

FOURTH COURT

Revan Kiosk

Sünnet Odasi
(Circumcision room)

Apartment of the Princes

Terrace of the Favourites

Pavilion of the Holy Mantle

THIRD COURT

Harem Garden

Library

Treasury

Throne room
(audience chamber)

Court of the Enderum

HAREM

Gate of Felicity

Armoury

Grand Vizier's Office

Divan

Palace Kitchens

SECOND COURT

Domestic Quarters

Royal Stables

Meyyit Kapisi

To Hagia Eirene

Middle Gate
(Salvation Gate)

**COURT OF THE JANISSERIES
(FIRST COURT)**

| 0 | 10 | 20 | 30 | 40 | 50 m |
| 0 | 10 | 20 | 30 | 40 | 50 yards |

march captured Konya from the Seljuks, but then in Cilicia, on the coastal plain, he fell accidentally into the Calycaduus river at Seleucia (Silifke) and was drowned. His discouraged army, decimated by sickness and desertions pushed slowly on to Antioch, by which time it had become so spent in force its remnant was disbanded.

Richard and Philip failed to recapture Jerusalem, but they did succeed in taking Acre from Saladin, which became the capital of Outremer until in 1291 it was taken by Baibars, the Mameluke Sultan of Egypt.

As has been noted, the Fourth Crusade was launched, under the instigation of Pope Innocent III, by Geoffrey de Villhardoin, but it was financed by Enrico Daudols, the Doge of Venice. It is unlikely the Doge had any more intention than capturing Constantinople, which happened, and setting up a kingdom under his control. The intention of Villhardoin had been to capture Egypt as a stepping stone to the recapture of Jerusalem. The result was the Latin Kingdom of Constantinople lasting from 1204 to 1261.

Pope Innocent IV instigated a Fifth Crusade in 1215, launched and fought unsuccessfully in Egypt.

Sights

Sultanahmet—The Old City

TOPKAPI PALACE
FIRST COURT

Sultan Ahmet III loved fountains and tulips. He became sultan in 1703 and each April held a Tulip Festival, at which time the Seraglio Gardens were decked with cages of canaries hanging in trees, and tortoises roamed freely with lighted candles on their backs. A fountain, erected in 1728 and decorated with marble tulips, stands outside the Royal Gate of his palace. Two years later Ahmet was deposed because of his extravagance.

Topkapi was built after the Ottoman conquest, between 1465 and 1478, on the site of the former city built by the Roman Emperor Septimius Severus in the early part of the third century AD, a section of the walls of which are still in place at the rear of St Sophia. After Mehmet II, other sultans made their contributions to its four courts. Ahmet was not perhaps among the more outstanding of the sultans, but he is cherished for his fountains, and during his reign—the Tulip Age—many beautiful buildings were erected in the city, and progressive ideas were furthered through the setting up of printing presses and paper factories.

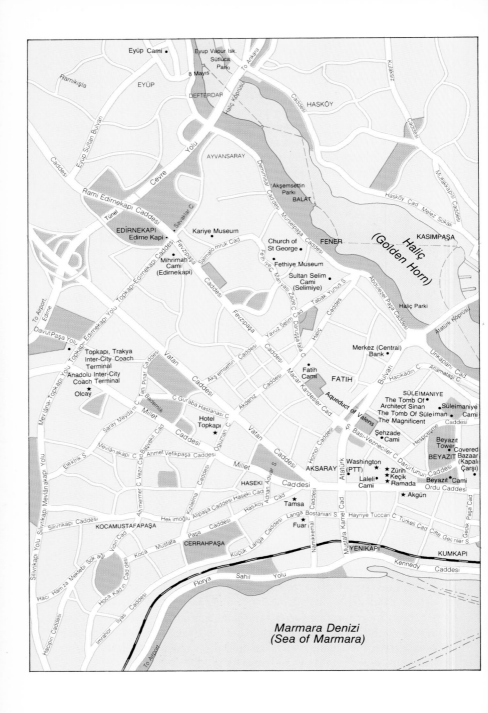

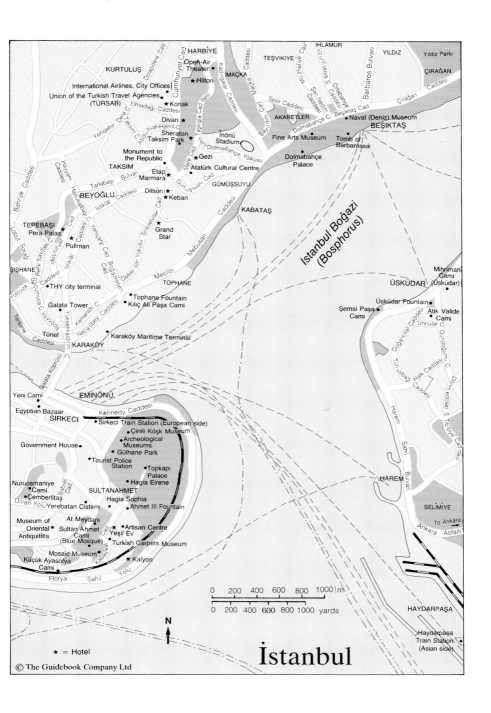

İstanbul

★ = Hotel

© The Guidebook Company Ltd

The **Royal Gate**, or Bab-i-Humayun, leads through the walls of Septimius Severus' rebuilding of Byzantium, which he called Antoninia after his wife. The gate opens on the First Court and entrance grounds of the palace.

Over to the left after entering is the Church of St Irene, **Hagia Eirene**, or Church of Divine Peace. The church was never converted to a mosque and is now a museum. An earlier St Irene had probably been built on the site of a temple to Aphrodite but was burned down in the Nika Riot, and afterwards rebuilt on a lavish scale. What can be seen today is the basilican plan of that rebuilt church— in rectangular layout with a semi-circular apse—with further modification and restoration following yet another fire and an eighth-century earthquake. Artillery armament once displayed on the grounds outside the church has been removed to the Askeri (Military) Museum at Valikonagi Sokak, at the northern end of Cumhuriyet Caddesi in Beyoğlu, where the main road forks to Nişantaşı.

THE JANISSARIES

Near St Irene stood the Mint, and in front of this building stands a great plane tree, known as the Tree of the Janissaries, the Ottoman Royal Corps of Guards. By tradition the Janissaries would assemble at this tree whenever they wanted to dispute their conditions of service or, more drastically, to depose a sultan. Their method of protest was to bang their cooking pots or kettles or, in a serious revolt, overturn them. Under Mahmut II (1808–39), the Janissaries became such a menace to the court and to public order that the sultan secretly deployed artillery units about the palace. When the Janissaries next overturned their kettles and called for the sultan's deposition, murdering the emissaries he sent to parley with them, the sultan mounted a white charger, unfurled the Banner of the Prophet and ordered the artillery to open fire on the Janissaries at point-blank range. Those who survived this onslaught took refuge in their barracks, which were then mercilessly pounded. A handful of survivors fled to the Basilican Cistern, where each was individually hunted down and killed. The Corps was never re-formed.

An **Executioner's Fountain** stands close to the Ortakapi, the Middle Gate and entry to the Second Court. The gate had a prison, and the executioner doubled as the palace head gardener. After execution the head of a ranking person was displayed on the Ortakapi but a less-privileged person had to be content with an ear or a nose set up outside the Royal Gate among the mass of the executed.

SECOND COURT

The **Middle Gate**, Bab-i-Salam, or Selam Kapisi (Salvation Gate), is a double one designed to prevent unlawful entry. Pay the entrance fee here; there is an additional charge for a visit to the Harem. In the vicinity of the gate, excavators have unearthed evidence of the Byzantine Magnaura Palace. On the right of this Second Court are the domestic quarters where the main kitchen with its enormous fireplace, huge cooking pots and cauldrons, as well as iron and copper kitchen utensils, can be seen. In another section is a large display of porcelain and china, gifts to the court from kings, queens and potentates; in other sections are copperware, glassware and silver.

On the west side of the court is the **Divan**, or Kubbealti (Council Chamber), in which the grand vizier, the empire's executive officer, conducted affairs of state. Until the time of Suleiman the Magnificent, the sultan himself used to preside at meetings here, but Suleiman constructed a room with access to his own quarters in the Harem, allowing him to overlook proceedings incognito. Ahmet III discontinued this use of the Divan, whereafter the grand vizier conducted meetings in his own quarters, outside the palace, which then became universally known as the Sublime Porte. There is a private entrance to the Harem behind the Divan; the public entrance is at the back of the Armoury, the next building up on that side.

THIRD COURT

The entrance to the Third Court is the **Gate of Felicity**, or Bab-us-Saade, and the building immediately inside the entrance is the sultan's throne room, or audience chamber. Ambassadors often had to wait on benches at the gate before being summoned to an audience. Here were the quarters of the White Eunuchs, who served the sultan and the palace and were therefore neutralized, not castrated as were the Black Eunuchs who served in the Harem and had their quarters there.

Under a colonnade on the right-hand side, there was a palace school for boys in the **Court of the Enderun**. On graduation the pupils first served the sultan as pages. The rooms here display royal clothing and ceremonial costumes. Next to it, in the former **Treasury**, is the royal collection of jewellery, along with jewel-encrusted daggers, swords, thrones, cots and gewgaws into which jewels have been indiscriminately embedded. The **Library** of Ahmet III, which is at the centre of the main court, has a collection of illuminated manuscripts.

The most sacred building in the Third Court is the **Pavilion of the Holy Mantle**, or Hirka-i-Saadet Dairesi, containing Mohammed's cloak, brought back along with his sword and standard by Selim I after his conquest of Egypt. These three sacred items conferred the title of Caliph on the holder, the highest religious office in Islam.

Lower down on the left of this court is the 15th-century **Ağalar Cami**, and behind it is the discreet **Küshane Kapisi** entrance to the Harem. The **Harem** complex consisted of 250 rooms situated on varying levels, and in the time of Suleiman the Magnificent there were 1,000 selected inmates, as well as other girls in training. Sinan designed part of the **Seraglio** for Suleiman, and a concealed passageway led

The Harem, Topkapi Palace

from that sultan's quarters to the room of his current favourite. The Valide Sultan, the mother of the Sultan, was nominally in charge of the Harem and had her quarters there. Another section consisted of the **Kafes** which was in fact a royal prison for the heir to the throne. Those who lived there were cut off from all contact with society outside the palace: Osman III spent 50 years in the Kafes prior to his elevation as sultan.

Mehmet II, the conqueror of Constantinople, on his accession promulgated the Law of Fratricide—given credence by Koran interpreters—whereby a newly elected sultan, as a safeguard against palace rebellion and conspiracy, had his brothers and other near relatives executed by means of a silken cord. A later sultan suspended this law and restricted action to confinement in the Kafes of only the immediate heir to the throne. In the 19th century, the mad Abdul Hamid II temporarily revived the Law of Fratricide.

FOURTH COURT
Notable in the Fourth Court is the **Baghdad Kiosk** (Bavğdat Köşkü) built by Murat IV and modelled on a building he had seen in Baghdad in 1638, when he captured the city. It has exquisite tiling and faience (decorated porcelain) work, and the rooms,

complete with divans, look out to a courtyard with a fountain and views of the Golden Horn. In the same court the **Revan Kiosk**, an earlier building, is again modelled after a building Murat had noted on campaign. This kiosk has for company the **Sunnet Odasi** of 1641, built by

Calligraphy Gallery, Topkapi Palace

Sultan Ibrahim for the circumcision ceremonies of princes. The **Mustafa Paşa Kiosk**, the Kara Mustafa Köşkü or Sofa Kiosk, was so named because of its low-set sofas in the window bays. Kara Mustafa was the grand vizier responsible for restorations at the

Tugra (monogram) of Suleiman the Magnificent, Topkapi Palace, İstanbul

palace. Pierre Loti, the French novelist of the late 19th and early 20th centuries, received the reigning sultan's permission to stay at this kiosk during his residence in İstanbul.

The pools, gardens and marble terraces of the Fourth Court make it an agreeable place to linger. Overlooking the Marmara Sea is a restaurant situated in a kiosk, once a favourite retreat of Abdul Mecit I. A gateway out of this fourth court leads to **Seraglio Point** where wayward and offending ladies of the Harem, tied into weighted sacks, were dropped into the Bosphorus.

Abdul Mecit (1831–61) ultimately abandoned Topkapi in favour of Yıldız Kiosk, near Beşiktas on the Bosphorus, on the other side of the Golden Horn. He lived there until the Dolmabahçe Palace at Kabataş was completely built.

In their Revolution of 1908 the Young Turks, whose political aim was to bring Turkey out of the dead past and into the 20th century, broke up the Harem and invited relatives of inmates to reclaim their kin. Circassia, in the Caucasus region, had been a favoured recruiting ground for girls, and many villagers arrived from Circassia, as from elsewhere, to claim their kin. Not every odalisque was so claimed, nor did every inmate welcome release from the security the Harem had provided. Unclaimed residents were given house room in the Eski Saray, the Old Palace near the Fatih Cami, which had been the Harem prior to Suleiman's day.

HAGIA SOPHIA

On leaving Topkapi, and passing Ahmet's fountain, **Ayasofya** (in Turkish) or **St Sophia**, the Church of the Holy Wisdom, is on the right. The church from this southeast side looks massive, partly because of the heavy buttresses that were erected during the Latin occupation at the beginning of the 13th century. The Belfry on the west façade is a Latin addition too. The ninth century saw the construction of flying buttresses in support of the main structure. After Byzantine reoccupation of the city in the 1260s, Andronicus II Palaeologos installed other buttresses against the main piers. On its conversion to a mosque, Mehmet II erected a wooden minaret on the southeast corner, later replacing it with a brick one.

Beyazıt II added a stone minaret at the northeast corner, and Sinan was employed by Selim II to erect another on the southwest, and finally in the cause of harmony Murat II added a fourth. Murat also donated two large alabaster urns taken from Pergamum to serve as a *sadirvan* (ablutions fountain) in the forecourt. To add to the mounting clutter, several large tombs were placed on the west side. In general, the exterior aspect of this great building could well discourage a visitor prior to entering it. Yet in fairness, the massive nobility of the entire structure is best seen from the Marmara on a ferryboat making its way to the Princes' Islands.

Constantine, or his son and successor Constantius, is thought to have erected a first church over what had been a temple to Artemis on a site sacred to even earlier deities. This church, as with St Irene, was among the buildings burned down in the Nika Riot of 532. Afterwards, Justinian commissioned Anthemius of Tralles and Isadore of Miletus to build a new and larger church, which was completed in 537. The unique feature of the new building was the round dome set on a square by use of squinches, pendentives and soffits. Twenty years later, weakened by earthquakes in 553 and 557, the dome collapsed; a new, higher one was erected by a nephew of Isadore of Miletus. In 986 the western arch collapsed, and the dome was rebuilt by an Armenian architect. The eastern arch fell in 1347, and this time three Italian architects were employed to undertake repairs that took seven years. In the 19th century, Sultan Abdul Mecit I commissioned Swiss engineers, the Fossati brothers, to place a precautionary iron girdle about the dome.

In magnificence of concept, Justinian believed he had built better than Solomon with his Temple at Jerusalem. Its priceless gold and silver, brocades and precious ornamentation are no longer here: much of it disappeared with the Latins. Its mosaics and frescoes have been plastered over and whitewashed under Islam, its windows boarded up or blocked. Kemal Atatürk ended its use for Muslim worship and declared it a museum, but the low-hanging chandeliers remain, as do the large

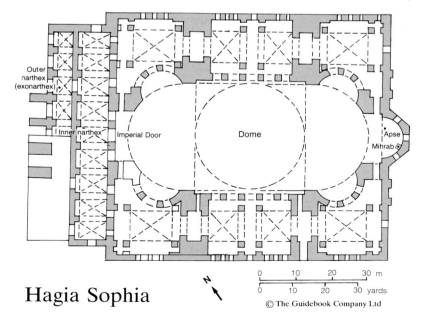

Hagia Sophia

0   10   20   30 m
0   10   20   30 yards
© The Guidebook Company Ltd

medallions with their calligraphic inscriptions of Allah, Mohammed and the first four caliphs.

The tall wooden structure with a stairway leading up to the *minber* (a pulpit) is Muslim, and in the apse is the *mihrab* (the shallow niche that represents the cave in which Mohammed hid from his pursuers on the night of his escape from Mecca). Aligned on Mecca, the setting of a *mihrab* in a converted church can often look off-centre, since the alignment of a church altar is not always built to face true east architecturally. The great dome, which spans 32 metres (105 feet), is supported on four main piers with arches between them and half-domes on the west and east. The eight pillars of the nave are of green Molossian marble and probably came from Ephesus. The porphyry columns of the porticoes are likely to have been cut in Egyptian quarries at Thebes.

Work on the restoration of the mosaics was begun in the 1930s by Thomas Whittemore and his team from the Byzantine Institute of America and was continued by Paul Underwood after Whittemore's death in the 1950s. The lunette (wall in which windows are set) over the main entry from the narthex—the vestibule between the church entrance and the nave—has a detail of Christ between roundels of the Virgin Mary and the Archangel Gabriel, with Leo VI a prostrate interceding emperor. In the lunette over the southwestern entrance to the narthex, Constantine offers his city to Mary, while to Justinian he offers his church. In a room over the southwestern porch, there is a mosaic of Christ between Mary and John the Baptist (St John Prodromos), and there are other portraits of Apostles and of patriarchs. The dome of the apse has a portrait of the Virgin. In the south gallery, the Empress Zoe and the Emperor Constantine IX Monomachus are on either side of an enthroned Christ. Near it another panel has John II Comnenus and his wife Irene in company with Mary, and in another damaged mosaic Christ is again with Mary and St John Prodromos. All these works date from between the mid-ninth and early 12th centuries.

Henry Dandolo, the blind Doge of Venice, the evil counsellor at the time of the Latin assault on Constantinople and its subsequent occupation, rates at least a modicum of sanctity in that an inscribed stone in the women's gallery commemorates him.

Two of the original bronze gates that stood at the southwest entrance have survived. Entrance is now by way of the exo-narthex and narthex on the north-western end.

SULTAN AHMET CAMI—THE BLUE MOSQUE

Go southwest from Ayasofya, through the open area of the former Augusteum to the site of the Hippodrome to arrive at the Blue Mosque; the entrance into the

Hagia Sophia, İstanbul

Blue Mosque (Sultan Ahmet Cami)

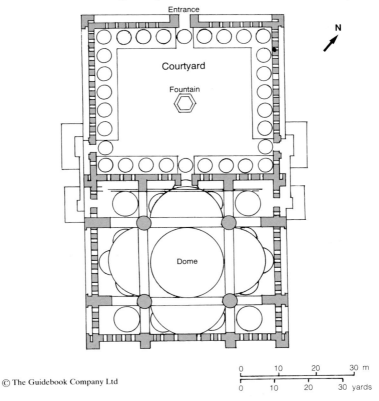

Entrance

Courtyard

Fountain

N

Dome

© The Guidebook Company Ltd

```
0        10        20        30  m
0        10        20        30  yards
```

walled forecourt is on the northwest side. If St Sophia is a paean to the revealed Wisdom of God, Sultan Ahmet is celestial illumination through blue and green İznik tiles: Allah is conveyed in a less-delineated form for the faithful than the son of God in Christian mosaic, portrait and sculpture. Four massive pillars support the 43-metre- (141-foot-) high dome, 23.5 metres (77 feet) in diameter, with half-domes on each side. The somewhat austere effect is set off by filtered and reflected light on the beautiful tulip-patterned tiling. Birds nest in the dome and are in almost constant flight, as in an enormous birdcage.

The mosque, begun under Ahmet I in 1609 and completed in 1616, was built over part of the ruins of the Byzantine Great Palace, the Daphne. Its architect was Sedefkar Mehmet Aga, a pupil of Sinan. From the fine, spacious forecourt with its elegant fountain on six pillars with floral carvings, the exterior mass of the building lightens impressively as it rolls back and rises in ascending curves to the dome. There are six slender minarets. An apocryphal story says that Ahmet was considered presumptuous in erecting six minarets since the only other mosque with six was the Ka'aba at Mecca, and so as not to jeopardize his hope of eternal felicity the sultan donated a seventh to Mecca, which in fact already had seven minarets.

For a Muslim, ritual ablution accompanies the five canonical daily periods of prayer. In the larger mosques, the *sadirvan* is in the mosque's forecourt, though in some, such as the Ulu Cami at Bursa, the fountain is inside the mosque; in a small mosque a tap above a basin in the wall near the entrance may serve as the *sadirvan*.

One must go shoeless into a mosque, and women are expected to be soberly dressed, with covered heads. At large mosques overshoes or slippers can be obtained at the entrance; they are not for hire, but a small tip can be given to the custodian when returning them. Shoes can be left in his care or carried. In general, no objection is raised to the discreet use of a camera inside a mosque.

THE HIPPODROME

The main gateway from the forecourt of the Blue Mosque leads into the **At Meydani** which was the site of the Hippodrome. The Daphne section of the Great Palace here had an entrance into the Royal Box, the Kathisma.

In Constantinople, chariot racing was the principal spectacle, not gladiatorial contests as in the Coliseum in Rome. This was interspersed with light entertainment—dancers, acrobats and singers—or heavier spectacles in the form of a public execution or the humiliation of a captive of distinction or perhaps a fallen emperor, as with Andronicus I. The display could be gruesome, as when Basil I blinded 15,000 Bulgarian prisoners, or idiosyncratic, as with Constantine V's alleged mustering of the city's monks and nuns and ordering them to copulate on pain of execution or blinding. The humiliation of a captive, however, not unusually might have ended with an act of clemency, such as granting permission to stay on in the city with accommodation and a job. Draperies were hung in the Royal Box to indicate the form of entertainment for the following day. The Emperor, the human being with the closest edge on divinity, adjudicated from the Kathisma.

Competing charioteers wore the colours of one or other of the factions, a legacy from Rome, though they seem not to have been politically organized at first. Later, the Greens were recruited from and supported by the lower social groupings; the Blues came from the better off. There had been Whites and Reds as well, but the Whites joined the Blues, and the Reds merged with the Greens. Inter-faction fighting was frequent, more often than not with casualties, even fatalities. Some

Blue Mosque towards dusk

civil responsibilities were expected of the members, such as serving as supplementary police or as standard bearers in civic processions or triumphal marches.

The Nika Riot lasted eight days and culminated in the Hippodrome, with a great part of the city destroyed, damaged or burning. According to the historian Procopius, Justinian's nerve, about to crack, was held firm only by the greater determination of Theodora, his empress. About 30,000 Greens were massacred by the imperial troops, and Justinian rebuilt the city.

Of the monuments that were set up along the centre spine of the Hippodrome, only three have survived. The one that attracts most attention is the **Serpent Column**, transferred by Constantine from its original site at Delphi in Greece where it had been placed to commemorate the victory of the Greeks over the Persians at Plataea in 478 BC. Only part of one head of three entwined serpents exists now, and this is in the Archaeological Museum. According to René Guerdon, this monument once dispensed wine, milk and honey through its three mouths, but the Patriarch Theophilus in his day considered it a source of evil and went out one night to axe the heads of the 'dragon'. He succeeded in destroying two before the night watch stopped him. The benignity of the serpents, though, was made manifest when one sultan, also considering the monument malign, had the remaining head removed, and the city afterwards became infested by snakes.

The **Theodosian Column** was brought from Karnak by Theodosias I (379–95). Carvings in relief with inscriptions in Latin and Greek at the base of the granite column record events of the emperor's career.

The **third obelisk** is one that was rededicated to Basil I (867–86) by Constantine Porphyrogenitus (913–59) in honour of the former emperor's reign. The gilded plaques that once adorned this monument were removed for their value by Dandolo's soldiers, as was the sculptured group of four Bronze Horses set up above the portal of St Mark's in Venice.

The fountain at the northeast end of the Hippodrome, the **Alman Çeşmesi**, or Kaiser's Fountain, was a gift from Kaiser Wilhelm to Abdul Hamit II in 1898.

At the rear of the Marmara University offices at the southern end of the At Meydani, excavation and reconstruction have established part of the Hippodrome's curved retaining wall, which had been built up to counter the steep slope of the hill at that end.

OTHER OLD CITY SIGHTS

On the opposite side of the At Meydani from the Blue Mosque is the **Museum of Oriental Antiquities**, housed in the former 16th-century Palace of Ibrahim Paşa, named for a grand vizier of Suleiman the Magnificent. Besides the exhibits, the building itself is of considerable interest.

The **Artisan Centre** (see Crafts, page 44) can be found on Kabasaçal Caddesi by going out of the open place in front of St Sophia at its southwestern corner. The courtyard of this restored *medrese* can be a cool, quiet place in which to rest. There is a fountain. Its workshops are under the arcade that surrounds the central court. Next to the Artisan Centre on Kabasaçal Caddesi is **Yeşil Ev**, a restored timbered mansion, which has been converted to a hotel and restaurant. The garden here has a marble pool, a conservatory and flowered arbours. Reconstruction of these two buildings was sponsored by the Turkish Touring and Automobile Club.

The **Basilican Cistern** is located on Soğukçesme Caddesi, which is off the roadway that runs downhill from the north side of St Sophia. It is on the line of the walls built by Septimius Severus. The cistern, which had been dry for a long time, has now been converted into an attractive restaurant, with its tables among the ancient columns. Beside it, and along Antoninia's ancient wall behind St Sophia, a row of timbered houses has been converted into an attractive pension, with accommodation and restaurants.

On the opposite side of the open place in front of St Sophia, the site of the former **Baths of Zeuxippus** has been refashioned and landscaped as a park. When the silkworm was first brought to the city from China by two Byzantine monks, the Baths were converted to an imperial silk factory. Beside the park on the southwestern corner of the open place, a former Turkish bath has been reconstructed and opened as a museum. The many rooms have been fitted out in keeping with their purpose, and throughout the building there is a display of fine Turkish carpets and *kilims*. In one section, carpets or rugs may be bought or ordered. The rear exit leads into Kabasaçal Caddesi. Entrance is free.

Beyond the northeastern end of the At Meydani and the Kaiser's Fountain is the entrance to the remarkable **Cistern of Philoxenos** or **Yerebatan Saray**, constructed in the time of Justinian. Water was brought to it via the aqueduct, built by the co-emperor Valens (364–78), which spans the valley between the city's third and fourth hills. The cistern has 336 columns supporting arched vaults in brick, and covers an area of 9,800 square metres (11,720 square yards). Effective floodlighting and a wooden walkway that surrounds the whole area have been installed. Most of the columns have their capitals still and most probably were brought here from pagan temple sites. At least two of the columns are set on carved Medusa heads that may well have been brought from Ephesus or Didyma. A café is in operation on a platform below the entrance stairway where the walkway starts. Above the cistern is a brick water tower, one of several in the city.

In Roman and Byzantine times the main street of the city was the Mese, which ran westward from the Augusteum and through the city walls at Hadrian's Gate to link up with the Egnatian Way, the great road east from Rome. The Milion was the post from which all road distances were measured. Alongside the entrance to the Yerebatan Cistern, at the start of Divan Yolu, an excavation has located the site of this milestone, part of which has been uncovered.

The former Great Palace, the crown of a vast complex of hillside buildings, pavilions, gardens, stairways and stoas, was very nearly a total ruin at the time the Blue Mosque (Sultan Ahmet Cami) was built there. What has survived are a number of fine mosaics of the sixth century, some of which are *in situ*; others have been moved and reset in what is now the **Mosaic Museum**. The museum is on Torun Sokak, downhill from the northwestern corner of the open place in front of St Sophia but also reached from the southeastern end of the Hippodrome. Entrance is in the arcade of the Arasta Bazaar, a reconstructed unit of tourist boutiques and carpet sellers.

The First Court of Topkapi Palace is part of **Gulhane Parki**, which is encompassed within the walls of Septimius Severus' city, and on the northern side runs downhill to the Bosphorus shore. From Ayasofya follow the line of the walls northeastwards down towards the Bosphorus to reach the entrance into the park and the **Archaeological Museum**. Exhibits include many from early and prehistoric periods as well as Hellenistic, Roman and Byzantine. A notable exhibit is the item known as the **Alexander Sarcophagus**, excavated at Sidon in the Lebanon and believed by some to be that of the Macedonian conqueror. It has fine relief carvings, including one of a hunt. A companion sarcophagus is that of the **Weeping** or **Mourning Woman**, which also has beautiful carvings and is assigned like the other to the fourth century BC. An exhibit from Cyprus is of a savage caveman-like Heracles with club.

In the close neighbourhood of the museum is the **Çinili Kiosk** of 1472, one of the very earliest Ottoman buildings in the city, where Mehmet II is said to have resided while the new Topkapi Palace was under construction. Its style is pleasing Persian with large open-fronted tiled and vaulted chambers know as *eyvans*. Now a tile museum, among its exhibits is a Seljuk *mihrab* from Karaman in dark-blue faience with traditional stalactite pattern.

Lower down in the park, towards the shore, the **Column**, known as that of the Goths, is of obscure origin. It has been attributed to Claudius II (268–70) but also to Constantine, though it may have been set up by Septimius Severus: an inscription of a much later date assigns it as a victory monument to the defeat of a Gothic incursion.

In the park is a small zoo, which contains a section of birds of prey that is not without its mesmeric fascination. Many visitors might feel outraged by the caged dogs on display.

VICINITY OF SULTANAHMET
ÇEMBERLITAŞ
Set off westward along Divan Yolu from the Milion. After several hundred metres, a little off to the right is the **Çemberlitaş**, or **Burnt Column of Constantine**, so called because of its having been damaged by fire.

In Constantine's day there was an oval forum situated here at what may have been the west gate of Antoninia. On its erection, the column of nine high drums was surmounted by a statue of Constantine as Apollo, and the orb he carried was said to contain a fragment of the True Cross. At the foot of the column was a sanctuary in which were relics claimed to be from the crosses of the two thieves who had hung with Christ on Calvary, the baskets from the loaves and fishes miracle, a jar belonging to Mary Magdalene and presumably used by her in the washing of the feet, the palladium of ancient Rome and a wooden statue of Athena from Troy.

In 1150 a gale blew three drums and Constantine's statue off the column. Bronze wreaths once covered the joins between the drums, but these were likely to have been taken as loot by the Latins, or perhaps lost in a fire. After the column had again been damaged, Sultan Mustafa II (1695–1703) made good the loss of the wreaths with iron bands.

A shopper's paradise, the Kapalı Çarşı (covered market) or Grand Bazaar

THE GRAND BAZAAR AND VICINITY

Between Constantine's Column and the Kapalı Çarşı, the Covered or Grand Bazaar, there are two mosques of interest, the **Atik Ali Paşa Cami**, which is one of the oldest in the city, and the **Nuruosmaniye** (Light of Osman). The Atik Ali was built in 1497 by a grand vizier of Beyazıt II. It is on the same side of the road as the Çemberlitaş. A little further on again, and off to the right, is the Nuruosmaniye, a mosque begun in 1746 under Mahmut I (1730–54) but completed by Osman III (1754–7). The interior is impressively uncluttered, and a multitude of windows let in light. One of the ten or more entrances to the Grand Bazaar can be reached down beyond the Çemberlitaş and the mosque. The main entrance to the **İç Bedesten** (Old Bazaar) is further along on Divan Yolu.

The bazaar is a complex of market areas. The İç Bedesten was in origin Byzantine; Mehmet II began extensions in 1461, and the complex grew. Fire has on more than one occasion destroyed whole sections, and there has been damage by earthquakes; repairs and reconstructions are undertaken on an almost permanent basis. Within the complex several main avenues and something like 100 cross streets or arcades exist.

A *bedesten* is a separate vaulted court, each a centre for a particular trade. The jewellers' is among those most advertised, but the merchants of fine rugs are numerous, as are those dealing in leather and suede. The *bedesten* for brocades is also an auction hall, where the items on display in the morning are for sale in the afternoon. A visit or two is required to become acquainted with those *bedestens* of your particular interest. You may harbour a belief that bartering and oriental bazaars go hand in hand, but fixed prices are more the order of the day now, although vendors can be found who enjoy a haggle for its own sake. If you happen to be in a hurry over the purchase of a leather garment and cannot find one off the peg, there are tailors who can measure and make one in a matter of hours, including a fitting. The bargain hunter should perhaps temper enthusiasm with the realization that a bargain is the exception rather than the rule, particularly regarding jewellery.

There are over 3,000 shops, including restaurants and cafés, in the covered market. Streets on the northeast side of the bazaar lead down, shops all the way, to the Mısır Çarşısı, the **Egyptian** or **Spice Bazaar**, which is situated just off the waterfront at Eminönü on the Golden Horn, close to the western egress from Galata Bridge.

Within the complex of the Grand Bazaar are several *hans*, or inns, in particular the **Valide Han**, built in 1651, and the **Zincirli** at the northwest corner. Throughout Turkey such *hans* provided accommodation for merchants, their animals and their merchandise, as well as for travellers. A *han* is a large rectangular structure that has an open central courtyard, off which are the stables for animals and storage space for merchandise; a balcony overlooking the court provides access to the rooms for merchants and travellers. Many abandoned *hans* are still standing. You may find some still in use, with few refinements but of agreeable ambiance.

SULEIMANIYE CAMI

This mosque is situated on a hill counted as İstanbul's third to the northwest of the Grand Bazaar. It was built by Sinan between 1550 and 1557 for Suleiman the Magnificent. In his ambition to create

Mosaic in the Kariye Museum (formerly the Church of the Chora Monastery), dating from the 14th century

Süleimaniye Mosque

0   10   20 m

0   10   20 yards

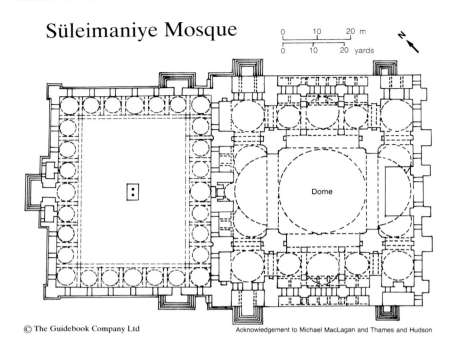

Dome

© The Guidebook Company Ltd

Acknowledgement to Michael MacLagan and Thames and Hudson

an individual Ottoman style this great architect had already built two mosques, the Sehzade and the Mihrimah, but for this new one he seemed to revert to that unassailable achievement, Hagia Sophia, as his model. There are resemblances of both buildings, though the Suleimaniye dome is smaller and set higher. Because the buttresses supporting the dome have been partially concealed within the walls they are less conspicuous than those of St Sophia, and the mass of the piers has been lightened by stalactite-patterned niches. Light comes from windows designed by an artist known as Ibrahim the Drunkard, whose method was to pour lime into clay moulds into which his glass was then set. Calligraphic inscriptions within the mosque are by Hassan Celebi. The *minber* is in carved marble with wood and inlaid mother-of-pearl, and the *mihrab* is in marble.

The courtyard of the mosque is as pleasing as the interior, with marble paving, columned porticoes all round and cupolas. There are four minarets, two on the east with three balconies each and two shorter ones on the west, each with two balconies. The number of minarets and the combined number of balconies are said to have significance in that Suleiman was the fourth sultan to reign in İstanbul but was the tenth in line from Osman.

Within the large complex of buildings surrounding the mosque, there are *medreses* including two that have been turned into a library, a former *imaret* or soup kitchen for the poor, a former hospital and a hostel. In the grounds is the octagonal red and white marble tomb of Suleiman. Faience tiling on the interior of the dome is dark red in colour and set with crystal roses with emerald centres. Nearby is the tomb of his favourite wife, Haseki Hurrem or Roxellana, revered as a woman of strong character, who may have been of Russian parentage. Sinan's tomb is also in this complex.

CHURCH OF ST SAVIOUR IN CHORA: KARIYE CAMI

Because it has outstanding mosaics and frescoes, a visit to this church, now a museum, is imperative. It is situated off to the right of Fevzi Paşa Caddesi as you approach the Edirne Gate in the Theodosian Walls of the city. An earlier church existed on the site, which at that time was outside the walls of Constantine's city. The church was rebuilt in the eighth century after the conclusion of the Iconoclast controversy, and again in the 12th century by Mary Ducaena, mother-in-law of Alexius Comnenus. Theodore Metochites (1303–26), the Grand Logothete of Andronicus II (1282–1328), rebuilt it again, adding not only the narthex, exo-narthex and south chapel but also commissioning every inch of wall and ceiling space to be covered with mosaic and fresco decoration. It was a late flowering of Byzantine art wherein Christian belief is illustrated through the depiction of Gospel stories and miracles, with apostles, saints and the holy family portrayed. All this remarkable work was hidden under plaster and whitewash until the building was declared a museum. Then Paul Underwood and his assistants from the Institute of Byzantine Studies in Boston, already mentioned in connection with the recovery of the mosaics of St Sophia, began the restoration work that has achieved such magnificent results. The museum is now the centre of a harmonious pedestrian complex with newly restored old houses and a pleasant hotel.

Admiring the mosaics at the Kariye Museum calls for a great deal of looking up, and a visitor might well consider it an advantage to take along a small cushion for sitting or lying on the floor, as well as opera glasses for appreciating details of the work.

BEYAZIT II CAMI

Divan Yolu (the former Mese) becomes Ordu Caddesi, and by continuing on beyond the Covered Bazaar you reach Beyazıt Meydani, which in Byzantine days was the Forum of Theodosius, or the Forum Tauri. On the right is the university campus. Just inside the campus is the **Beyazıt Tower**, built for fire-watching by Mahmut II (1808–39) to replace an original wooden tower.

The Kariye Museum (formerly the Church of the Chora Monastery) lies just inside the city wall. The superb mosaics and frescoes date from the 14th century

Beyazıt II's mosque (Sultan Beyazıt 1481–1512) is one of the earliest Ottoman constructions, modelled perhaps on St Sophia, with Seljuk overtones. Its former large paved courtyard was an assembly centre for pigeons, and there is a story that a poor widow once presented the sultan there with a brace of pigeons, whereupon the pigeons afterwards obtained the protection of the mosque. English writer and novelist Robert Liddell maintained that by feeding the pigeons at this mosque you invariably got news of absent friends. As a consequence of roadway reconstruction, the courtyard is now gone.

The mosque has been incorporated into a park, with the sultan's tomb in the garden, as well as that of his daughter, and the tomb of notable 19th-century statesman Mustafa Resat Paşa. East of the mosque in an enclosed court is Sahaflar Çarşısı, the secondhand book market. An 18th-century *hamam* here is no longer in use as a bath, but at the entrances to the Grand Bazaar are two reconstructed *hans*, or inns, the Hasan Paşa and the Simkes. The Beyazıt tower, a fire-fighting construction, stands inside the University grounds. Two large, underground shopping malls lie on this widened roadway running to the road junction at Aksaray.

CHURCH OF SAINTS SERGIUS AND BACCHUS: KÜÇÜK AYASOFYA

By going downhill from the southern end of the At Meydani, past Torun Sokak and the Arasta Bazaar, you can find Küçük Ayasofya near the Marmara sea walls on Küçük Ayasofya Sokak. You may have to locate the warden to open up, but almost inevitably a small boy of the area will appear and run to fetch the warden or at least bring back the key.

The architects of the church, now in use as a mosque, were those chosen for the larger Hagia Sophia. The church, known as the Little St Sophia, was dedicated in 527, earlier than the greater church, and may well have been its model. Sergius and Bacchus were soldier converts to Christianity, martyred under Diocletian and Maximium (284–305). Justinian believed these two saints had interceded successfully on his behalf when he was under sentence of death after being implicated in a plot against the Emperor Anastasius.

The church—an octagonal shape within an irregular quadrilateral—has a dome set without the use of pendentives. Columns stand back from the centre and contribute to semi-circular recesses; 18 columns in the gallery are connected by arches. A frieze running below the gallery has an inscription to Theodora, praising her charitable activities, and includes a reference to St Sergius. Monograms of Justinian and Theodora are set on some columns.

Below, the railway runs along the line of the sea walls. Against the walls was the **Bucoleon Palace** built by Theodosias II (408–50). Only three windows with their carved balcony supports remain. On the man-made harbour was the sculpture of a bull in conflict with a lion. When Rhodes fell to the Turks, the lion, it is said, turned its head defensively to the east. Justinian restored this palace. One of its pavilions was known as the Porphyra, and a child born there of a reigning emperor was called Porphyrogenitos (born in the purple), as was Constantine VII. Nicephoros Phocas (963–69) restored the palace, only to be assassinated here. Manuel I Comnenus (1143–80) brought back a porphyry slab on which he believed Christ's body had lain after being taken down from the cross, and carried it on his back up the long stairway from the quayside.

CITY WALLS

Long stretches of the **Theodosian walls** of the city exist in surprisingly intact condition, and in a sense still control the city's entrances and exits as they did in the days of Byzantium. A recent mayor of İstanbul has tried to tidy up the past by reconstructing sections of the walls and the city entrances, as well as the roadway intersections, particularly between Hadrian's Gate and the Yedikule Tower on the southern Marmara section. Alas, this has not been done with strict fidelity to the antique model, even though the convenience of today's citizens has been enhanced.

Walls were built by Septimius Severus (193–211), enclosing his city of Antoninia, that area now occupied by Topkapi Palace, At Meydani, the Baths of Zeuxippus and Gulhane Park. Restored sections of this old wall survive. When Constantine decided to build New Rome he paced out the boundary of the city himself, drawing the line of his new walls with the tip of his spear, claiming that an invisible guide was walking ahead of him. His walls have not survived. The **Aqueduct of Valens** (364–78), which stands in such prominent majesty still at Unkapani, a city entrance, may have replaced an aqueduct of Constantine's time. It was built perpendicular to the line of Constantine's walls which ran along present Atatürk Bulvarı from the Yenikapi (New Gate) on the Marmara through the Aksaray road junction to the Atatürk Bridge.

In 413, Anthemius, the regent for Theodosius II (408–50), built new walls, the present ones, to the west of Constantine's, stretching from the Marmara to the Golden Horn. Anastasius (491–518) built additional walls even further to the west, running for 105 kilometres (65 miles) from the Marmara to the Black Sea. Although there are no walls there, this line is now a recognized feature of current Turkish defence strategy.

Topkapi, or **Cannon Gate**, the St Romanus Gate for the Byzantines, was the focal target of Mehmet II's assault on the city. Ordu Caddesi, which becomes Millet Caddesi after the Aksaray junction, runs to it. Here, because the gateway was in the valley of the Lycus River the attackers on the hills had an advantage of height over the defenders on the walls. A huge cannon designed and built by Urban, a Hungarian engineer, pounded the walls here. It took two months to haul this piece the 250 kilometres (155 miles) from Edirne. Loading the cannon took two hours, which gave welcome respite to the defenders and the opportunity to repair damage, and the gun had to be doused with gallons of oil after firing. After only a limited use the cannon blew up, killing Urban himself and many members of the gun crew. Mehmet, however, had other smaller cannons at work on the walls. The last Byzantine emperor, Constantine XI Dragases, died at this gate on the final day of the siege.

The next major gate to the north of Topkapi is the towered **Edirne Kapi**, the exit through the walls on Fevzipaşa Caddesi. It is the principal gate in today's reconstructed road system. However, this was the Byzantine Charisios Gate, named after the leader of the Blues when an emergency wall construction programme was undertaken by the city prefect, Constantine Cyrus. The walls are at their highest elevation here, before descending to the Golden Horn. North of the gate is **Tekfür Saray**, the Byzantine palace of Constantine VII Porphyrogenitos, of which some good stonework and brickwork is left. Another gate in the walls here, the **Kerkoporta**, reportedly was left open by mistake after a Byzantine sortie, enabling a small body of Turks to gain entrance. By all accounts the incident need not have been disastrous, except that defenders elsewhere seeing the standard raised by the Turkish infiltrators panicked, believing the walls had been irrevocably breached, and their resistance crumbled. The walls from here to the Golden Horn now include that of the outer wall of **Blachernae Palace** favoured by the Comneni emperors, and its gate the **Karsios** or **Oblique Gate**, outside which Alexius III Angelos allowed the army of the Fourth Crusade to camp, from where they successfully attacked the city.

At the Marmara end of the Theodosian walls was the **Golden Gate**. The present road from İstanbul's airport, Florya Highway, running along the Marmara, enters the city near this former gate. Triple-arched, the gate was used by royalty, for whom the central, taller arch was reserved. The suburb of Hebdomon and the military Campus Martius lay outside the walls. Hebdomon had a port, and a palace where an emperor returning from an overseas campaign stayed prior to his triumphal entrance into the capital. If he was a newly elevated emperor, acclaimed by the troops on the Campus Martius, his exaltation would be confirmed at the monastery church of **St John in Studion** inside the walls. The meagre ruins of that church, protected by fencing, still can inspire appreciation. Between the Golden Gate and the shore was the Postern of Christ, said to have borne his monogram. What has survived of the Golden Gate is now incorporated in a fort known as **Yedikule**, or the **Castle of the Seven Towers**, an Ottoman construction. The Byzantines had a prison at the Golden Gate, where an ambassador or a plenipotentiary might sometimes be imprisoned, as was Luidprand, the Bishop of Cremona, and the Ottomans used Yedikule for similar purposes.

The main city wall was four metres (13 feet) wide and 13 metres (43 feet) high. It had 96 towers—square, pentagonal or octagonal—20 metres (66 feet) high. Ahead of this wall were protection ramparts with their towers, a moat and a sentry platform.

The Golden Horn

For an excursion up the Golden Horn, a ferry service starts from Eminönü in the old city. It calls at stations on either side of the waterway, which is now spanned by three bridges. Atatürk Bridge crosses from Unkapani on Constantine's line of walls to Azapkapi on the Galata side. Above Atatürk Bridge some of the ferry stations have historic connotations, such as Fener (on the left bank) which was the Phanar district where many Greeks settled after the conquest of the city and became known as Phanariotes. The **Church of St George** here became the seat of the Greek Orthodox Patriarch; it was rebuilt in 1720. Kasimpaşa (on the right bank) is likely to have been the place where Mehmet II relaunched his boats after they had been hauled overland from the Bosphorus. The Byzantines had closed the Golden Horn with a chain stretching from Seraglio point to Galata, and Mehmet, his navy having failed to force an entry by direct attack, hit upon this arduous surprise tactic, thereby completing the city's encirclement.

Roadway reconstruction has opened up the western side of the Golden Horn, and Fener (Phanariot), Ayvansaray and Eyüp are now easily accessible by road; the former sea walls and ancient buildings along it can be seen to full advantage.

Hasköy, higher up on the right bank, was the quarter of the Sephardic Jews, given sanctuary here after their expulsion from Spain.

On the western or left bank, Ayvansaray was the quay for the Blachernae Palace, where the land walls met the sea walls, the latter running all the way down the Golden Horn to Seraglio Point. In a street near the quayside is the **Ağhiasma of Mary**, the most holy Byzantine shrine in the city. Mary's robe was kept here to serve as a talisman, and was displayed whenever the city was threatened by assault. During the course of the annual celebration of Mary's Day, on 15 August, an emperor would plunge three times into this sacred pool. The **Koça Mustafa Cami** here was formerly the Church of St Peter and St Mark, wherein the holy robe had been kept prior to its transfer to the Ağhiasma.

THE BIRDS OF FLORYA PLAIN

*T*he boys were always up very early in the morning, but even before they had woken, at the first glimmer of dawn, Tugrul would be there already. How many times had I seen him rushing along the fringe of the wood towards the poplar tree, as though fearful of missing something, and then, if the boys were still asleep, he would draw a deep breath and slump down in his accustomed place in front of the barbed wire, resting his chin on his knees.

On Florya Plain, the bird hunt was in full swing now. So it is each year when October comes, when the north wind is blasting, ice-cold, keen as a razor's edge, or when the sea is churned into a furious foaming mass by the lodos that blows from the south. Then, clouds of tiny birds are tossed hither and thither, tracing zigzags in the air, flurrying down over the thistles, only to rise again in the same instant, veering swiftly over the sea, on to Cekmece Lake and back to the wood, grazing the crests of the trees, a scatter of many-coloured specks in the sky, vanishing from sight and appearing again. But on warm sunny days, they swarm down over the thistles in thousands, twittering madly, and devour with frightening rapacity the seeds of the dried shrubs that, in the summer, had flowered bright yellow, dyeing the whole plain saffron.

Ever since ancient Byzantium, through Ottoman times to this day, these tiny birds, coming no one knows whence and going no one knows where, have sojourned here, on Florya Plain, from October to the end of December. And ever since, the people of Istanbul town have set all kinds of snares to capture them. They capture them, and then sell them, in front of churches if they are Christians, synagogues if they are Jewish, or mosques if they are Moslems. 'Fly little bird, free as the air, and meet me at the gates of Paradise.' And so, all over Istanbul town, the sky will be swarming with little birds delivered from captivity by those who wish to ensure a place in Paradise cheaply. Children especially, and also the very old...

Many years ago, it must have been when I first came to Istanbul, I had seen in Taksim Square a very old gentleman, wearing a fur-collared coat, and a little boy of six or seven. From a barefooted youngster they were buying tiny wild-eyed yellow birds and casting them up into the air.

They would take it in turns, first the old gentleman, then the little boy, and at every throw the three of them would cry out in pure joy. And there was that cat huddling in the bushes under the plane trees... Every now and again, one of the small birds, unable to take wing, would fall to the ground and flutter off into the bushes. No sooner there than that monster of a cat would pounce on it, tear it apart with claws and teeth, and devour it greedily. Then, licking its chops, the cat would lie in wait, quite still, its eyes on the air, for its next prey.

Nowadays, it is only in the courtyard of Eyup Mosque that children manage to sell a bird or two to be set free. So they prefer to take them to the bird market in Eminonu where the dealers select a few of the finest out of hundreds, in order to sell them at a high price to bird fanciers. And the children go back home, weary, disappointed, toting their cages still filled to the brim, wondering what to do with all these birds.

If the chroniclers of Istanbul city neglect the history of these birds and of the fowlers on Florya Plain, then their work, according to me, will not be worth much. Indeed, it will all have been in vain. The joy of millions of little birds set free in front of churches, synagogues and mosques for hundreds of years, and the joy of so many people too... Is that an adventure of small importance? One day, I know it, some person, imaginative, wise, pure of heart, will come forward and write the fine history, full of hope and gladness, of the birds of Florya Plain, and then Istanbul city will be a more beautiful, a more enchanting place. Is the magic of Istanbul only in its sea and sky, its rivers and monuments? And what of the Florya birds then?

Yashar Kemal, The Birds Have Also Gone

EYÜP

The third bridge, the newest in construction, crosses the Golden Horn just above Ayvansaray; it links up with the Bosphorus bridges that carry traffic from Europe directly into Asia. Justinian had a bridge constructed about here which was called the Callinicus, and Mehmet II spanned the Golden Horn with a bridge of barrels. Passing under today's Halic Bridge, you reach the last quay on the left bank, Eyüp. This is a place of graves, from the tombs of sultans and princes to the tombstones of the humble and the meek. The **Eyüp Cami** here is dedicated to the Companion and Standard Bearer of Mohammed, who was killed during the Arab siege of Constantinople in 672, but whose burial place was discovered only after Mehmet II's capture of the city. The mosque was built in 1458, and as the saint was again laid to rest, Mehmet himself was present and ceremoniously accepted the Scimitar of Osman. It became the practice for each newly acclaimed sultan to go to Eyüp to pray at the mosque and to receive the scimitar in confirmation of his role as spiritual and military champion of Islam.

The mosque was damaged during an earthquake in the early 1800s and was reconstructed. Light is admitted onto marble and carved ivory through lattice-patterned windows. The inner of two courtyards holds the saint's tomb, little more than a niche in a tiled wall, behind a grille through which a pilgrim may offer his prayers or beg a spiritual favour. In the vicinity of the mosque is a Sinan tomb built for Sokollu Mehmet Paşa, a grand vizier. Mehmet V (1909–18), the last sultan to die within Turkey's borders, also has his tomb at Eyüp.

Climb up the hill at Eyüp on a pathway through a forest of tombstones to a café on the crest. This is a café that Pierre Loti visited often, and it is named after him. In his day it would have offered a clear view of the Golden Horn as it opens up to the Bosphorus, or inland to hills, to the Forest of Belgrade and the Sweet Waters of Europe with their Ottoman aqueducts.

Beyoğlu—The New City

TAKSIM SQUARE

Taksim is the centre of the new city. Buses run to it from the THY air terminal, but it is not all that far to Taksim from there, taxi fares are low, and taxi drivers adhere strictly to the meter.

The **Monument to the Republic** in Taksim Square was erected in 1928 under the guidance of an Italian architect. Between it and the lower end of the square is a railed garden, and beyond this is the **Atatürk Cultural Centre and Opera House**. Standing with your back to the Opera House, the Marmara Hotel is on the left-hand side. On the right-hand side is the stairway entrance to **Taksim Park**, above the bus terminals for various city districts.

From the top end of Taksim Square, by the monument, Cumhuriyet Caddesi (Republic Street), one of the two principal thoroughfares of Beyoğlu, leads off to the right, a broad twin-avenued thoroughfare with a central spine of trees, railed at the Taksim end to restrain haphazard pedestrians from erratic crossings. Along Cumhuriyet, following the line of shops on the right-hand side, is the Intercontinental Hotel opposite the more recently constructed Hyatt International. Further along, beyond the Divan Hotel is the Hilton. On Cumhuriyet, too, between the Hilton and Taksim Square, on both sides, are the offices of the major airline companies, some of the larger restaurants and *pavyons* (nightclubs), and many boutique-type shops selling tourist souvenirs.

İstiklâl Caddesi is a pedestrian thoroughfare leading out of Taksim Square, and is the leading shopping street at the centre of Beyoğlu, with fashion shops, restaurants, cafés, snack bars, cinemas, patisseries, tailors and book shops, most having been recently restored and renovated. The convenient tramway runs down the centre, to Tünel, and as you near the post office, the popular Çiçek Pasaj, once an attractive plebeian, a covered alleyway of beer booths and snack bars next to the flower, fruit and vegetable market, has up-marketed itself into one of the restaurants. The expanded and tidied-up covered market is still there.

While the French Consulate is at the Taksim end of İstiklâl Caddesi, the consulates of the former Soviet Union, The Netherlands and Sweden are further down. For Britons and Americans, consulates can be found by turning right about halfway down İstiklâl Caddesi just after passing the Post Office, and then left immediately into Mesrütiyet Caddesi. The British Consulate is a large rail-enclosed building on the corner, and the American Consulate can be found on the right by following this street for several hundred metres. Mesrutiyet Caddesi leads to Tepebaşı, the district in which the hotel Pera Palas is located, and so on to the THY air terminal at Sishane.

In the very lowest reaches of İstiklâl is the entrance to Tünel. Built in 1877, it is at present the city's only underground railway line—really more of a funicular— and runs down to Karaköy on the Golden Horn waterfront near Galata Bridge.

Tarlabaşı Caddesi, running out of Taksim on the western side, is an old street that has been transformed into a new highway, a principal thoroughfare in the revamped road system between Taksim and Galata. Yet another street leading out of Taksim, in a southeasterly direction, is Siraselviler Caddesi, where there are several medium-range hotels. Off the lower eastern end of Taksim, on the right of the Opera House as you face it, Gümüssüyü Caddesi runs downhill to the Bosphorus waterfront near the ferry station at Kabatas and the Dolmabahçe Palace.

Atatürk, who chose to stay in this palace whenever he visited İstanbul, died there in 1938; all the clocks in the palace were stopped at the exact time of his death.

At its northern extremity, Cumhuriyet Caddesi becomes two prongs of a fork: the lower prong leads through Nişantaşı, and the upper one passes through Osmanbey to Şişli (an inland route to the upper reaches of the Bosphorus and the Black Sea). Osmanbey and Nişantaşı have developed as rival centres to İstiklâl for fashion shopping.

GALATA DISTRICT AND TOWER

Galata, or Pera, was the area of the merchants, the Genoese in particular. Under the Byzantines, the Venetians enjoyed greater and often exclusive trading privileges, with warehousing facilities on the western shore of the Golden Horn. In their mercantile rivalry, the two Italian republics were quite frequently at war with each other in these waters. Still the commercial, banking and shipping centre of the city, Galata stretches along the quays at Karaköy from Atatürk Bridge to the docks on the east side of Galata Bridge and up the narrow and hilly streets that rise above the waterway here. The most conspicuous building in the area is the **Galata Tower**, built with a fire-watching post up top by the Genoese in 1348 when timbered structures were the architectural order of the day. Originally of wood, the tower was rebuilt in 1423. Reconstructed again in the 19th century, the tower had its more recent facelift a few years ago when its top section was converted into a restaurant and nightclub. Sixty-eight metres (223 feet) high, the tower may be climbed by way of the spiralling stone stairway, or ascended by lift. The views from the top will repay the small fee, even if you decide against eating there.

The Bosphorus and the European Shore

Taking Dolmabahçe Palace as the starting point, a tree-lined avenue, Dolmabahçe Caddesi, runs for about a kilometre (0.6 miles) north to Beşiktas. Two Ottoman palaces on this section of road, **Yıldız Kiosk** and the **Çirağan Palace**, have been revitalized: Yıldız with its pavilions and lake as a public park; and Çirağan as an exclusive luxury hotel and restaurant on the waterfront. At Beşiktas the **Tomb of Barbarossa**, designed by Sinan, is situated in a small garden near the ferry station. The notorious, red-bearded pirate became famous and successful as an admiral under Suleiman the Magnificent. Also nearby, sailing ships of many ages are the fascinating exhibits in a **Naval Museum**.

At Ortaköy, the newly developed pedestrian quarter, a little to the north of Beşiktas, the road passes under the western stanchions of the first Bosphorus suspension bridge to reach Arnavutköy, the first of the waterway's residential villages, a place of elegant timbered houses.

Bebek is the next village, developed as a substantial suburb with good restaurants and several *gazinos*. In Turkey a *gazino*, or casino, is a blend of restaurant and music hall—with singers, raconteurs and dancers—catering in general to family eating and entertainment, and unlike a *pavyon* (nightclub) where the show can be considered *risqué*. On the hills above Bebek is the campus of the Bosphorus University, which in origin was an American foundation, Robert College. The grounds are lovely and offer fine views of the waterway.

The castle at **Rumeli Hisar**, erected in three months by Mehmet II and 3,000 workmen, was a principal item in his eventual plan for capturing the city. The walls and towers still stand sound, and the castle is used frequently as a theatre, particularly during the annual İstanbul Arts Festival. The second Bosphorus Bridge most elegantly spans the waterway from a little beyond Rumeli Hisar.

Emirgan has a modern harbour with a dry dock. It was Sosthenion for the Byzantines. The Argonauts built a temple here to a winged mentor who had come to their assistance in a crisis; Constantine built a church, dedicated to the Archangel Michael. Daniel, a notable stylite saint, occupied a column here.

Yeniköy was Neapolis, where a former Byzantine palace on the waterside became a gambling casino, the first one in the city, until a manager, it was said, absconded with the profits. The casino then moved to the Hilton Hotel, the palace becoming a private bathing club and restaurant. The waterside Carlton Hotel is nearby. Today numerous licensed casinos and machine-gambling saloons are scattered throughout the city.

Tarabya has an attractive bay and yacht marina, as well as a multitude of quayside restaurants, all serving indescribably good seafood. It was Therapeia in classical and legendary times when the blind king Phineas was tormented here by the Harpies. On the northern arm of the bay is the large Grand Tarabya Hotel with its casino.

Büyükdere, a village of very fine timbered buildings, has its waterside restaurants too. **Sarıyer**, a little to the north of it, has developed far beyond the rusticity of its simple village origins, having large waterside restaurants, *gazinos* and a sizable fish market as well.

Beyond Sarıyer is Rumeli Kavaği, from where it is unlikely you will be allowed further north along the shore without the permission of the military. Before reaching Rumeli Kavaği (Roman Poplar), **Tellibaba** has the shrine of a Muslim saint, whom infertile wives petition for the blessing of fecundity. **Rumeli Kavaği** has the ruins of a Byzantine fortress, and a public bathing beach at **Altınkum**. From the heights here, the Clashing Rocks of Homer, the gateway to and from the Black Sea, can be observed.

Rumeli Kavağı is some 16 kilometres (ten miles) from Taksim, from whose square you can catch a bus or minibus to the waterside village of your choice, the waterway a perpetual pleasure to travel along, or to sit beside. Restaurants abound, their cuisine of a high standard, though it could be wise to remember that less gaudily canopied eating places are not necessarily less worthy than their flamboyant neighbours, and are certainly less expensive.

Ferryboats no longer ply the Bosphorus regularly, zig-zagging from shore village to shore as once upon a time. This is partly due to roadway construction and introductions, and has deprived some villages of their ferry stations. There is a service from Eminönü to Sarıyer and one or two of the villages. The ferry station on the west side of Galata Bridge. However, this Eminönü service is a diminutive one, with the ferryboats replaced in part by smaller water buses, plying the route to designated stations, which like *dolmuş* wait for a certain number of passengers to board before setting off. Freshly caught, newly fried or grilled fish are for sale from boats moored along the Eminönü quayside.

A good way to enjoy the Bosphorus is to take a ferry boat to Rumeli Kavağı, then return by minibus to one or other of the ferry stations to select a restaurant, preferably one with a waterside view.

Due to the notorious strength of the undertow, the Bosphorus is not an exceptional place to take a spontaneous plunge. It is advisable to use one of the established facilities along its shores. **Kilyos** on the Black Sea, however, has a long sandy beach, full bathing facilities, camping, hotels and other accommodation. It can be reached on the inland route from Taksim by taxi, bus or minibus, or from Büyükdere on the Bosphorus.

Other bathing beaches near İstanbul are on the Marmara Sea at Florya, Ataköy and a little further west at Yeşilköy, a pleasant residential suburb close to the international airport.

Üsküdar—İstanbul's Asian Shore

KIZ KULESI OR MAIDEN'S TOWER

This tower set in mid-stream in the Bosphorus has been erroneously associated with the legend of Leander and Hero, the true location of this event being the Hellespont at the southern end of the Dardanelles, to the southwest. At the time of the Athenian Empire in the fifth century BC a toll post on this rock exacted dues on all shipping passing through the Bosphorus. Later in history the rock acquired a lighthouse, and is now a signals station.

ÜSKÜDAR

This was Scutari at the time of the Crimean War (1853-56) when Britain, France and Sardinia were allies of Turkey against the Russians. At a much earlier date it was Chrysopolis, the Golden City, which was plundered by the Goths in the third century. Prince Igor's Russians held it for a time in the tenth century until driven out by the Byzantine Emperor Romanus Lecapenus. There were Seljuk Turks serving as mercenaries in the army of Nicephorus Botantiates during his attempt to seize imperial power in 1078, offering at least some Turks a chance to observe the potential prize of Constantinople across the water.

A little way back from the quayside, and to the left of it, is the **Mirimah Cami** built by Sinan in 1547, and on the waterside is a fountain erected by the tulip-loving Ahmet III. On the right of the quay is the **Semsi Paşa Cami** of 1580, now a library, and beyond this is the **Yeni Valide Sultan Cami** of 1583.

There are two ferry stations on the quayside: the larger is for the main ferry service from Eminönü and Sirkeci to the Bosphorus stations; the smaller, to the south crosses between Kabatas, near the Dolmabahçe Palace, and Üsküdar, with sailings every half-hour from early morning until 8.30pm. There are other ferry services from Eminönü to Harem Quay close to Üsküdar, and from Karaköy to Haydarpaşa station.

The quayside at Üsküdar skirts the Yeni Valide Sultan Cami and becomes a long esplanade stretching for over a kilometre (0.6 miles) to Harem Quay, and on to the *otogar* (bus station) from where there are coach services to most destinations in Anatolia. For travel by coach into Anatolia it is preferable to use this *otogar*, crossing the Bosphorus from Kabatas and taking a taxi to the terminal, than by risking the frenzy of the *otogar* at Topkapi Gate.

From Üsküdar's quayside you can go by the town road out to the **Selimiye Barracks**, in whose hospital Florence Nightingale worked as a nurse during the Crimean War. Among the cemeteries in this area is one for the Allied dead.

Kadiköy, beyond the Selimiye Barracks and where the Haydarpaşa railway station is, was the city of Chalcedon, founded by Megarans. Their leader Byzas later decided to found Byzantium on the opposite shore. The earlier Megarans were of course sneered at for choosing a site inferior to that of their rival, but they may not have been so stupid after all, since the climate of Kadiköy is far more equable than that of İstanbul. Septimius Severus, in punishing the citizens of Chalcedon for their opposition to him, demolished the city's wall, using the stone for his own project of Antoninia. In 451, the Fourth Ecumenical Council of the Church held at Chalcedon declared the Monophysite Christian doctrine a heresy.

THE EASTERN SHORE

Urban villages are fewer along the eastern shore of the Bosphorus than along the western, and the roadway sometimes leaves the waterfront, or is diverted inland by the road reconstruction system. There are, however, pleasures to be derived from an excursion up the shore, not least to note a number of old timbered houses, many of which have been pleasingly reconstructed.

Beylerbeyı, where the first Bosphorus bridge touches land on the Asian shore, has a castle built by Sultan Abdul Aziz (1861–76). The mad Abdul Hamit II, who while occupying Yıldız Kiosk carried a pistol everywhere and threatened those he believed were plotting against him, was exiled here in 1909, bringing only his cat, the single being he appears ever to have loved. An interesting baroque-style mosque here dates from 1778.

Eight kilometres (five miles) north of Beylerbeyi, at **Kandirli** are two streams, the Kücuksü and the Göksu, known as the Sweet Waters of Asia. There is an organized bathing establishment on the Bosphorus shore here. In the vicinity is an elegant waterside *yali*, an 18th-century timbered villa. An ornate gateway leads into the 18th-century **Göksu Palace** grounds, in which there is a handsome fountain. In the 1850s the meadows through which the Kücuksü ran was a picnic area for the fashionable of İstanbul, and a trysting place. Ladies accompanied by a eunuch or chaperone would stroll on one side of the stream while on the other the gentlemen would pass. By an exchange of wordless expressions, and gestures such as tossing a flower across the water, affections and desires were exchanged.

A little north of Kücuksü is **Anadolu Hisar**, a fort built by Beyazıt I. Unlike the Rumeli Hisar of Mehmet II, its opposite number on the European shore, Anadolu Hisar, is pretty much of a ruin, if a picturesque one. The road system of the second Bosphorus bridge has had its effect on the landscape here. **Kanlıca** to the north is noted for its yoghurt, and there is a mosque built by Sinan for a grand vizier of Suleiman the Magnificent. Another lovely timbered *yali* just to the south of Kanlıca is of 17th-century construction.

The palace at **Çubüklü** was built for the Khedive of Egypt in 1900. **Beykoz**, three kilometres (two miles) to the north, must be considered the most urbane of the eastern shore villages, with an 18th-century fountain in the main square and at least one restaurant over the water. It was here that the Argonaut Pollux wrestled with and killed Amycus, the king who until that time had boxed with and killed any and every stranger who landed on his shore. Out of Amycus' grave grew a bay tree with leaves said to induce madness if chewed.

Further north at **Hunkar iskelesi**, the palace is in use as a hospital. Beyond the Tokat valley and inland a little, on top of **Yusa Tepesi**, or Hill of Josua, there is a grave 12 metres (40 feet) long known as the **Bed of Heracles**. The next and last ferry stop is **Anadolu Kavaği**, whose fortifications, as with those of Rumeli Kavaği on the western shore, were built by the French.

POLONEZKÖY

A day trip from İstanbul could be made to Polonezköy, or it could be included as part of a two-day trip to Üsküdar and the villages on the eastern shore. Lying inland from Beykoz, Polonezköy can be reached by road from Çubüklü or Beykoz, with an overnight stay planned. Polonezköy is not so much a village as an area settled by Polish refugees who were given land to farm by a reigning sultan because of their service to him during the Crimean War. The inhabitants have created a little Poland in lifestyle, and in landscape with its individual farmhouses. Polish home-cooking can be enjoyed in any one, and rooms are available for brief or longer stays, Inevitably, the rapid development of tourism in Turkey has had an ill effect here.

ŞILE

The western Bosphorus has its popular bathing spa on the Black Sea coast at Kilyos, and the eastern Bosphorus has Şile, also on the Black Sea, which is not quite so accessible from İstanbul but is likely to be less crowded as a resort. Its beach is a good one, with accompanying bathing facilities, accommodation and a ruined **Genoese castle**. It can be reached from Beykoz, 73 kilometres (45 miles) away, or by road 020 that branches off the E5 after it has crossed the Bosphorus bridge and is about to join the coastal road south of Üsküdar. The distance by the latter route is 54 kilometres (34 miles).

Other Mosques and Churches

The **Fatih Cami** (Mosque of the Conqueror), begun in 1462, was the first to be built in the city after the conquest. It is on the fourth hill, to the northwest of the Aqueduct of Valens. This was the site of the Church of the Holy Apostles founded by Constantine I but completed by Constantius, his son and successor. Constantine was buried here, but was afterwards disinterred and reburied at Hereke. Justinian enlarged the church, and it became the burial place of a succession of emperors, whose tombs were looted during the Latin occupation of 1204–61.

Mehmet II installed Gennadius as Greek Patriarch here, but in 1461 the patriarchate was transferred elsewhere when the building of the mosque was begun. The architect of the mosque is said to have been Atik Sinan (no relative of the great Sinan), but the structure is also attributed to a Greek architect named Christodoulou, which may well have been Atik Sinan's name prior to a conversion to Islam. The mosque was badly ruined in an earthquake of the 1800s, to be rebuilt. According to a 16th-century travellers, the original mosque had a central dome, and a half-dome above the *mihrab* and above each lateral, suggesting that the design was founded on the earliest Ottoman mosques of Bursa and Edirne. St Mark's in Venice is said to be modelled on the original church of the Holy Apostles.

The **Yeni Cami** (New Mosque) is the impressive-looking mosque with twin minarets that you see as you cross Galata Bridge towards Eminönü and the old city. It was begun in 1592 for the mother of Mehmet III, Safiye, but building was stopped in 1602 on the death of the sultan, renewed again in Mehmet VI's reign and completed for his mother, the Valide Sultan, in 1663. A feature of the exterior is a second *mihrab* in the east wall outside the mosque, for use by latecomers or in the event of a full mosque. The fountain is a fine feature of the forecourt.

MOSQUES BY THE ARCHITECT SINAN

The **Sehzade Cami** is one of Sinan's first constructions, built by Suleiman the Magnificent for his son, Prince Sehzade, who died young in 1543. It is close to Valens' Aqueduct. Supporting the central dome are four half-domes instead of two as at St Sophia and the Suleimaniye. There is fine tile decoration on the prince's tomb.

Construction of the **Mihrimah Cami** may have followed that of Sinan's work on the Sehzade. Mihrimah was the sister of the young prince and was married to the Grand Vizier Rustem Paşa. The mosque (1566) is on the sixth hill up near the Edirne Kapi (Edirne Gate). In this construction Sinan dispensed with half-domes, replacing them with walls and corner turrets in support of the squinches.

The **Rustem Paşa Cami**—a major work of Sinan—stands to the right of the Yeni Mosque, near the waterside, and is dated 1561. The building is constructed on a terrace, with two enclosed stairways leading up to the forecourt. There is fine İznik tiling on the exterior and interior of the mosque. The dome is supported on four pillars, with half-domes replacing the pendentives. The *sadirvan* (ablutions fountain) stands in its own enclosure.

You can find your way to the Sinan **Sokollu Mehmet Paşa Cami** by going downhill from the Hippodrome (At Meydani), past the street with the **Mosaic Museum**, and on towards the **Küçük Ayasofya Cami** (Sts Sergius and Bacchus) but moving gradually to the right. Construction was begun in 1571. The architectural innovation here is the hexagonal support for the dome, having four laterals buttressed by half-domes. A fine doorway enhances a porticoed court, and İznik tiles grace the interior. Sokollu Mehmet was an admiral of Selim II, son of an Orthodox priest and convert to Islam. He married Esmekham, a daughter of the sultan, said to have been a dwarf.

Sinan began the **Piyale Paşa Cami** in 1573 at Kasımpaşa on the northeastern shore of the Golden Horn. As Grand Admiral of Selim II's fleet, Piyale Paşa was defeated by a combined Christian navy under the Venetian Andrea Doria. The design of this mosque is simple in comparison with the architect's more ambitious projects, and broke with tradition with placement of a single minaret at the centre of the façade and not on the right of the entrance, as was customary.

The **Kiliç Ali Paşa Cami** is the mosque of yet another admiral, this one serving under Murat III. For Sinan, this commission came late in his career, in 1580. The mosque is at Tophane, close to the Bosphorus in Galata. To Sinan, the influence here could have been a reversion to the plan of St Sophia, with the architect's installation along both aisles, and the *mihrab* set as though Sinan had an apse in mind while designing it.

The **İskele Cami** or **Büyük Cami** (Grand Mosque) on the quayside at Üsküdar lies beside the ferry station. Built on a platform, it dates from 1547, when Sinan was in middle-age. It is dedicated to Princess Mirimah.

The **Sinan Paşa Cami** was built for an unrelated Sinan, a sailor and brother of the Grand Vizier Rustem Paşa. This mosque is at Beşiktas, on the western shore of the Bosphorus, where the first suspension bridge crosses the waterway. The mosque's exterior has good brick and stone work.

The **Sultan Selim Cami** (the Selimiye) was built for Selim I by Suleiman the Magnificent, his son, on his succession. This early Sinan mosque is on the fifth hill of the city at Yavuz Selim, northwest of the Fatih Cami. The central area has a dome with two adjoining cupolas, and the portico is an impressive one. Again, there is excellent tile and inlay decoration. From the courtyard there is a fine view of the Golden Horn.

Go south on Millet Caddesi, beyond the Aksaray road junction, and to the west. In 1539, Suleiman commissioned Sinan to build the **Haseki Cami** for Roxellana, his favourite wife.

EARLY MOSQUES BY OTHER ARCHITECTS

In Aksaray near the road junction west of Beyazıt Square, the **Murat Paşa Cami** is an early mosque of 1466. Built on a T-shaped ground plan it was erected by Murat Paşa, a grand vizier of Mehmet II. The mosque's central area has two domes above it, and the vestibule runs below cupolas.

In Cerrah Paşa on the Marmara seaboard, the **Cerrah Paşa Cami** stands about halfway to the walls in the area of the Golden Gate. This mosque was built in 1594 for a grand vizier of Mehmet III. The Roman Forum of Arcadius was here, and the base of a column erected for that emperor in 404 in still *in situ*.

18TH- AND 19TH-CENTURY MOSQUES

Near the Dolmabahçe Palace and the ferry station at Kabatas is the **Dolmabahçe Cami**, built in 1853 by Sultan Abdul Mecit. It has the most slender minarets of all the mosques in the city.

In Koçamustafa, west of Cerrah Paşa, the **Hekimoğlu Ali Paşa Cami** was built for Mahmout I in 1735, by architect Araboğlu Meliton Kalfa.

Lâleli is a district east of the Aksaray junction, and the **Lâleli Cami** is on the north side of Ordu Caddesi, the road that extends from Divan Yolu to the city walls. Dating from 1763, except for its minarets, it is not an especially distinguished mosque, but the large courtyard is a most pleasing feature, as it is in many mosques with ablutions fountains.

MOSQUES THAT WERE FORMERLY CHURCHES

On the fifth hill at Yavuz Selim, the **Ahmet Paşa Mescidi** was **St John Prodromos in Trullo**, located near the Selimiye. The Church of St John Prodromos (John the Baptist) is a 12th-century construction, and its semi-circular apse is of smooth construction, in contrast to the more usual angled apse.

The **Fethiye Cami** was the **Church of the Pammakaristos**, also on the fifth hill, a little to the northwest of the Ahmet Paşa, and overlooking the Phanariote (Fener) area of the Golden Horn. A monastery church, it was reconstructed in the 14th century as the Church of the All Blessed, the Pammakaristos. It became the seat of the Orthodox Greek patriarch after the patriarchate was moved from the Church of the Holy Apostles. It was converted to a mosque in 1586, under Murat III. The dome was added after its conversion. There are some very beautiful mosaics uncovered by the restoration team from the Institute of Byzantine Studies in Boston.

In proximity to the Golden Gate, **St John in Studion**, now **Imrahor Cami**, was a notable Byzantine theological centre. Newly elected emperors received ceremonial confirmation of their elevation here, and more than one emperor, either deposed or having relinquished office, retired to St John's to end his days in prayer and contemplation. The St John of the title is John the Baptist, and the monastery's most precious relic was the Baptist's severed head, to which each emperor paid due homage on the anniversary of the saint's execution by Herod.

The Patriarch, Studios, founded the monastery in 463, which became known as that of the Akoimetai, or sleepless ones, the liturgy being celebrated unceasingly by relays of monks. A late seventh-century abbot, Theodore, brought fame to the monastery through his reforms and by the attainment of a high standard of theology, music and calligraphy. A vigorous opponent of iconoclasm, Theodore was ultimately exiled to Büyük Ada in the Princes' Islands, where he died in 826, by the iconoclastic Empress Irene.

St John's was built in true basilican form, with a long rectangular columned hall with aisles, the semi-circular apse, and the entrance by porch and narthex. On its conversion to a mosque, a *sadirvan* was installed in the court. The building was damaged by fire in 1782, by an earthquake in 1894 and by fire again in 1920, after which it was closed to the public. Visible only through a paling, this peaceful area reveals slender columns with lightweight capitals. Note the verd-antique columns of the north aisle, and the narthex colonnade with its architrave and Corinthian capitals. There is part of a mosaic pavement contributed by Michael VIII Palaeologos on his return to the capital as Byzantine emperor after his expulsion of the Latin usurpers.

Located in the Koçamustafa district northwest of Cerrah Paşa is **Koça Mustafa Paşa Cami, St Andrew in Krisei**—if indeed this is St Andrew's. The church was built under Basil I (867–86) over an earlier church. It was rebuilt or modified in 1284, and further structural changes took place when it was made a mosque. Koça Mustafa was a grand vizier to Beyazıt II (1481–1512).

Standing west of the Fethiye Mosque, the **Boğdan Sarayi** may have been the **Church of St Nicholas**. If so, it could have been founded by an Anglo-Saxon of the Varangian Guard, that elite Corps of the Byzantine Court, like the British Brigade of Guards or the American Marine Corps. The members of the Varangian Guard were recruited from northern Europe, with Swedes prominent among men from Scandinavia, though Anglo-Saxon recruits later became numerous in its ranks. The Corps was a forerunner of the Ottoman Janissaries.

The **Gül Cami**, or **Church of St Theodosia**, is at Balat, lying above Fener on the Golden Horn. It is ninth century in origin, with later 14th-century brickwork, while the dome and minarets were added after its conversion to a mosque. The mixture of styles could be called an early example of post-modernism. There is uncertainty about its true identification. Mehmet broke through into the city on St Theodosia's day, and according to legend this church is said to have been packed with people and deco-rated profusely with roses, hence its name, Gül (Rose) Cami.

Situated in the area of the Fatih Cami, the **Eski Imaret Cami**, or **Church of Christ Pantepoptes, the All-seeing**, was built by the mother of Alexius I Comnenus (1081–1118). The interior has lost little of its original identity, though it has been in use as a school. Some very attractive brickwork remains on the exterior of the south side.

Arap Cami, or the **Dominican Church of St Paul and St Dominic**, is in the Galata district. There could have been a mosque here when the Arabs occupied this quarter during their 717 siege of Constantinople, and it may later have been rebuilt, or the earlier building was converted for use by the Dominican Friars. It seems to have reverted to a mosque in 1455 to serve Arab refugees from Spain. In 1808 the building was badly damaged by fire.

The **Zeyrek Kilise Cami**, or **Church of Christ Pantocrator, the All-ruling**, is northwest of the Fatih Cami, standing near the Aqueduct of Valens and above the Atatürk Bulvarı. This monastery church—the monastery founded by the Comnenian Empress Irene or by her husband John II (1118–43)—is in fact a composite of two churches and a chapel. On the northeast side is the original church; the other on the southwest is a larger, late 12th-century building, with a funerary chapel in between, which may have been built by Manuel I (1143–80) to house the tomb of his father, John II, and where later Comneni were buried. The marble slab on which Manuel believed Christ's body had lain, which he had carried up on his back from the Bucoleon harbour to the palace, was placed in this chapel. During the Latin usurpation the Icon of St Demetrius, patron saint of Thessalonica, was kept at the Pantocrator for safekeeping, as was the image of the Panaghia Hodighetria from Blachernae, an icon believed to have been a creation of St Luke's. When Michael VIII returned to Constantinople in 1261 the Panaghia was carried at the head of his triumphal procession through the Golden Gate. Gennadius (George Scholaris) was confined to the Pantocrator by Constantine XI, the last emperor, because of his opposition to the latter's policy of agreement to unification with the Roman Church. On his release after the fall of the city, Mehmet II appointed him Orthodox Patriarch.

The **Bodrum Cami** is in the Zeytinburnu district of the city, southwest of Beyazıt Meydani. This is considered to have been part of the monastery complex of Myrelaion, which Romanus Lecapenus (919–44) established. There are doubts about this identification however, for it could have been built as a monastery or convent of the sixth century and rebuilt under Romanus. Two churches stand one above the other; the lower a basilica of the seventh century, the upper of a later date was built on a cross-in-square pattern. Conversion to a mosque occurred in the 16th century.

The **Sancaktir Mescit** (the Standard Bearer) is situated in Samatya, the district bordering the Marmara to the south of the Fatih area. The site is thought to have been that of the **Gastria**, a monastery built under the Emperor Theophilus (829–42). St Helena, mother of Constantine I, is said to have brought back plant cuttings from the Holy Land and planted them here, hence the district's title Gastria—a *gastra* in Greek is a plant pot. Mehmet II's standard bearer, Hayrettin, is buried here.

On the third hill of the city, to the northwest of the Aqueduct of Valens, the **Vefa Kilise Cami** was **St Theodore in Tiro**. The building was restored in the 14th century, although the façade retained its sixth-century structure, three domes covering the narthex. There are remnants of mosaics. There is some doubt concerning the correct identification of this structure.

The **Kalenderhane, Kalender Cami**, or **Church of Christ Akataleptos**, is southwest of the aqueduct. Christ the Incomprehensible is the designation of this monastery church. Built in the ninth century, it has undergone a number of rebuildings and reconstructions.

Fenari Isa Cami, or **St Mary Panachrantos, the All-immaculate**, is on Vatan Caddesi where this approaches the military postern gate in the walls near Topkapi Gate. It is a two-church structure, with a common narthex. Constantine Lips, a court official of Constantine VII Porphyrogenitos, dedicated the first church; he died in 917. The second church was built by Theodora, widow of Michael VIII. Both structures were badly damaged by fire in the 1920s. Close by is the **Column of Marcian** (470–77), the Kiztasi or Maiden's Column, so named because of a carving of Aphrodite on the column. Five metres (16 feet) high, it has a Corinthian capital, and there are carved eagles on its pediment.

CHURCHES

Other than the Church of St Irene in the First Court of Topkapi Palace, the most important church that has never been converted to a mosque is **St Mary of the Mongols** at Fener. Mary was the daughter of Andronicus I (1282–1328). In order to secure an alliance treaty with the Mongol Great Khan against the Turks, the emperor offered Mary to the Khan as his bride. The account tells that by the time Mary reached the Mongol court the Great Khan had died, but his successor, Abaka, accepted Mary and married her. As her husband was shortly afterwards poisoned by his brother, Mary returned to Constantinople. There is, however, some doubt about her parentage; some claim that she was the bastard daughter of Michael VIII. The church was dedicated in 1265, during Michael's reign, yet Mary's journey seems unlikely to have taken place prior to the late 1270s, and by the time Andronicus had come to the throne both the Great Khan and Abaka were dead, which may also indicate that an existing church was rededicated to Mary.

The church at Fener of St George's has already been mentioned as the seat of the Greek Orthodox patriarchate.

AN AUTOCRAT AT THE HAMAM

Now and then, usually about once in a week, my grandmother had a sociable turn of mind and when these moods came upon her she invariably went to the Hamam. Hamams, or the Turkish Baths, were hotbeds of gossip and scandal-mongering, snobbery in its most inverted form and the excuse for every woman in the district to have a day out. Nobody ever dreamed of taking a bath in anything under seven or eight hours. The young girls went to show off their pink-and-white bodies to the older women. Usually the mothers of eligible sons were in their minds for this purpose for these would, it was to be hoped, take the first opportunity of detailing to their sons the finer points of So-and-so's naked body. Marriages based on such hearsay quite frequently took place, but whether or not they were successful few of us had any means of knowing.

In the hot rooms of the Hamams little jealousies and rivalries were fanned into strong fires and very often fights took place between the mothers of attractive daughters vying for the favours of the same young man.

As against the mothers of daughters the mothers of sons took pride of place. There was a sort of sharp dividing line drawn between them and it was quite easy for a stranger to tell which of the plump, matronly ladies had the best wares for sale. For whereas the mothers of daughters were inclined to laugh a lot, to draw attention to their family groups, the mothers of sons lay aloof on their divans—too conscious of their own superiority to contribute to the general noise and scandalizing. They would lazily nibble fruit, eye the simpering, posturing young girls critically and sometimes accept the offer of having their backs washed by some ravishing young creature but with such condescension that immediately the wildest speculations were engendered in the other female breasts as to why such an obvious favour had been shown at all. The backwashing concluded, the ravishing young creature would be dismissed and one by one the mothers of the ignored daughters would sidle up to the devilish old autocrat who had just had her back washed and whisper the most damning things about the character of the recent, elated, now vanished back-washer.

Irfan Orga, Portrait of a Turkish Family

Marmara Sea and North Aegean Region

The Bosphorus separates the Black Sea from the Sea of Marmara, which on its eastern extremity becomes the Gulf of İzmit. Nine islands, the Princes' Islands or Kızıl Adalar (Red Islands), lie in the Marmara Sea south of the eastern shore of the Bosphorus, their Turkish name derived from the red earth common to them all. A traveller has little reason to linger here other than to tip a hat to the memory of the Emperor Diocletian, whose capital Nicomedia once lay here.

Koçaeli (İzmit) is a modern industrial port at the head of the gulf, and the first major city to be reached after leaving İstanbul on a road journey into Anatolia.

İznik is a walled city with over 100 towers, with three of four gates standing. Many of the city's Byzantine buildings now lie under İznik Lake, whose water level has risen over the years.

Though evidence of Ottoman beginnings is scant, Sogut, southeast of İznik, has been the starting point for the Osmanli tribe's later expansion into an empire. Lying below Uludağ—Mount Olympus to the Mysians—on a shelf above a fertile, well-watered plain that stretches away to the north and east, Bursa became the first capital city of the Ottomans. A little to the west is the spa of Çekirge with its health-giving springs and baths.

Down from the North Aegean coast, from Thrace (Trakya) stretches the Gallipoli peninsula, forming one arm of the Dardanelles, the narrow waterway that joins the Aegean Sea to the Sea of Marmara. During World War I the Western Allies unsuccessfully waged the Battle of Gallipoli here, of special significance to Australians, whose contingents fought heroically. A visit to the battle site can be made from Çanakkale on the mainland opposite.

Travelling south from Çanakkale one can reach ancient Troy (Truva). A visitor today would find it hard to run round the walls of that tragic city as Hector did, chased by Achilles, not because of the distance to be covered, but because of the uneven fall of land about it. There is an absence of impregnable walls or towers, and in fact little to encourage a visitor's imaginings of events that took place at Priam's city throughout ten years of war, as Homer recorded them in *The Iliad*.

Further south from Troy, at Bergama, is the site of Pergamum. The ancient acropolis of Pergamum is to the northeast of the town's centre; the Asclepium (Sanctuary of the Healing God) is off to the west.

Getting There

There is a regular daily ferry service to the largest of the Princes' Islands, Büyük Ada, leaving from Eminönü at the shore of the Golden Horn at the western side of Galata Bridge. After stopping at the islands, the ferry continues across the Gulf of İzmit to Yalova on its southern coast. Seventeen kilometres (ten miles) south of İstanbul, there is a ferry at Kartal to Yalova, from where İznik (Nikaia), Bursa and Troy are easily reached by road.

From Üsküdar it is possible to use the old Ankara road to Kocaeli (İzmit), the road for a time running alongside the railway, and passing through the villages of Hereke and Gebze, and so avoid some of the unattractive aspects of the new highway that runs as a viaduct sometimes above its ancient partner. Kocaeli is some 93 kilometres (58 miles) from Üsküdar.

İznik is 68 kilometres (42 miles) south and east of Yalova, at the eastern end of the Lake of İznik, or İznik Gölü. On a road which passes through Yenişehir and Bilecik, 90 kilometres (56 miles) to the southeast of İznik, is Sogut.

There is a good bus service from Yalova to Bursa, a distance of 74 kilometres (46 miles) through attractive hill and mountain country. If travelling by car, you may want to take a detour to see Mudanya on the way. This is the Marmara Sea coastal resort for Bursa, 26 kilometres (16 miles) north of that city.

Çanakkale is close to Troy and can be reached from Bursa by way of the Marmara coastal route on road 200 through Bandirma to Lapseki, then southwest down the Dardanelles to Çanakkale (on the E24), a total of 300 kilometres (186 miles). Or you may choose an inland route on road 545: 162 kilometres (101 miles) through Balikeşir to Edremit, along the shore of the Gulf of Edremit to Ayvaçik, 83 kilometres (52 miles), and then north to Ezine and Çanakkale (E24), 136 kilometres (85 miles).

An alternative route by road from İstanbul is to go west to Tekirdağ on the E25, cross the wide neck of the Gelibolu Burnu (Gallipoli Peninsula) to Kesan, then go south, down the peninsula to Eceabat (E24), 333 kilometres (207 miles), and cross by ferry to Çanakkale.

From Çanakkale the E24 runs south to Intepe, ten kilometres (six miles) away. After another eight kilometres (five miles), you turn seaward for five kilometres (three miles) to reach Troy. The site Alexander believed to be Troy is on the coast further south. Take road E24 to Ezine, a distance of 22 kilometres (14 miles), cross the Scamander River and turn coastwards for Geyikli, a further 15 kilometres (ten miles). Among the trees stand Hellenistic columns and arches to which Alexander must have contributed, as well as Roman and later remains.

Continue south 26 kilometres (16 miles) on the E24 to Ayvacık, but then take a minor road to the port of Behramkale. Assos occupies a cone-shaped mass of basalt rock with its citadel on the flat top, and terraced buildings on the seaward slopes.

From the harbour you climb back to the citadel to pick up the E24 for Bergama (Pergamum). Edremit, at the eastern head of the gulf, is the chief town of the *vilayet* (provincial government) and its museum has an interesting display of weapons from early times to the present. It is 45 kilometres (28 miles) to Ayvalik, a town situated attractively on a lagoon that is very nearly wholly enclosed, with sandy bathing beaches at Çamlık and Samsakli. Within the lagoon are the Alibey Islands.

With a ferry service is Cunda, the largest island, noted for its cheese, honey, fish and wine. The Seytan Sofrasi (Devil's Dinner Table), on the heights near Ayvalik, offers felicitous views of the gulf, the mountains and the island of Lesbos, all of which can be enjoyed while eating. At Dikili, 33 kilometres (20 miles) south of Ayvalik and four kilometres (2.5 miles) off the E24 to the west, there is a ferry service to Lesbos during the summer months. Bergama is 16 kilometres (ten miles) inland from the E24 turnoff to Dikili and then north off the main road for about a kilometre (0.6 miles).

Historical Background

To the Byzantines, Kızıl Adalar were the Princes' Islands, favoured by royalty, and at other times used as a place of exile. Methodius, Patriarch of Constantinople, an icondule supporter, was exiled to the island of Burgaz for several years during the second Iconoclast period, during which pictures and images were banned from churches.

The great Carthaginian general Hannibal lived as an exile at Gebze, committing suicide there after the Romans defeated the Selucid, Antiochus III, whom Hannibal had advised, at Manisa in 190 BC. His tomb is here. Mehmet II is said to have died at Hereke, and Constantine I seems to have had a preference for the village, which is set among orchards.

Nicomedia (İzmit, now renamed Kocaeli), the principal city of Bithynia, was Diocletian's administrative centre for the eastern part of the Roman World after he divided it in two.

İznik was Nicaea. Lysimachus, a ruling heir of Alexander, gave it his wife's name after his victory there over Antigonus, yet another of the Alexander heirs. Following an earthquake, Hadrian (117–38) rebuilt the city. In the sixth century Justinian restored the walls (on which it is possible to walk over a greater part of their circumference), as did Leo III (717–41), who added aqueducts, baths, a bridge and several churches.

The First Ecumenical Council, convened by Constantine, was held here, resulting in the condemnation of the Arian heresy (adherents of a doctrine which denied the full divinity of Christ) and the promulgation of the Nicene Creed, a formal statement of Christian belief. It was also the initial location for the Seventh Council at which the Iconoclasts (who were against the use of the human form in religious worship) were denounced.

The first Osmanlis (tribe of Osman), about 50,000 under the command of a Suleiman, who had entered Anatolia ahead of the advancing Mongols, seem to have settled initially in Armenian territory. As a result of repeated Mongol threats, part of the tribe under Ertogrul (father of Osman) moved westward and may have taken service under the Seljuk Sultan of Konya, a service later rewarded by the allocation of land in Bithynia, at Sogut.

Nikaia became the first capital of the Seljuks after their entry into western Anatolia following the battle of Manzikert in 1071. It was recaptured in 1097 during the First Crusade and by agreement given back to the Byzantines. In 1204, after the Latin capture of Constantinople, it became the capital of the exiled Byzantine emperors until Michael VIII's return to Constantinople in 1261.

On the disintegration of the Seljuk Sultanate of Rum after its defeat by the Mongols at the battle of Mughar, near Konya, in the mid-13th century, its possessions fell to a number of independent emirs, some 48 in all, though many such emirates were little larger than the village in which the emir had his residence. The Osmanlis began their expansion by defeating or absorbing those emirates within the vicinity of Sogut, Bursa surrendering to Orhan, the son of Osman, in 1326; this news reached Osman on his deathbed. Timur sacked Bursa in 1402, but since he seldom lingered in the places he had subdued it was subsequently reoccupied and rebuilt. After the death of Beyazıt, whom Timur had defeated, a civil war broke out between that sultan's sons and Mehmet I Celebi, the ultimate successor.

Çanakkale was Abydos and, along with Sestos (Eceabat today), controlled all shipping through the Dardanelles and levied dues. It was here, at the narrowest crossing of the Hellespont, that Leander swam nightly to Hero. Byron swam it in emulation of Leander, and in this century there have been other distinguished crossings, notably by the writer Patrick Leigh Fermor, a feat made difficult by the contrary tides of the channel and the strong undertow.

In 480 BC, Xerxes bridged the Hellespont with boats, just to the north of Çanakkale, a crossing Alexander led in reverse 150 years later when he set out to destroy Persian power.

Schliemann (1822–90) identified Troy and recovered the treasures and jewels he believed had belonged to Priam's royal house. Digging at Schliemann's site in the 1930s, Carl Blegen, an American archaeologist, recorded 46 levels of occupation going back to 3000 BC. Schliemann himself came to acknowledge that the city had existed 1,000 years prior to the one he believed had been Priam's. Dorpfeld, Schliemann's assistant and successor, established level VI as being the most likely one of Homer's Troy, but this was subsequently amended to level VIIA.

Schliemann found his treasure at level II, and Blegen was to find hundreds of gold beads at the time of his excavations. The city of level VI was built by a people who introduced the horse into this area. After a long period of stagnation during which living standards fell to an extremely low level, the city was destroyed by an earthquake around 1240 BC. Level VIIA, built on ruins after the earthquake, fell to assault about a century later.

A most dramatic and tragic episode in *The Iliad* is when Hector, arriving at the city gate after other battling Trojans have gone in, stops and turns towards an incensed Achilles, bounding across the plain of the Scamander towards him. It is as if Hector is aware that the coming encounter will be decisive, that it is his destiny to die, yet he resolves manfully to face the challenge. His courage falters, though, and he runs. Achilles chases him three times round the walls of the city before Hector's courage revives, and he stops at the gate and in the ensuing combat is killed.

Xerxes sacrificed bulls at Troy, and Alexander arrived with a copy of *The Iliad* annotated by Aristotle. Julius Caesar had plans for building, and Constantine set up a gateway as a preliminary to the city he intended. In time the fallen columns, marble blocks and carved metopes were carted away to become incorporated in buildings erected by Romans, Byzantines and Turks.

Assos has an Aeolic foundation; it was colonized by immigrants from the islands of Lesbos, Chios and elsewhere in the north Aegean region. The Attalids of Pergamum rebuilt it after 190 BC, masters at constructing on the steep sides of hills, as is wonderfully evident at Pergamum. Aristotle spent three years at Assos and, if Strabo's information is correct, was married there.

Pergamum was a fortress in Alexander's time. It was there that Lysimachus, one of his successors, stored a considerable amount of treasure acquired during Alexander's conquests. Lysimachus put Philaeterus, a Paphlagonian, in charge of the treasure, but when Lysimachus lost his war against Antiochus (a Seleucid), Philaeterus, who had switched loyalties during the conflict, was confirmed in his role as guardian of the fortress and the treasure. In 263 BC, Philaeterus was succeeded by his adopted son, Eumenes, who opted for independence from the Seleucids, and Attalus I, his successor, made himself king of Pergamum. Attalus

Worshippers leave the Yeni Cami (Yeni Mosque) after Friday prayers, İstanbul

allied himself first with Rhodes, then with Rome, and set about expanding his kingdom. Eumenes II was the ally of Rome in its war against the Seleucids, and, on the defeat of the last Seleucid king in 190 BC, Rome, in gratitude, gave Pergamum control of all Seleucid possessions in Asia Minor.

In 133 BC, the last Pergamene king, Attalid III, bequeathed his kingdom to Rome, and it became part of the Roman Province of Asia. Marc Anthony gave the Pergamene library to Cleopatra to replace losses when the great Library of Alexandria was destroyed by fire, but the Emperor Augustus later restored the books and manuscripts to Pergamum. *Charta pergamene* (parchment), a replacement for Egyptian papyrus, was invented at Pergamum.

Galen (130–200), the first great surgeon and physician, was born at Pergamum and for a time practised there. He wrote treatises and commentaries on Hippocrates and contributed medical documents to the library.

For the Byzantines, Pergamum's importance was strategic rather than civic. In the early eighth century the Arabs sacked it. Leo III (717–41) restored it. The city held out against the Seljuk Turks but fell eventually to the Ottomans. After Timur's defeat of Sultan Beyazıt at Ankara in 1402, the Mongols decimated the population. The Ottomans, in their subsequent reoccupation, ignored the citadel and the city's past in favour of their new town of Bergama.

Sights

THE PRINCES' ISLANDS (KIZIL ADALAR)

Büyük Ada is 13 kilometres (eight miles) in circumference and among its attractions are imperial-style wooden houses, flower gardens, pine trees and the leisurely pace of its horse-drawn phaetons. A phaeton tour of the island takes about one and a half hours.

Burgaz, too, has pines and can offer exceptional views to those who climb to its plateau. The sites of two monasteries and a ninth-century church, St John Prodromos (John the Baptist), are on this island.

Copper was mined on **Heybeli**. Queen Elizabeth I appointed Sir Edward Barton as her unpaid ambassador to the court of Sultan Murat III; the ambassador, whose tomb is on Heybeli, died in 1597. The naval school here was a convent founded by the wife of John VIII Palaeolagos. Heybeli can be covered in about an hour.

İZMIT (NICOMEDIA)

With a history of occupation dating back to 712 BC, İzmit—now renamed Koçaeli—has little to show for it. All that can be seen today among the vast expansion are the remains of a Byzantine citadel on the acropolis hill and, from the Ottomans, a mosque designed by Sinan for a vizier of Suleiman I.

İZNIK (NICAEA)

You arrive at the **North** or **İstanbul Gate**, which Vespasian may have restored. The **East Gate**, the **Lefke**, is probably Hadrian's, beyond which are the aqueducts (restored by Orhan). The **South** or **Yenişehir Gate** has an inscription of Claudius II (268–70). The **West Gate** is under the lake.

To the northwest of the Lefke is the 14th-century **Yeşil Cami** with its green-tiled minarets. Over to the west is an *imaret* (a Muslim soup kitchen) of 1388, one of the first of its kind, now a museum.

Two main streets intersect the town, and at the crossroads is Justinian's **Hagia Sophia**, converted to a mosque under the Seljuks and then restored and decorated by the Osmanlis in the 14th century. In the southeast area is the 11th-century **Koimesis Church** (The Dormition of the Virgin). There are several early-style Ottoman mosques: the **Mahmoud Celebi Cami, Hacı Hamza, Hacı Özbek** and the **Suleiman Paşa Medrese**.

The town is congenial to storks, who have chosen it as a breeding centre, and the lake has an abundance of fish. Outside the city walls on the lakeside are the hotels, motels, restaurants and *pensions*.

İZNIK TILES

U nder the Ottomans, İznik's artistic importance was established when Sultan Selim I imported potters from Tabriz in Persia and set them to work here. Their tiles subsequently decorated many of the country's finest mosques and other buildings. Three periods of artistic achievement are recognized: 1490–1525, 1525–55 and 1555–1700. Other potteries were established later at Kutahya (still active) and, in the 18th century, in İstanbul.

SOGUT

Osman, the eponymous founder of the Osmanlis, was born at Sogut. One can reach this town from Kocaeli by travelling further along the Ankara Highway to Adapazari—now renamed Sakarya—then by turning south to Bilecik. Sogut is 28 kilometres (17 miles) southeast of there and can be reached by way of a regular half-hourly minibus service. There is the tomb of Ertogrul, Osman's father, who died here, but little else in auspicious commemoration of the start of a great empire, though there is a substantial monument to Kemal Atatürk, the founder of the current Turkish Republic. Osman's tomb is in Bursa, an Ottoman capital and the first major conquest of Orhan, Osman's son, whose tomb is also there. Sogut lies in fertile surroundings, with vineyards and orchards among the mountains, and the Sakarya river nearby.

BURSA

It is said that Hannibal persuaded the Bithynian king Prusias (228–180 BC), who founded the city, to give it his name. In AD 111 Pliny inspected the baths and agreed with the citizens that a rebuilding was necessary. Justinian built a palace, as well as additional baths.

The city is built on more than one level, and distances on foot can be longer than one might expect from looking at a map of the city. The *otogar* (bus station) is in the plain on the north, some two kilometres (1.25 miles) from the higher level city centre at Heykel where the restored covered market and the Ulu Cami (Grand Mosque), the largest mosque in the city, can be found. Alongside the Ulu Cami on Atatürk Caddesi, as well as at the Koza Han are entrances to the covered bazaar. The shops of the Koza Han arcade include a tourist information office.

The **Ulu Cami** was begun about 1395 by Beyazıt I (1389–1402), but the mosque was not completed until the reign of Mehmet I Celebi (1413–21). It has 20 domes connected by pointed arches on 12 supporting piers, but there was a modification of design after an earthquake in 1855 damaged 18 of the domes. The *sadirvan* is set in the entrance hall, with an opening in the dome above it. The interior has a grand but austere appearance, with decoration confined to beautiful calligraphic inscriptions on the walls.

To the east is the **Orhan Cami**, built in 1338 on the site of a Byzantine church. An inscription on this mosque is dated 1417, but this may refer to a reconstruction. The building suffered damage in the 1855 earthquake, subsequently repaired.

The rebuilt covered bazaar extends behind the Ulu Cami and the Koza Han. It was damaged in the 1855 earthquake and almost totally destroyed by a fire in the 1960s. Bursa is a traditional centre of the silk industry. Cotton towelling, too, is a speciality, and you ought at least to be tempted into buying a bathrobe. Bursa

The town of Bursa, rising up the hillslope

Tomb of Mehmet I, Bursa

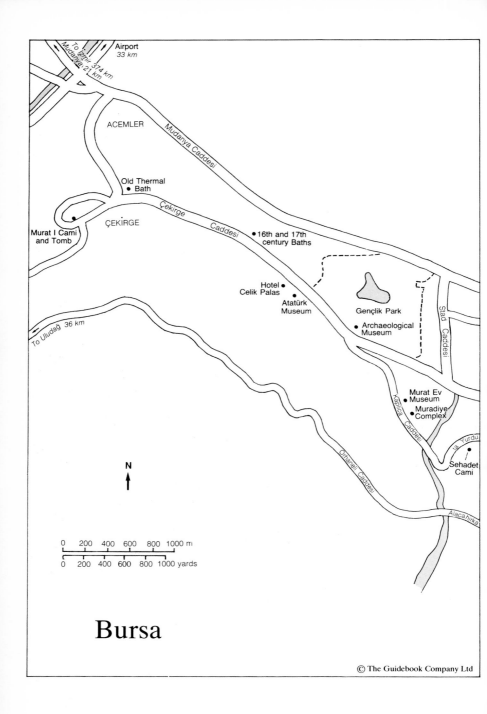

Airport
33 km

To İzmir 374 km
Mudanya 21 km

ACEMLER

Mudanya Caddesi

Old Thermal
● Bath

Çekirge   Caddesi

ÇEKİRGE

Murat I Cami
and Tomb

● 16th and 17th
century Baths

Hotel ●
Celik Palas

● Atatürk
Museum

Gençlik Park

● Archaeological
Museum

Stad Caddesi

To Uludağ 36 km

Orhaneli Caddesi

Murat Ev
● Museum

● Muradiye
Complex

Kaplıca Caddesi

la Yurdu

● Sehadet
Cami

Alacahirka

N

0   200   400   600   800   1000 m

0   200   400   600   800   1000 yards

Bursa

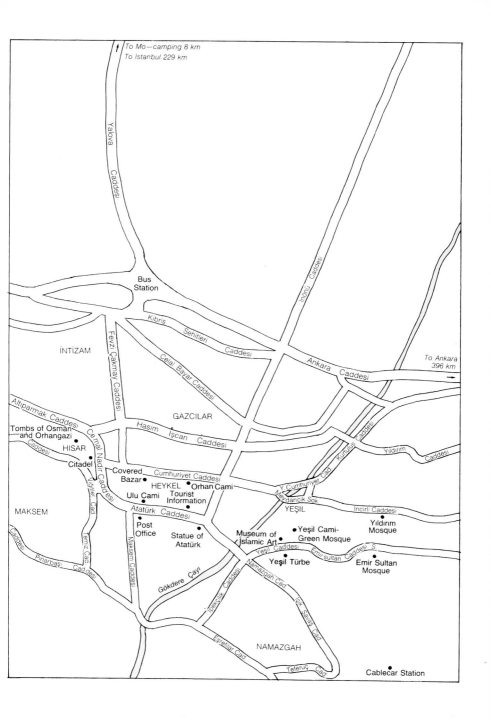

To Mo—camping 8 km
To Istanbul 229 km

Yalova Caddesi

Bus Station

İNTİZAM

Fevzi Çakmay Caddesi

Kıbrıs

Şehitleri Caddesi

Celal Bayar Caddesi

İnönü Caddesi

Ankara Caddesi

To Ankara 396 km

Altıparmak Caddesi

GAZCILAR

Hasim İşcan Caddesi

Cemal Nadir Caddesi

Tombs of Osman and Orhangazi

HISAR

Caddesi

Citadel

Yiğitler Cad

Covered Bazar

Cumhuriyet Caddesi

HEYKEL

Orhan Cami

Ulu Cami

Tourist Information

Kurtuluş Caddesi

Yıldırım Caddesi

Y. Cumhuriyet

Meydancik Sok

YEŞİL

İncirli Caddesi

MAKSEM

Atatürk Caddesi

Post Office

Statue of Atatürk

Temiz Cad

Maksem Caddesi

Caddesi

Pınarbaşı Cad

Gökdere Çayı

Museum of İslamic Art

Yeşil Caddesi

Yeşil Cami- Green Mosque

Emir sultan Caddesi S.

Yıldırım Mosque

Yeşil Türbe

Emir Sultan Mosque

Namazgah Cad

İnekçilik Caddesi

Işık Sokak Cad

NAMAZGAH

Eşreflar Cad

Teteruç Cad

Cablecar Station

peaches, incidentally, are large and luscious. Besides the fruit, visitors should sample İskender or Bursa kebab—beef carved from a rotating upright grill, served on squares of unleavened bread, spread with yoghurt and doused with melted butter.

Going east a kilometre (0.6 miles) or so from the Ulu Cami, crossing the **Gökdere Çayi** (stream) by a high bridge, and then turning north on Yeşil Caddesi, you reach the **Yeşil Cami**. This mosque is among the first of the structures to achieve a distinct Ottoman style, with an open hall containing the *sadirvan*, a wide recessed section for the *mihrab* (niche in a mosque indicating the direction of Mecca) with the *minber* (mosque pulpit) alongside, and two domed recesses on either side of the entrance. *Yeşil* means green, and the mosque gets its name from the dark green, dark blue and turquoise tiling. It was begun by Mehmet Celebi between 1422 and 1424.

Over the road from the mosque is the **Yeşil Türbe** (Green Mausoleum), the octagonal tomb of Mehmet I Celebi. The original tiling on this tomb was destroyed in a fire, and the present green tiling dates only from the 19th century. On the south side of the Yesil Cami is the **Museum of Islamic Art**. To the east is the **Emir Sultan Mosque**, built on the site of an older mosque in the early 19th century. Emir Sultan was the spiritual advisor to Beyazıt I.

In the same area, to the north, is the mosque of **Sultan Beyazıt Yildirim**. This is believed to date from the late 1390s, or a year or two before that sultan's defeat by Timur at Ankara in 1402. Its interior design is similar to that of the Yeşil Cami, for which it may have been the model. Its tiled decoration has been seriously depleted by time and earthquakes.

Back at the Ulu Cami, go west along Altiparmak Caddesi for almost a kilometre. Shortly before you reach the roundabout road junction, a wide high stairway climbs the escarpment on the southern side of the road. Turning right at the top of the stairway, you come to the enclosure within which are the tombs of Osman, the dynasty's founder, and Orhan (Orhangazi), who captured Bursa. On foot it is then a walk of two or three kilometres (1.25–2 miles) up and then down into a valley to reach the **Muradiye** complex. A bus or a taxi can be taken however from the Heykel area. The Muradiye is a large enclosed multiflowered garden in which, as well as the **Mosque of Murat II** with its distinctive tiling, built between 1424 and 1427, and a *medrese*, there are eleven impressive tombs including that of Murat. His tomb has a decorated, carved wooden canopy. A smaller chamber contains the tombs of four of his sons. An attendant will open these tombs and several others, including that of **Prince Cem** (1494), notable for its rich faience panelling, and that of **Mustafa**, son of Suleiman the Magnificent, with its black and turquoise tiling and an inscribed border of light blue and white on dark blue. A restored 17th-century house in a central square is known as the **Murat Ev**.

The backstreets of Bergama

The citadel is in the Hisar area, on a higher level than that of the tombs of Osman and Orhan, which are close to the **Hisar Kapisi**. There are three other ancient gateways, the **Kaplica Kapisi**, **Zindan** and **Yerkapi**, and there are sections of original walls among those of both Byzantine and Ottoman rebuildings. On the way to the Muradiye from the Osman and Orhan enclosure, you pass the small **Sehadet Cami**, then the city hospital which has been erected on the foundations of a Byzantine palace.

ÇEKIRGE AND ULUDAĞ

Near the stairway to the Hisar area and tombs of Osman and Orhan, walk west from the road junction. Another kilometre (0.6 miles) on the road to Çekirge will bring you to **Gençlik Parki** (Youth and Culture Park) that spreads on the right down to a lower level and contains restaurants, *pavyons* and other facilities. The **Archaeological Museum** is located in the park. Left of the roadway entrance to the hotel Çelik Palas are the sites of the 16th- and 17th-century baths, the **Yenikaplıça**, **Karamustafa**, **Kaynarca** and **Eskikaplıça** which incorporate original Byzantine features. The hotel too has its baths, a reconstruction of an earlier establishment.

At Çekirge, a spa several kilometres to the west, the hotels have the curative waters piped into their bathrooms and washbasins. The **Murad'i Hudavendigan Türbe** here was commissioned by Nülifer Hanum, the mother of Murat I. Murat was assassinated on the battlefield after his victory over the Serbs at Kosovo, 15 June 1389. His son, Beyazıt I, avenged his father's death by executing those princes and nobles whom he was holding captive, and brought the body of his father back to Bursa for burial. The **Murat I Cami** opposite the tomb dates from the 1360s.

The road up Uludağ (Mount Olympus) starts from Çekirge. Uludağ, 2,328 metres (7,635 feet) high, is a winter sports centre, with alpine-style hotels among other kinds of accommodation. There are ski-lifts, and viewing pavilions on precipitous heights. You can also mount by *téléférique* (cable car); the station is on the east side of Bursa, well signposted.

ÇANAKKALE

The military cemeteries of the Allied and Turkish dead of the 1915 Gallipoli campaign are to the south of this town. The fortress, rebuilt by Mehmet II, is used by the Turkish military and has a **Museum of Military Ware**. Its companion fortress at Eceabat on the opposite, western side—the waterway is at its narrowest here—is another Mehmet construction. The **Archaeological Museum** has a collection of recoveries from sites in the locality, dating from pre-Hellenistic times to the present.

TROY

The site is signposted, with arrows indicating a route to be followed. A Cyclopean-type wall of huge rounded stones, along with a carriage ramp, are assumed to be of Mycenaean times (1500–1100 BC). There are the remains of a theatre and a bouleuterion (council chamber), and remnants of towers and gateways.

Most impressive is a megaron (a hall or building of the type Homer describes), consisting of a large chamber with a central hearth at which visitors were given pride of place.

The plain where the many single combats and battles were fought is under cultivation, with no obvious evidence of the streams of Scamander and Simois, locations that were so strategic to the battle. There are mounds near the shore, though, that might well conceal the charred bones of heroes. Strabo said that he saw funeral mounds on the shore here at the end of the first century BC. Mount Ida somehow seems a little too distant for Zeus, or Hera or Athena, to have been able to keep so constant an eye on the progress of the battle, but they were after all divine. The island of Tenedos lies just off the coast, to which the Greeks feigned to retire as part of their deceptive strategy with the wooden horse, and is now Turkish Boscaada.

ASSOS

There are many fourth-century BC buildings on the acropolis, including the citadel towers and substantial city walls. On the roadway down to Behramkale are the terraced Pergamene stoas and other buildings. The attractive little harbour, isolated on the northern shore of the Gulf of Edremit, has been privately and modestly developed, while at the entry to the gulf lies the Greek island of Lesbos.

PERGAMUM (BERGAMA)

The town has one very long main street that ends eventually in the old centre. Development has brought new hotels and a number of *pensions* into existence. The Ministry of Tourism's Information Office is on that main street about one kilometre (0.6 miles) before the *otogar*, or bus station, is reached. Continuing on the main road from the bus station, you come to the museum on the left where the rise has been landscaped, next to the *belediye* (town hall).

Among the museum's exhibits are models of the **Altar of Zeus** and the **Demeter Temple** and stoa (large colonnaded porch); both sites are on the acropolis. A mosaic floor with a depiction of the Medusa, a statue of Hadrian, terracotta statuettes from Myrina and a *kuros* (young man) from Candarli are also here. There is an ethnographic section.

THE ASCLEPIUM
To reach the Asclepium, continue on from the museum and take a signposted turn to the left (the post office is on the other side of the main road). If you are on foot, the walk is a fair distance from the turn-off. Finally, you follow the perimeter of a large barracks to reach the car park and entrance to the site.

*Decorated carts, Bergama. Artistic transport
is now being replaced by pick-up trucks*

The Cult of Healing was brought
to Pergamum from Epidaurus in
Greece in the fourth century BC. The
Sanctuary of the Healing God was
built over an earlier one to Telephus (a
son of Heracles), the founder of the
city, and from the centre of the main
temple court a hidden tunnel led to a
temple to Telephus, in which the
curative rites were performed. Activity
at the sanctuary reached its highest
level during the second century.

From the car park entrance and ticket office, you step into a colonnaded street
running in a northeasterly–southwesterly direction. The first section has lines of
square and round columns, the next section has round columns with a retaining
wall on the right. On the left is a section of wall behind a semicircular platform
with an olive tree, and next to it a circular structure—the site of a pool or an altar.

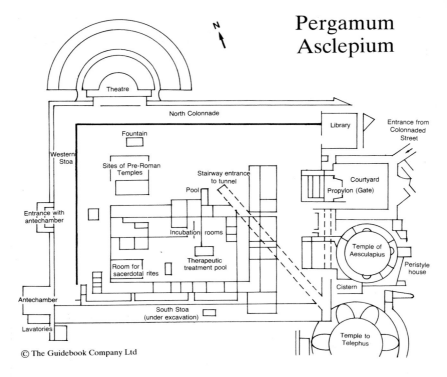

Pergamum
Asclepium

Theatre

North Colonnade

Library

Entrance from
Colonnaded
Street

Fountain

Western
Stoa

Sites of Pre-Roman
Temples

Stairway entrance
to tunnel

Pool

Courtyard

Propylon (Gate)

Entrance with
antechamber

Incubation rooms

Temple of
Aesculapius

Peristyle
house

Room for
sacerdotal rites

Therapeutic
treatment pool

Cistern

Antechamber

South Stoa
(under excavation)

Temple to
Telephus

Lavatories

© The Guidebook Company Ltd

The centre of the paved way has a covered conduit which may have brought water
to the sacred pool. If this was the Sacred Way to the sanctuary, it could have run
from the stadium, away to the northwest of the site, past a Roman theatre, then
through a gateway, and most likely would have had shops along it. It leads to a
courtyard and the propylon (gate), erected during the reign of Antoninus Pius
(130–61). On the left of the stairway to the court are some reconstructed columns
and a section of architrave, backed by a wall.

Now you enter a large square, which from the evidence of column bases, standing columns and steps would have been surrounded by stoas. On the right of the
propylon is the library, and the museum's statue of Hadrian may have occupied a
principal niche here. The colonnade running along that northeast side, part of
which was rebuilt after an earthquake in AD 178, brings you to a Greek-style
theatre cut out of a steep hill. Over on the left from the propylon is the **Temple of
Aesculapius**, cylindrical in shape and domed, built about AD 150 and modelled on
the Pantheon in Rome. Towards the centre of the area, in front of the theatre is a
spring and pool, and evidence of shrines. Near the pool is the entrance to a tunnel
that leads under the site to emerge at a double-storeyed building in the south
corner, beyond the Temple of Aesculapius. The tunnel leads into a paved outer way

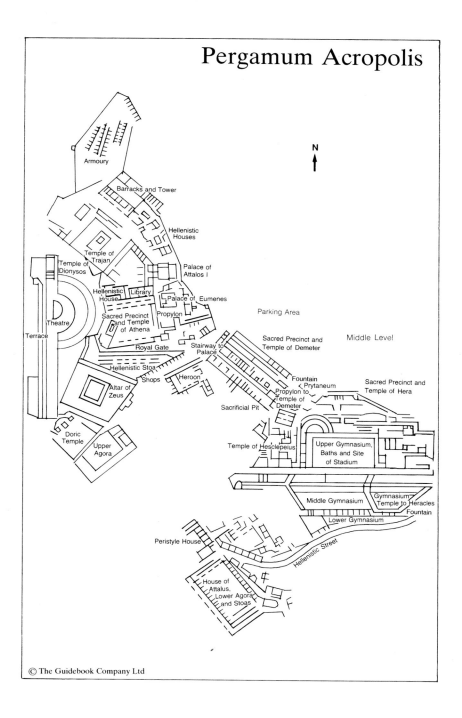

Pergamum Acropolis

N
↑

Armoury

Barracks and Tower

Hellenistic Houses

Temple of Trajan

Temple of Dionysos

Palace of Attalos I

Hellenistic House

Library

Palace of Eumenes

Sacred Precinct and Temple of Athena

Propylon

Parking Area

Theatre

Terrace

Royal Gate

Stairway to Palace

Sacred Precinct and Temple of Demeter

Middle Level

Hellenistic Stoa

Shops

Heroon

Fountain

Prytaneum

Propylon to Temple of Demeter

Sacred Precinct and Temple of Hera

Altar of Zeus

Sacrificial Pit

Doric Temple

Upper Agora

Temple of Hesclepeius

Upper Gymnasium, Baths and Site of Stadium

Middle Gymnasium

Gymnasium, Temple to Heracles

Lower Gymnasium

Fountain

Peristyle House

Hellenistic Street

House of Attalus, Lower Agora and Stoas

© The Guidebook Company Ltd

that circles the structure, with arched openings into the interior section, and to the hub that is walled up. This was probably the site of the early temple to Telephus. Between this structure and the Temple of Aesculapius is a cistern, and above this latter shrine is a peristyle house. The stoa along the southwestern side of the main site is under excavation. On the rear wall of the total enclosure is a stepped, columned entrance that was excavated in 1967, and at the southwestern corner are ancient lavatories, much admired by visitors.

Outside the area of the Asclepium, west of the stadium is a large amphitheatre that was used for aquatic entertainments; its water was supplied through conduits

(above) A farmer tasting his olives before selling them in the local market, Bergama
(opposite) Exclusively male enclaves, cafés provide backgammon, coffee
and hubble-bubble pipes, Bergama

from the nearby Selinus River, or Bergama Cayi. Between it and the theatre, on the Sacred Way, is the site of a temple to Athena.

Going via the narrow streets of the town's centre, you will find that the acropolis is a fair distance from the healing sanctuary. On the way to the acropolis hill is a large impressive building known as the **Kız Avlu** (Red Courtyard) because of the colour of the brickwork; foundation arches of one section span the Selinus River. In origin, this may have been a temple to Serapis, later converted by the Byzantines into a Christian basilica.

THE ACROPOLIS

From near the Kız Avlu, the roadway to the acroplis ascends for nearly six kilometres (four miles) to a parking place on the northeastern side, below the main acropolis buildings situated on a number of levels. The summit is 440 metres (1,444 feet) above the valley of the Calicus River, or Bakır Cayi.

From the car park you go up on foot to the **Royal Gate**. From here, moving towards the northwest, you come to the site of the library, and further on to the northeast, against the acropolis walls, are the remains of two palaces. North of these are Hellenistic houses, followed by a barracks and then an armoury. Northwest of the palaces is a **Temple of Trajan**. Moving round to the west and south you reach the truly magnificent theatre with its auditorium curving down the very steep hillside to a buttressed terrace or promenade where the stage was located. There is a **Temple of Dionysos** on this terrace. Back from the rear of the theatre, a **Temple of Athena** stands on its own terrace to the west of the Royal Gate.

A pathway running down from the Royal Gate reaches a high plinth on which stood Pergamum's most famous monument, the **Altar of Zeus** with its sculptured frieze of battling gods and Titans, built by Eumenes II. German archaeologists first excavated Pergamum and carried out restorations. Important recoveries were taken to Berlin prior to 1945 and are in the Pergamum Museum there; among the items is a reconstruction of the Altar of Zeus that incorporates sections of the excavated finds, including a wide marble stairway which leads up to a columned stoa-like structure with a winged extension on either side. The great carved frieze runs round below the stylobate (a continuous base supporting a row of columns).

To the east, and on a terrace below on which the altar stood, is the upper agora (marketplace). Follow the pathway, down past the *heroon* (shrine) of Pergamene kings, to the level of the **Temple of Demeter**; the setting here is a particular delight. Lower down, to the east, is a **Temple of Hera**, then to the south of this is a three-sectioned, three-levelled gymnasium (school), a complex that includes a palaestra (exercise ground) and the site of a stadium. Continue down to arrive at the lower agora.

BETWEEN A ROCK AND A HARD PLACE

*O*n my own childhood, polygamy and its results produced a very ugly and distressing impression. The constant tension in our home made every simple family ceremony seem like a physical pain, and the consciousness of it hardly ever left me.

The rooms of the wives were opposite each other, and my father visited them by turns. When it was Teizé's turn every one in the house showed a tender sympathy to Abla, while when it was her turn no one heeded the obvious grief of Teizé. It was she indeed who could conceal her suffering least. She would leave the table with eyes full of tears, and one could be sure of finding her in her room either crying or fainting. Very soon I noticed that father left her alone with her grief.

And father too was suffering in more than one way. As a man of liberal and modern ideas, his marriage was very unfavorably regarded by his friends, especially by Hakky Bey, to whose opinion he attached the greatest importance.

He suffered again from the consciousness of having deceived Abla. He had married her when she was a mere girl, and it now looked as if he had taken advantage of her youth and inexperience. One saw as time went on how patiently and penitently he was trying to make up to her for what he had done.

Among the household too he felt that he had fallen in general esteem, and he cast about for some justification of his conduct which would reinstate him. 'It was for Halidé that I married her,' he used to say. 'If Teizé had married another man Halidé would have died.' And, 'It is for the child's sake I have married her father,' Teizé used to say. 'She would have died if I had married anyone else.' Granny took the sensible view. 'They wanted to marry each other. What has a little girl to do with their marriage?'

The unhappiness even manifested itself in the relation between granny and Hava Hanum. The latter criticized granny severely for not *having put a stop to it before things had gone too far, and granny felt indignant to have the blame thrown upon her by a dependent for an affair she so intensely disliked.*

Teizé, with her superior show of learning and her intellectual character, must have dominated father at first, but with closer contact, the pedantic turn of her mind, which gave her talk a constant didactic tone, must have wearied him. For in the intimate companionship of every-day life nothing bores one more than a pretentious style of talk involving constant intellectual effort. Poor Teizé's erudition and intelligence were her outstanding qualities, and she used and abused them to a maddening degree. When, after her dull and lonely life, she gave herself, heart and soul, to a man, the disillusionment of finding herself once more uncared for rendered her very bitter; and she either talked continually of her personal pain or else of some high topic, too difficult to be understood by the person she was talking to. Somehow her efforts to dethrone her rival from the heart of her husband lacked the instinctive capacity of the younger woman's, and it was only granny and poor me that sympathized and suffered with her in a grief which did not interest anyone else.

The wives never quarreled, and they were always externally polite, but one felt a deep and mutual hatred accumulating in their hearts, to which they gave vent only when each was alone with father. He wore the look of a man who was getting more than his just punishment now. Finally he took to having a separate room, where he usually sat alone. But he could not escape the gathering storm in his new life. Hava Hanum not inaptly likened his marriage to that of Nassireddin Hodja. She told it to us as if she was glad to see father unhappy. The Hodja also wanted to taste the blessed state of polygamy, and took to himself a young second wife. Before many months were out his friends found the Hodja completely bald, and asked him the reason. 'My old wife pulls out all my black hairs so that I may look as old as she; my young wife pulls out my white hairs so that I may look as young as she. Between them I am bald.'

Halidé Edib, Memoirs of Halidé Edib, 1926

Central Aegean Coast

İzmir, lying at the head of a deep gulf, is Turkey's third city. As Smyrna—its ancient name—it was destroyed at the conclusion of the Turkish–Greek conflict of 1920–22. The present city is modern, with a long waterfront and tree-lined avenues, and pleasant enough to be a base for exploration outside the city. An International Trade Fair is held here each September in the Youth and Culture Park, and a visitor without an advance booking might find difficulty getting a room, in spite of the increase in accommodation in recent years. In general, the hotels, led by the Buyuk Efes, Etap İzmir and Kismet, are of a high standard, and there is a wide choice of medium-range accommodation. Restaurants are located principally along the harbour and on Atatürk Caddesi, the extended waterfront. The headquarters of NATO's Southeastern Command is at İzmir, with its display of members' flags in almost perpetual flutter at the premises on the waterfront. West of İzmir are beaches and archaeological sites, and at Çeşme there is a 15th-century castle.

Selçuk, the location of one city of Ephesus (for as with Smyrna there were more than one), has developed as a pleasant tourist centre in its own right and could be a convenient base for visiting Ephesus as well as other archaeological sites on this section of the Aegean coast.

An alternative to İzmir or Selçuk as a base for exploring this section of the Aegean coast is the port of Kuşadası. Its tourist facilities have been extended considerably along its coasts to the north and south, and its amenities include a yacht marina as well as an enlarged harbour. Throughout the summer there is a passenger and car ferry service from Çeşme to the Greek island of Samos. To visit the sites of Priene, Miletus and Didyma from Kuşadası, allow a minimum of one full day, but at least two days are recommended.

Getting There

Roadway reconstruction on the edge of İzmir has created not so much a spaghetti junction as a macaroni one, with many underpasses and dual carriageways. The *otogar* for long-distance coaches and minibus services is on this perimeter, and services are frequent. The Adnan Menderes Airport is about 12 kilometres (eight miles) from the bus station.

It is 80 kilometres (50 miles) by road from Konak Square in İzmir to Çeşme.

The town's beach facilities are unexceptional but within easy reach are hotels, holiday complexes and camping facilities on good sandy beaches, and every amenity of a popular and flourishing holiday resort catering to international and national visitors.

Leaving İzmir for Selçuk, take the E24 south to Aydin. To visit Ephesus, take the Kuşadası road out of Selçuk for about one kilometre (0.6 miles), turning left by the Tusan Motel. After another kilometre, the entrance to the site, lying between Mount Coressus and Mount Pion, can be reached. You go through the line of the Byzantine walls to reach the car park. If you are travelling without a car, then a minibus or taxi can be taken from the Selçuk *otogar*, which is on the main İzmir-Aydin road.

Kuşadası is 22 kilometres (14 miles) from Selçuk. Visitors to Kuşadası can make a day trip to Samos, a Greek island, since at least three Turkish boats make the two-hour journey at 8.30am and 3.30pm, though sailings are less frequent outside the summer months.

If you are staying in Kuşadası, you will want to see the sites of Priene, Miletus and Didyma. If you are based in Selçuk, there is a daily tour from the *otogar*, first taking in the archaeological sites there, and then paying visits to the three sites. Again from Selçuk it is possible to take a bus to Didyma, and work your way back by minibus to Akköy, near Miletus, and then towards Söke to see Priene. However, the lack of established transport can cause difficulty by this route, as Miletus is four kilometres (2.5 miles) from Akköy, and Priene 11 kilometres (seven miles) from a turn-off two kilometres (1.25 miles) out of Söke. The distance from Selçuk to Didyma is 62 kilometres (39 miles); from Miletus to Söke is 32 kilometres (20 miles).

If you are driving, two kilometres (1.25 miles) after the road has left Söke going south, take road 525, which branches off southwest for ten kilometres (six miles) to where a roadway runs northwest for one kilometre (0.6 miles) to Priene. To see Miletus, go back to the Söke road junction and continue south for 22 kilometres (14 miles) to Akköy; the site of Miletus (or Milet) is four kilometres (2.5 miles) further. Didyma is a relatively short trip away from the gateway at Miletus; the Sacred Way once ran for nine kilometres (six miles) to the precinct of the Temple and Oracle of Apollo at Didyma.

Historical Background

The founders of Smyrna were Aeolians, probably from the Aegean Island of Lesbos. By establishing themselves here during the migrations of Greeks from the

Greek mainland and archipelago around 1000 BC, they drove the indigenous inhabitants inland. Later the immigrants allowed Ionians from Colophon, an inland town, to settle in Smyrna, and the story has it that the latter took control on an occasion when the Aeolian residents were out on the hillsides celebrating a Dionysian feast.

Like other cities on this section of coast, Smyrna has had to change its location more than once due to the action of the Hermus River; deposits of silt collected at the river mouth constantly change the coastline and access to the sea. This happened with the Maeander and Caister rivers of the region too. (Even in our present century the silting of the Hermus has threatened İzmir and the river had to be diverted into one of its older beds.)

In the seventh century BC a new, planned and strong-walled city, oval in shape, was constructed at what is now the district of Bayraklı, four kilometres (2.5 miles) to the north of present-day İzmir. This city was taken and sacked in 600 BC by the Lydian king Alyattes, who had a siege mound constructed to assist in the breaching of the walls. In time this became a hill surmounted by an acropolis, and survives today as Tepeküle, at the foot of which is a tomb said to be that of Tantalus, the legendary king of the region. By Alexander's time (the fourth century BC) the city was in such a pitiful condition because of the silting that Lysimachus ordered a rebuilding elsewhere, his city sited on Mount Pagus.

During the time of the Crusades, Smyrna was occupied by the victorious Franks after they had defeated its independent Turkish emir. The Crusaders held it for 60 years, until Timur sacked it. After the Mongol's departure it reverted to the independent Emir of Mentese, who had been restored by Timur, but ultimately it became Ottoman. In 1920, the invading Greeks made it their principal base in the war against Atatürk's new Turkey. When they were ultimately evicted in 1922, the city of wooden buildings was left inexplicably burning.

Ephesus was initiated when Ionian settlers built a city on Mount Pion at the mouth of the Caister River. A century or two later, when the Lydian king, Croesus, subdued all the Ionian cities except Miletus, the river's silting had rendered the principal harbour useless, so Croesus built a new city on the east side of Mount Pion. Croesus was a generous benefactor, and he contributed largely to the construction of a new Temple to Artemis, the city's patron goddess. He seems to have wanted to emulate, if not surpass in size and magnificence the Labyrinth, Polycrates' great Temple to Hera on the island of Samos. The new temple was begun in 550 BC but had still to be completed some 14 years later when Croesus lost his throne to Cyrus, the Achaemenid Persian king. There were 127 columns with sculpted pedestals, and a sculpted frieze surrounded the outer portico, running just below the roof. Xerxes paid homage at Ephesus on his way through to his fifth-century BC assault on mainland Greece. In 365 BC, Herostratus, a citizen, set fire to the temple for no explicable reason other than notoriety; it burned to the ground.

The building of a new temple had begun when Alexander arrived. His contribution was to make the Ephesians pay into the building fund those taxes that they would have paid to the unseated Persian satrap. Alexander might even have been willing to donate a sum personally had the citizens been willing to rededicate the edifice to him and not to Artemis, which they were not.

Once again the city fell victim to the Caister, and Lysimachus rebuilt it on the western slopes of Mount Pion; its walls were connected to Mount Coressus, and a new harbour was built on the southwest. The isolated temple now became part of a separate sacred precinct, outside the new city's walls.

Ephesus became the capital of the Roman province of Asia when Attalus III of Pergamum bequeathed the Romans the city in the second century BC. During the first campaign of Mithridates VI of Pontus against Roman domination (88 BC), the Ephesians, siding with the king, butchered the Romans living in the city, and on the king's ultimate defeat the Romans rescinded the privileges attached to Roman citizenship. By the third century AD the city's unending struggle with the Caister concluded in yet another defeat, and its maritime importance ended.

In the sixth century, Justinian the Great built a new citadel on a hill to the northwest of the temple precinct. He also erected a great church, that of St John Theologos. He used columns from the Artemisium in constructing the latter and transported other columns to Constantinople for inclusion in the building of St Sophia there. Ephesus became known as Agios Theologos, which today's Turkish inhabitants know as Ayasolük.

Miletus resisted Lydian domination, and after the fall of Croesus, its elders struck a deal with Cyrus that enabled the city to maintain its comparative independence. In 499 BC, after instigating an Ionian revolt against Persian rule resulting in a Persian victory, the city was razed and the majority of its citizens exiled to the Persian Gulf.

When Alexander came, the Persian garrison withdrew into the citadel and hoped to hold out until the Persian fleet should come to its rescue. But Nicanor, Alexander's admiral, forestalled Persian naval intervention by anchoring the Macedonian ships off the Island of Lade at the entrance to the harbour. The garrison sued for terms of surrender, but as those offered were unacceptable, the Persians defied Alexander and were annihilated—an outcome their fleet was powerless to prevent. Miletus began its independent life again.

The Maeander, though, as well as the Persians, seemed determined to immobilize Mileus, and the river's silting eventually joined Lade to the mainland, gradually

Old men at a tea house

filling the city's four harbours with sand, contributing to the decay of its economic prosperity—fine quality wool having been among the principal exports.

Intellectually, Miletus was the leader of the Ionian world, counting the philosophers Thales and Anaximander among its distinguished sages, as well as Hecataeus the geographer and Hippodamas the architect.

Miletus founded colonies on the north Aegean, Marmara and Black Sea coasts, as well as in Syria and at Naucratis on the Nile delta. It supported Athens in that city's long struggle with Sparta—Pericles of Athens married Aspasia, a girl from Miletus—and was duly humiliated by Sparta after its eventual victory. Miletus became Roman through the legacy of Attalus III of Pergamum. St Paul preached here. Its ultimate decline came under the Byzantines, though two of its harbours were still open. Following the Seljuk entry into western Anatolia, the city fell to the independent Emir of Mentese, and later to the Ottomans, by which time silting had not only closed the harbours but also the inlet of the sea that had helped to form the peninsula on which Miletus had been built, thereby creating the inland lake of Bafa.

It has been said that Milesian women and girls do not sit at table with their men: when the Ionians invaded in the first millennium BC, those Greeks who founded Miletus are said to have killed all the males of the territory they occupied, taking by force the wives and daughters of their victims. For this reason the women vowed never to eat with their abusers, or ever speak to them.

From the Milesian port of Panormos, a disembarking point for pilgrims and petitioners it was seven kilometres (four miles) to Didyma. The Oracle of Apollo at Didyma was second in importance only to that of the Delphic Oracle, though excavations at Claros, to the south of İzmir, and a re-reading of texts in the light of the discoveries made there, could well place its Oracle of Apollo on an equal footing with that of Didyma.

The site had been a sacred one long before the arrival of the Ionians. An earlier temple was at least partially destroyed when the Persians razed Miletus. At that time the oracle was in the keeping of the Branchidae, a priestly family who abandoned Didyma after the Persian victory. Either they took the cult image with them and set up a Shrine to Apollo at Sogdiana, or the Persians took the statue and then invited the Branchidae to establish the shrine. When Alexander came to Didyma, he made a sacrifice at the temple and ordered a rebuilding, a project that was continued on and off over the next 500 years, and in fact has never been completed. When Alexander defeated Darius, the Branchidae were hunted down and killed, and Seleucus, one of Alexander's generals, arranged for the return of Apollo to Didyma. The Goths sacked the temple in AD 256, and in early Byzantine times the adytum, or sacred chamber, was converted to a church.

Sights

İZMIR

Konak Square, south of the harbour, is modern İzmir's centre—as it was in the last of Smyrna's ancient cities—with the Town Hall, Opera House, Museum of Modern Art and a landmark in the form of a 19th-century clock tower of Moorish design. The bazaar occupies a network of streets off the east side of Konak Square, starting on Anafartalar Caddesi. A little to the east of it is the **Archaeological Museum**, which contains a rich display of exhibits from excavated sites in this region of the Aegean coast.

Among the notables is a statue of Poseidon from the second century BC and a bronze Demeter from the fourth century BC. There are sections of the sculpted frieze from the Temple of Aphrodite at Aphrodisias, if they have not been removed to the site museum, whose curator has claimed them. There are collections of jewels, coins and glassware. The **Ethnographic Museum** stands opposite.

To the north of the museums is the ancient agora, which Marcus Aurelius rebuilt after an earthquake in 178. On the west side is a section of a portico with 13 columns, all with their capitals, still standing. To the left of this is the entrance to a gallery, which would have had shops. On the north side are the remains of a basilica-style building on vaulted foundations. The entire site has been landscaped as a public garden. Mosques in the agora area are the Ottoman 16th-century **Hisar** and **Kemeralti**, both of which have undergone more than one restoration, as has the 18th-century **Sadirvan Mosque** with its external ablutions fountain. Dominating the city at its southeastern exit is **Mount Pagus**, upon which stood the ancient acropolis and where the Ottoman citadel **Kadifekale** now stands. Its medieval walls and towers were constructed on the substantial remains of the original citadel constructed by Lysimachus, one of Alexander's successors.

The city's main railway station is at Basmane on the north side. At Tepeçik, two kilometres (1.25 miles) south of the railway station, on the Melez Çayi, and where there is a lake whose water comes from several springs, are the remains of a **Roman Baths**; up river from here are aqueducts of Roman origin that were substantially rebuilt by the Byzantines and subsequently by the Ottomans.

OUT OF İZMIR

The choices for an excursion are manifold, and will naturally depend on time available to the visitor. Bathers, unless they can be content with the pool at the Buyuk Efes or other hotels, will be looking for a sandy beach. Such are to be found on the peninsula that stretches out westward into the Aegean Sea from south of the city, where sea bathing can be combined with archaeological exploration. If you use public transport, take a taxi, minibus or local bus from Konak Square going in the general direction of Çeşme.

İnciralti is a popular beach resort with restaurants, cafés and accommodation. Historically, it is a place of sulphur baths, and, archaeologically, its ancient curative establishment is the Agamemnon Kaplicalari, or **Baths of Agamemnon**, named for the leader of the Greeks during the Trojan War.

From Güzelbahçe, beyond İnciralti, take a road running southward across the peninsula to the site of **Teos**. This was one of 12 Ionian cities that combined to form a mercantile and naval federation. After the Persian conquest of the sixth century BC, the people of Teos, rather than endure Persian hegemony, removed themselves to Thrace in the north Aegean, where they founded the city of Abdera. Democritus, a pioneer of atomic physics, was born at Abdera. Anacreon, the poet, was a citizen of Teos. The remains of a Hellenistic **Temple to Dionysos** stands near the walls on the west of the lower part of the site, and on the south side of the acropolis hill is a theatre. There remain parts of an original square tower on a section of the ancient walls, and on the northeast are the ruins of a gymnasium and an odeon (recital hall). South of Teos is Myonessos on a rocky peninsula, another of the Ionian foundations, and to the north at Gümüldür is yet another, Lebedos. These sites deserve

a visit because of evidence offered of a high standard of civilization that existed in small communities.

Cross back over the peninsula to the north and continue westward from İnciralti to Urla. The ruins of the first city of **Clazomenae** lie on a small bay. Its citizens supported a revolt led by Miletus in 499 BC against Persian rule, but on the defeat of the Milesians, and to avoid reprisals, the Clazomenaeans transferred themselves *en bloc* to an island in the Gulf of Smyrna. Clazomenae was noted for its pottery and gave its name to a distinctive style of ceramic decoration. After Alexander had defeated Darius, the Clazomenaeans returned to the peninsula and built a new city. There is little to be seen, though excavators recovered examples of pottery that are on display in the İzmir museum and elsewhere. Anaxagoras, the natural scientist and tutor to Pericles, Athenian ruler of the classical period, was from Clazomenae.

West of Urla, the peninsula opens out to the north to form the western arm of the Gulf of İzmir. At İlidir, on a small bay a short distance along the coast, is **Erythrae**, another Ionian League site, though there is a claim that this city was founded by victorious Greeks after the conclusion of the Trojan War. There is evidence of early town planning here. The manufacture and export of millstones was a principal industry of the Erythraeans.

An outstanding feature of the port of Çeşme is its 15th-century **Genoese castle**. The Genoese had a self-governing colony at Phocaea (Foca) on the western arm of the Gulf of Smyrna. The castle was rebuilt by the Ottomans, who added a double wall with towers, a moat and an artillery terrace. Entrance is on the west side, facing the sea, where you cross the moat to a gate in the outer wall, then go left and through the inner wall. The Greek island of **Chios** lies to the west of Çeşme, only a short boat trip away. During summer months regular ferries operate for both passengers and cars; service is less frequent outside the summer season.

(opposite) Curetes Way, Ephesus. Hadrian's Temple fronts this extension of the Sacred Way (above) Column detail, Ephesus

EPHESUS (EFES)

SELÇUK

At Selçuk is the **Ephesus Museum**, which contains among its mass of interesting exhibits a **statue of Diana**, unearthed in 1966. This is considered to be the cult image that was buried by temple priests in the fourth century, following the edict of Emperor Theodosius for the destruction of all pagan temples. An angled road runs from the İzmir–Aydin dual-carriageway to the Kuşadası road, and on this, on the right, is the museum, with the Ministry of Information Office on its left.

The citadel hill is on the right as you enter Selçuk from İzmir. A paved roadway leads up the southern side of the hill, passing the site of a small temple with its ruins and a paved car park, to reach the impressive towered citadel entrance called—erroneously it seems—the **Persecution Gate**. A wide stairway mounts between high walls to the platform or plateau on which the Church of St John Theologos is built. Reconstruction of the church, and excavations on the site are being carried out by the Turkish Ministry of Culture and Information and the George B Quatman Foundation of Lima, Ohio.

Much of the city wall has been restored or reconstructed. On the west side of the hill is evidence of domestic and civic buildings. At the crown of the hill, the fortress walls and towers have been reconstructed. The main entrance is on the west side. In the interior, you can walk the steps leading up to a sentry walk just below the battlements. Within the fortress is a ruined mosque, a conversion from a Byzantine church, and another Byzantine structure. There are ancient cisterns, and, at the main gateway, what appears to be a guardroom.

Down below the wall is the restored İsabey Mosque, still within the city complex but appearing to be outside it; restoration has revealed its Byzantine origins. The high wall of the large rectangular court here is particularly impressive. From the walls on that western side of the citadel hill, other Byzantine structures can be noted, and the site of the Artemisium, the great temple, can be observed about two kilometres (1.25 miles) to the southwest.

The tiered and arched entrance to the **Church of St John Theologos** has been restored. On the west side is a chapel with apse, on the east side an apsed chapel with a mosaic floor and an altar. The pivotal interest is the restored baptistry, having an entrance at each cardinal point of the compass, and four arched recesses in the form of a four-leaved clover. At the centre is the font or baptismal pool permitting total immersion.

By taking a street opposite the car park below the Persecution Gate, you can walk down through the old part of city, wherein many houses have been converted into *pensions*, and stumble on a ruined Byzantine church. By this route you can also emerge on the Kuşadası road and, turning right, take a short parallel road to the

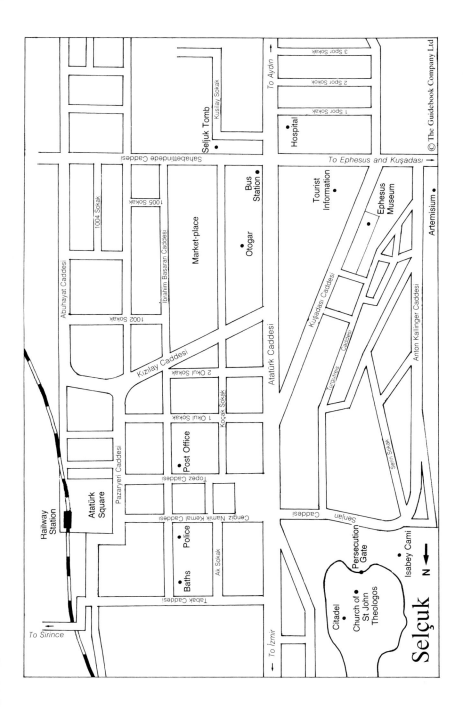

Railway Station

To Sirince

To İzmir

Atatürk Square

Pazaryeri Caddesi

Tabak Caddesi

Cengiz Namik Kemal Caddesi

Topaz Caddesi

Ak Sokak

Baths •

Police •

Post Office •

Abuhayat Caddesi

1004 Sokak

1002 Sokak

Kızılay Caddesi

1005 Sokak

İbrahim Basaran Caddesi

2 Okul Sokak

1 Okul Sokak

Koçak Sokak

Sahabettindede Caddesi

Market-place

Otogar •

Bus Station •

Kuşlay Sokak

Selçuk Tomb •

Atatürk Caddesi

To Aydın

3 Spor Sokak

2 Spor Sokak

1 Spor Sokak

Hospital •

To Ephesus and Kuşadası →

Tourist Information •

Kuşadası Caddesi

Turgutreis Caddesi

Ephesus Museum •

Anton Kallinger Caddesi

Artemisium •

Serin Sokak

Serin Caddesi

Citadel •

Church of St John Theologos •

Persecution Gate •

İsabey Cami •

N ↓

Selçuk

© The Guidebook Company Ltd

Artemisium—no entrance fee. The excavators have drained the marsh round the foundations of the great temple, once counted among the seven wonders of the ancient world. Aside from contemplating what was once here, there is little physical evidence to excite the observer. One column has been re-erected however, and the archaeologists may yet reveal other recoveries on site.

An aqueduct brought water to Justinian's city, and a number of the stanchions of this ruined edifice can be seen in the re-vamped market area of the town, near the railway station. In this section of Selçuk are some modest-class hotels and a number of *pensions*, as well as several restaurants. The streets are closed to traffic at nightfall, allowing visitors to sit out eating and drinking. On the south side of the bus station, a small public garden houses a neat Seljuk cone-topped *türbe*, as well as a Byzantine structure and an octagonal tomb, dated 1455, of a Muslim holy man from Sivas.

EPHESUS (EFES): THE EARLY SITES

A thorough exploration of Ephesus could occupy more than one day. Austrian archaeologists, working over many seasons, have excavated and restored the various sites.

In the area of the entrance there are restaurants, cafés and tourist boutiques. Faced with a number of options, it would be as well to follow a southerly itinerary from the entrance.

On the right is an arcaded **Verulaneum**, on the left a gymnasium with an arcaded court. Moving further on you reach the **Arcadian Way**,

Cornerstone of winged figure from a building on the Acropolis

a wide, paved and arcaded road that runs for 500 metres (1,640 feet) east–west from the great theatre to a silt-stolen harbour. Emperor Arcadius (395–408) constructed the roadway over an earlier one. Statues once stood on the pedestals located along its sides, and many of the columns that supported the covered arcades are still in place. At the western end, and flanking it, are the harbour gymnasium and harbour baths.

The theatre is built into the flank of Mount Pion. It was begun under Claudius (41–54) but completed only in Trajan's time (98–117). St Paul, who preached in it, spent three years in Ephesus, imprisoned for the greater part of that time. The city's silversmiths petitioned the governor for his execution, claiming that his anti-pagan teaching was crippling their trade in Diana-engraved mementoes and votive items for sale to pilgrims. There are enclosed stairways to the upper tiers. The façade was three-tiered but has only one tier now with niches in which statues once stood. The structure on the west side could have been a Hellenistic nymphaeum (fountain house).

Southwest of the theatre is a spacious Hellenistic lower agora with its porticoes and remains of shops. From here a colonnaded street ran west, with a gateway at each end. On the south side of the agora, a stairway leads to a platform or stylobate on which stands a **Temple of Serapis**, the Greek-Egyptian god. This structure with its Corinthian-style columns was converted to a church when pagan worship was abolished by Theodosias I.

On the agora's east side is the stylish, marble-paved **Marble Street**, which in origin had probably run from the Coressus Gate, situated northwest of the entrance to the site. Statues were set along this, and the medallions of gladiators can still be seen. Holes in the paving were for drainage.

At the southern end of the marble-paved street, on the right, is the **Library of Celsus**. Celsus was a governor of the province in the second century, and his son built the library to his father's memory. The fine two-tiered building has been reconstructed, along with its niches for manuscripts and parchments. In one of the niches is the coffin of Celsus.

A little below the library, the marble-paved street connects with the **Street of the Curetes**. This begins at the gate where there is a reconstructed ornamental fountain. Over from the street, to the right, is a group of Hellenistic houses which probably included those of the *curetes* (temple priests). On the left of the street is the brothel, and then comes a reconstructed **Temple of Hadrian**, alongside which is the **Scholastica Baths**, in which much of the conduit piping for heating and drainage can still be seen.

Beyond the baths, still on the left, and in the following order are a **Fountain of Trajan**, the **Gate of Heracles**, a monument ascribed to Memmius, and then a complex of buildings that include a hydreion (water tower), after which the area of the upper agora is reached. On the northern side is the prytaneum (the city prefect's administrative quarters) and a neat, reconstructed odeon (recital hall) of the second century, seating 1,400 and built by Publius Vedius Antoninus, a prefect and magistrate. Much of the original seating is in place.

Within the upper agora is a **Temple of Isis**. On the western side is the **Fountain of Pollio** and, still on the west, a **Temple to the Emperor Domitian**, erected during his reign (81–96), part of which now houses a **Museum of Inscriptions**.

Outside the area of this itinerary are some other buildings of interest. The House of the Virgin Mary, the **Meryemana** or Panayi Kapulu, east of the upper agora, can also be reached by going seven kilometres (four miles) along a direct roadway from Selçuk. Mary is said to have lived in Ephesus, having arrived there accompanied by the disciple John. Identification is of a comparatively recent date, attributed to the vision of a 19th-century German nun, but more than one Pope has since given credence to the fact by visiting the house at Ephesus. St John may have returned later to Ephesus, to write his gospel and to die there. His bones were later exhumed and reburied in the foundations of Justinian's church on the citadel hill in Selçuk.

There is a **Church of the Virgin Mary** to the west of the main entrance to the site, which is in fact a double building. The first church was erected in the fourth century over a pagan basilica and became the rendezvous for the Third Ecumenical Council of 431. Then, in the seventh century, a domed church was constructed within the first one. Today both churches harmonize as a single ruin.

One Ephesian legend is that of the **Seven Sleepers**. To avoid persecution, a group of young Christian men in the second century hid in a cave and fell asleep; they were rediscovered alive in the fifth century, in the time of Theodosias II. On their eventual deaths after a normal life span, this cave became their burial chamber and a church was constructed; this became a place of pilgrimage. A cave associated with the legend was discovered in the 1920s.

North of the site's main entrance, as you approach on the road from Selçuk, a second-century **Gymnasium of Vedius** with its porticoed court stands on the lower slope of a hill on the left. Further down on the right is a **Temple to Hera**, and over on the left (near where the Coressus Gate was) is the site of the stadium, built in the time of Nero (54–68), with its seating on one side cut into the hillside.

On the left, before reaching the car park and entrance, is a Byzantine building that was sited on a Hellenistic or early Roman predecessor. One of its chambers has niches for statues, while another room has an apse-like end wall and may have been a refectory.

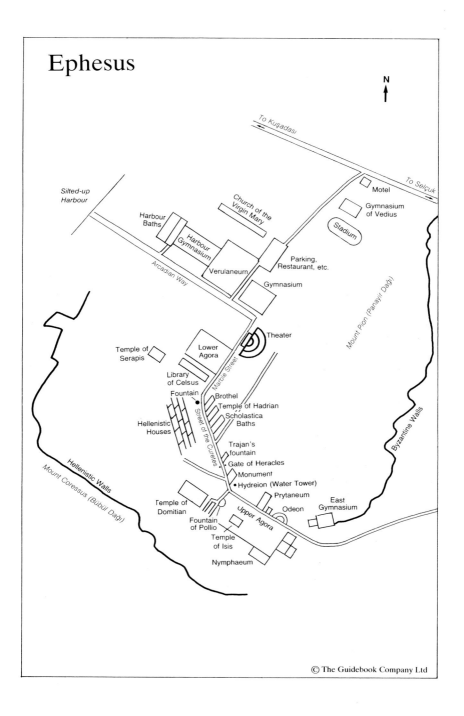

Ephesus

N

To Kuşadası

To Selçuk

Silted-up Harbour

Motel

Gymnasium of Vedius

Church of the Virgin Mary

Harbour Baths

Harbour Gymnasium

Stadium

Verulaneum

Parking, Restaurant, etc.

Arcadian Way

Gymnasium

Mount Pion (Panayir Dağı)

Temple of Serapis

Lower Agora

Theater

Marble Street

Library of Celsus

Fountain

Brothel

Temple of Hadrian

Scholastica Baths

Hellenistic Houses

Street of the Curetes

Trajan's fountain

Gate of Heracles

Monument

Hydreion (Water Tower)

Byzantine Walls

Hellenistic Walls

Mount Coressus (Bübül Dağı)

Temple of Domitian

Fountain of Pollio

Upper Agora

Prytaneum

Odeon

East Gymnasium

Temple of Isis

Nymphaeum

© The Guidebook Company Ltd

KUŞADASI

As with most tourist centres on the Aegean and Mediterranean coasts, Kuşadası has developed enormously. Its central streets have become a pedestrian enclave, and the old town gate is now almost lost among tourist boutiques selling carpets, leather goods, jewellery and souvenirs. There are good restaurants near the quayside and smaller, less expensive ones in the town. A causeway leads to an island in the harbour, Güverçin Ada or Pigeon Island. A castle there is an Ottoman rebuilding of an earlier Byzantine one, with modifications by the Genoese or Venetians, as both republics enjoyed trading rights here, granted them by the sultan in İstanbul.

There are a growing number of hotels, motels, camping sites and *pensions* on the approach roads from Selçuk. However, the most intense development is on the southern side of town, over the hill to the south on Kadinlar Plaj. The road to Söke mounts this hill, and after a kilometre or two, it branches off to the *plaj* (beach). There is another road running west from the Kuşadası harbour that eventually links up with the *plaj* road.

PRIENE

This fourth-century BC city was designed on a grid pattern by Hippodamas, the town planner of Miletus. It was built on the ascending lower ledges of Mount Mycale, which rises to 400 metres (1,313 feet). Only parts of the walls of the citadel on the crest remain. From the heights, the fall to the plain on the side facing the coast is almost sheer, and from up here the result of the Maeander River's silting activity can be observed. The sea is out of sight some 12 kilometres (eight miles) away, and former beds of the river turn and twist like serpents across the marshland. Priene had more than one harbour and its longshoremen were noted for their professionalism, even though they were often in dispute with those of Miletus over operating rights in the narrows. The harbours are lost somewhere under the silt.

The public buildings and the agora are located in a proximity which would have been most convenient for the citizens, and the principal streets were paved and arcaded. The line of the walls extends for over two kilometres (1.25 miles) along the base and up on the east and west sides to the citadel. The upper sections with their towers are Byzantine.

Enter through the **Fountain Gate** on the southeast. Along the lowest ledge, following the curve of the hill, is the stadium, built or reconstructed in the second century BC on an earlier one. It has seating only on the hillside because of the width of the terrace. Its length is 191 metres (627 feet), and the starting line for runners is marked. Adjoining it on the west is the lower gymnasium with its colonnaded court, changing rooms and washroom with lion-headed taps and stone baths. The walls of the room alongside are mottled with name-carvings, ancient graffiti.

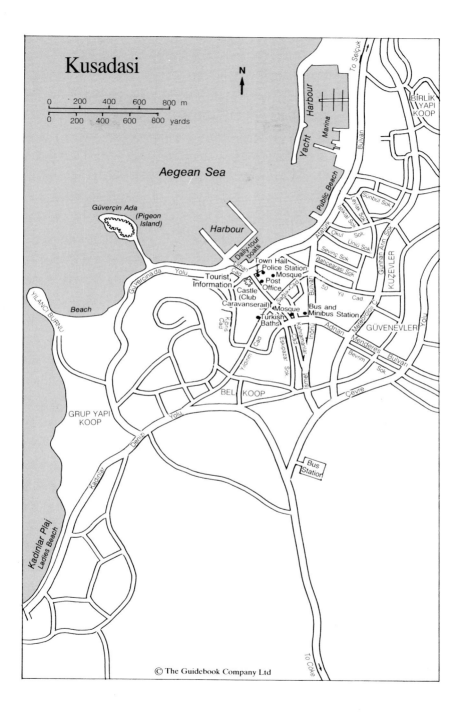

Kusadasi

N

Aegean Sea

Güverçin Ada
(Pigeon Island)

Harbour

Yacht Harbour

Marina

To Selçuk

BİRLİK YAPI KOOP

Public Beach

Bulvarı

Leylak Sok

Işıklar Sok

Sünbül Sok

Atatürk

Okul Sok

Ünlü Sok

Günhan Arin Sok

Güvercinada Yolu

Daily-tour boats

Town Hall
Police Station
Tourist Information
Castle
(Club Caravanserail)

Mosque
Post Office

Bahçearası Sok

Sevinç Sok

KUZEVLER

Kıbrıs Cad

Mosque

Turkish Baths

Bus and Minibus Station

50 Yıl Cad

Barbaros Cad

Bulvarı

YILANCI BURNU

Beach

Yıldırım Cad

Eskipazar Sok

İsmet İnönü Cad

Kahramanlar Cad

Adnan Menderes Bulvarı

Bevrim Sok

GÜVENEVLER

Yolu

Çevre

BEL KOOP

GRUP YAPI KOOP

Deniz Yolu

Kadınlar

Bus Station

Kadınlar Plaj
Ladies Beach

To Cöke

© The Guidebook Company Ltd

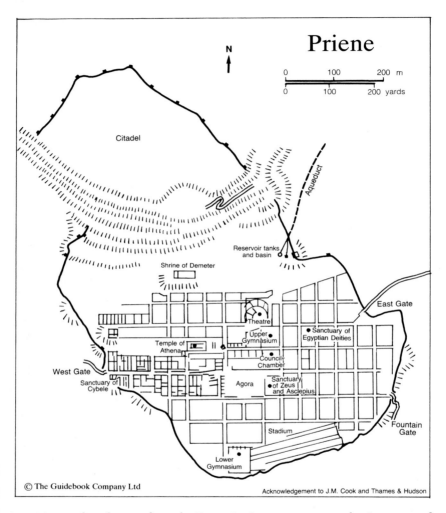

Priene

Moving directly west from the Fountain Gate, you come to the **Sanctuary of Zeus and Asclepius**. To the west is the agora with its public stoas, and, in the southwest corner, the market. Between here and the **West Gate** are the streets of houses, and on the south side of the gate itself a **Sanctuary of Cybele**.

On the terrace above, running along the north side of the agora, is the bouleuterion (council chamber) with its banks of seating on three sides and a carved stone altar at the centre. Its accompanying buildings were probably the

The ruins of Priene at Mt Mykale

civic offices. To the west of here, on a high terrace above it, is the Ionic **Temple of Athena** designed by Pytheos of Halicarnassus, and a stoa with Doric columns running along one side. The cult image, towards which Alexander is said to have contributed money, stood on a plinth in the forecourt. It was modelled on the one Phidias sculpted for the Parthenon in Athens. On the next level, and east of the temple, is the upper gymnasium, to the east of which is a **Sanctuary of Egyptian Deities**.

From the upper gymnasium, you climb a steep, stepped street to the theatre. Here the seating in the first row at the centre includes throne-like marble seats that were surely installed for distinguished citizens or visitors, and there is a marble altar, too, for ceremonial occasions. There are the changing rooms for performers, with a doorway into the stage or proscenium for every three rooms. The façade is of Doric half-columns; statues once stood in niches in the upper part of the entablature.

On the hillside above, near the walls on the east, is a **Shrine of Demeter**, along with cisterns and the remains of an aqueduct.

MILETUS

The ruins are strewn over a large area that includes the village of Balat, where some houses have made use of fallen items of marble. The **Roman theatre** is by far the most impressive building on the site. It was reconstructed under Trajan (98–117) on what in all probability was a Hellenistic rebuilding of an even earlier one. It held 25,000 people, the seating rising to 30 metres (100 feet). The lower tiers are in such good condition still that you might well be tempted to explore the crevices between the seats for ancient sweet wrappings. The width of the façade is 140 metres (460 feet). Above, the walls of an eighth-century Byzantine fort are merged into the theatre's upper gallery, though a previous fort probably existed here. Columns and blocks from a destroyed pagan temple or a fallen building have been incorporated into the structure, and there is evidence of Turkish rehabilitation subsequent to the Byzantine.

From the theatre's upper tiers the areas of two of the city's former harbours can be identified. To the northeast the **Lions Bay** had sculpted lions to guard it, and these still stand as sentinels on the dry sands. On the theatre's east side a rounded plinth was the base for a quayside sculpture erected by Augustus to celebrate a naval victory.

To the south and east of the naval monument is the northern agora with its surrounding stoas and shops. On the northeast corner is a **Sanctuary of Apollo**, the **Delphinion**, in which valuable inscriptions on blocks and votive offerings were found. To the north of the Delphinion, on the eastern edge of the former harbour

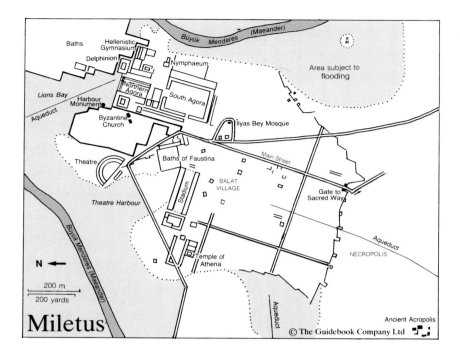

Miletus

and in a residential area, are the baths. Another residential area lay between the northern agora and the theatre.

The northwest corner of the northern agora has a restored Ionic-columned stoa standing on a stylobate of six steps, southwest of which is a Byzantine church that was probably built over a **Temple to Asclepius**. South of the Delphinion is a Hellenistic gymnasium, to the east of this a Roman baths dating from the time of Claudius (41–54). A Roman governor who may have built this could also have been responsible for the Ionic stoa.

Immediately south of the northern agora is the bouleuterion, and further south is the main entrance to the southern agora, whose two-tiered, three-arched, columned structure of Diocletian's time was reconstructed and moved to Berlin. On the top east corner of this agora is a first-century nymphaeum, once fed from an aqueduct south of the city. On the western side of the agora stands a **Temple to Serapis**, and a long building here could once have been a warehouse, perhaps for wool.

Return to the theatre and the area of its harbour. On the southernmost edge, 220 metres (720 feet) from the theatre's southern arm, is the large and extensive **Baths of Faustina**, named for the daughter of the Emperor Antoninus Pius and wife of

Marcus Aurelius (161–80), with a **mosaic of the River God** in its main pool. To the west are the remains of the stadium.

Northwest of the stadium is the site of a third agora, and on its southwest side is the sixth-century BC **Temple of Athena**, found by German excavators in the 1960s, along with evidence of Mycenaean and Carian occupation. To the east of this, in a courtyard of what could have been a large house, are the remains of a **Temple to Eumenes II** of Pergamum.

From the Baths of Faustina, a street runs southwest to the line of the ancient walls and a gateway leading out to the Sacred Way that ran to Didyma. An inscription of AD 100 found here dates a restoration to the time of Trajan. There are some sections of Hellenistic walls here, and outside the gateway is a necropolis.

The head of Medusa, from the Temple and Oracle of Apollo at Didyma

On the summit of **Kalabak Tepe**, a hill beyond, was the acropolis of Miletus prior to 494 BC. South of the hill is a section of that early city's walls of about 650 BC.

The **Mosque of Ilyas Bey** is an early 15th-century structure with a fine dome. Built during the Emirate of the Mentese, the mosque was constructed with material incorporated from the Ionian city. Not far from the mosque, on the street running to the Sacred Way, is the site museum.

DIDYMA

The Sacred Way was colonnaded throughout its length, with shops along it, and over the last 350 metres (1,150 feet) were marble lions at intervals, alternating with sphinxes and seated figures, all terminating in a sacred wood. One lion still lies in place within the temple enclosure, near the entrance. Much of the recovered sculpture that was excavated during the mid-19th century, though, is in the British Museum.

An earthquake in 1456 took a heavy toll on the temple. One column has been left as it fell, opened up like a pack of cards set for choice of dealer. As with the temple at Sardis, the column bases have fine and varied carvings.

Only three columns of the temple are standing fully erect, two with their Ionic capitals supporting a section of carved architrave. From the foot of the wide stairway leading up to the stylobate and the columned pronaos, however, there is

Cotton harvesters, Miletus

an impression of a complete temple, since parts of almost all the 122 columns are there, standing at varying, truncated heights.

The orientation of the structure is northeast–southwest. At the northeast end, there is a semicircular terrace dating from a period earlier than the time of the present structure. Within the temple a walled court contained the innermost sanctum, the adytum. This is set seven metres (23 feet) below a seven-stepped stylobate, and entrance was gained via tunnel-like passageways on either side leading down to the lower level. A wide seven-stepped marbled stairway leads up from the adytum to a columned chamber with an entrance on either side. Petitioners were probably not allowed beyond this chamber, access to the oracle being confined to the priests and initiates. A sacred olive tree stood within the sanctuary, which is surrounded by high walls supported by pilasters on which were gryphon-headed capitals; many of these stand on the floor of the adytum. The roped-off oracle section of the shrine contains the circular hole over which the priestess inhaled vapours from the sacred trance-inducing spring that ran below. A petitioner would have his request transcribed in verse by an official priest, and the reply would be in verse, pronounced in the antechamber and more often than not couched in ambiguous terms, as was the reply to Croesus at Delphi. A bronze cult image of the god stood in a separate sacred chamber.

A circular sacrificial altar stands in front of the main stairway to the temple. To the right of this, on the embankment at the entrance, near the lion, is a carved head of the Medusa, which was part of an original main frieze. To the right of the altar is a sacred well.

Games were held at the shrine, with its gymnasia, baths and accommodation for participants. On the southeast side are the remains of marble seating installed for spectators. On the steps along the stylobate are non-professional carvings of circles and squares that may have been boards for dicing whereby waiting petitioners could try to predict the result of their requests. To the left of the main stairway, a broken section allows entrance to what appears to be a small chamber, enclosed by a block with a Greek inscription.

Excavation continues outside the enclosure. North of two restaurants about 500 metres (1,600 feet) along, there is what appears to be the site of a smaller temple and an arched entry, plus sections of an aqueduct, an agora and an area of private dwellings.

Nine kilometres (six miles) south of the Temple of Apollo, at the end of the peninsula, is the holiday destination of **Altınkum** with its fine sandy beaches. Hotels, motels and a marina are found on this bay. There is ribbon development along a wide roadway, and the *plaj* is one favoured and promoted by Western European package-tour operators.

THE UNVEILING

*M*y mother was rebelling against life too—but for a different reason. Her rebellion was, unexpectedly enough, against wearing the veil, for she had noticed that none of the foreign women wore them and that even a few of the more daring Turkish women from good families had ceased the practice also. She used to complain about it to my grandmother, declaring she was sick and tired of keeping her face covered, and I would interrupt, with lordly ten-year oldness, saying I would not have her going about the streets with her face open. I would chastise her too for her many goings-out.

'You are never at home,' I would declare and although usually I was told to mind my own affairs, one day I was very surprised when my grandmother actually agreed with me.

'It is quite true,' she said heatedly. 'You are always out these days. And it is not right for you to complain that you have to wear the veil. Why, many women are still behind the kafes and they never see the colour of the sky, excepting from behind their veils. But at least you cannot complain of that for you tore the kafes from here and it is a wonder to me that you were ever accepted in this street, for you behaved exactly like a fast woman looking for another husband or like a prostitute. Yes, you did!' she assured my mother's astonished face. 'And now you talk of leaving aside your veil. Why, I lived for thirty years with my husband and I never went out without his permission and I had to keep my face covered all the time. If I went out in the carriage with Murat, immediately all the windows were closed and sometimes the blinds were drawn too. I say it is a scandal that women are today revealing their faces. God will punish them! Do not let me hear another word from you, my daughter, for surely the sky will open on you for such impiety.'

Never had I heard my grandmother talk at such length or with such obvious passion. My mother replied:

'You are talking a great deal of old-fashioned nonsense, mother! My place is not in the home these days. If I were to sit at home all day, or you either for that matter, who would go to market for us? Do you expect me to stay here all day, reading the Koran and wearing my veil for fear the passers-by should see me from the street? I tell you again, from now on I shall go without my veil!'

And she angrily tore the pretty veil from her face and threw it petulantly on the floor.

My grandmother lifted her hands to heaven.

'I never thought I should live to see this day,' she said.

'Times are changing,' said my mother.

'They will say you are a prostitute!' wailed my grandmother, genuinely distressed, totally incapable of accepting such a fierce gesture as the 'opening' of the face.

'If they do, it will not worry me,' retorted my mother. 'Their words will not bring bread to me. And from now on, you will throw aside your veil too, mother.'

'Oh no, no, no!' said my grandmother in superstitious horror. 'God forbid I should invite punishment upon me!'

But the next morning when my mother went into Beyoglu, with a box of embroidered articles under her arm and her lovely face naked to the world, she was stoned by some children near Bayazit and received a nasty cut on the side of her head. After that she was cautious about going anywhere alone, but was adamant about not re-veiling herself; Mehmet or I would go with her to Beyoglu, my grandmother steadfastly refusing to be seen with her. The reaction to her in the street was mixed. The older ones were stricken with horror, more especially since they had always recognised my mother as a good woman, and now their faith in her was sadly battered. She was still young and attractive—she was twenty-five— and despite the shadows that lingered now and then in her eyes, was so unusually beautiful that people could not help but stare at her, and certain sections of the street wondered if she were trying to catch a husband. They came in their droves, the old men as well, to remonstrate with my grandmother, urging her to put a stop to this terrible thing, and my grandmother, thoroughly enjoying herself, would groan to them that she had no authority left in this wayward family of hers. But the younger women sided with my mother, and some of them even began to follow her example. Their fathers, however, in the absence of dead husbands, took a stick to them muttering piously that no woman in their family would so disgrace themselves. So they put on their veils again in a hurry.

Irfan Orga, Portrait of a Turkish Family

Diversions Inland

If İzmir is your chosen base, a two-day journey inland to Manisa and Sardis could be made before moving south. Manisa is set neatly on a plain at the edge of a mountain. The Hermus river flows through the plain between Manisa and Sardis, on its way to the Gulf of İzmir; this is an area of orchards and vineyards. Near Sardis the burial tumuli of kings are conspicuous over a wide area.

Pamukkale, and the ruins of Hierapolis, can be found inland from Kuşadası on a plateau 100 metres (330 feet) above the plain. At Pamukkale the water from a thermal spring, flowing over the plateau's lip to the plain, has formed remarkable travertines, or irregular shelves. Calcareous deposits have contributed a veneer of translucent crystal to them, hence the Turkish appellation of Cotton Castle.

A number of motels and hotels here have channelled the hot spring water into constructed pools on their premises. The oldest of the pools is at the Pamukkale Motel, where you can float over fluted drums, capitals and sections of architrave. Here at the source of the spring sacred to Apollo, you can be certain of the god's blessing in water at a temperature of 37°C (98°F).

Although the city of Hierapolis was either founded or built up by the Attalids of Pergamum, the ruins at Pamukkale are predominantly Roman and Byzantine. Should you decide to stay in one of the motels on the ridge, or down in the nearby village, an excursion to Aphrodisias could be taken, as to other neighbouring sites such as Laodicea, Nyssa, Tralles and Magnesia on the Maeander.

Getting There

Leaving İzmir, take the Bornova road for Manisa, 36 kilometres (22 miles) to the northwest. To go from Manisa to Sardis, take road 250 for 27 kilometres (17 miles) to its junction with the E23. Turn left through Türgütlü to Salihli, another 44 kilometres (27 miles): the site of Sardis, or Sart, is five kilometres (three miles) to the west of Salihli, the E5 from İzmir in fact intersecting the excavations.

A second diversion inland could start from Kuşadası or Selçuk by taking the E24 to Aydin. The road continues along the Maeander valley through Sultanhisar, Nazili and Saraköy to Denizli, 165 kilometres (103 miles) from Selçuk. Pamukkale, 19 kilometres (12 miles) from Denizli, is reached on a main roadway, the Celal Bayer Bulvarı, that runs north from a roundabout at the east end of the town. The Denizli *otogar*, for those travelling by bus, is off to the right of the E24, shortly before reaching the roundabout. You will find the *dolmuş* stand at the side of the road. Pamukkale village, on the left of the road as you approach the site, is developing as a tourist centre with hotels, motels and *pensions*. Continue for another kilometre (0.6 miles) to the main square and the ruins of Hierapolis.

The minibus for Aphrodisias leaves Pamukkale village at 10am and takes approximately two hours, going east on the Isparta road before turning south and then west through Tavas and Karaçasu. Three hours are available for visiting the site; the bus departs for Pamukkale at 2.30pm. Another route to Aphrodisias is from Nazili, a town on the E24 road from İzmir. Twelve kilometres (eight miles) east of Nazili, a road turns south for Karaçasu.

On returning from Pamukkale to Denizli, the road to Laodicea, or Ladik, is signposted after nine kilometres (six miles). Nyssa is to the north of Sultanhisar, 25 kilometres (16 miles) west of Nazili. Another 30 kilometres (19 miles) west near Aydin, Tralles is situated on a hill. The E24 passes through the ruins of ancient Magnesia on the Maeander at Tekke, near Ortaklar, 19 kilometres (12 miles) west of Aydin.

Historical Background

At Manisa in 190 BC the Romans defeated Antiochus III and put an end to Seleucid (Hellenistic) rule in Asia Minor. Magnesia was given to Rome's ally, the then reigning king of Pergamum (Bergama on the map, to the north of Manisa).

After Alexander died at Babylon in 323 BC, the territory he had conquered became a battleground of his immediate successors, each of them wanting to inherit his extensive empire, for the next 133 years.

During his last hours Alexander, unable to speak, gave his signet ring to Perdiccas, and this general became Regent for the as yet unborn child of Roxane, Alexander's Persian wife. She gave birth to a son, Alexander IV, but Meleagev, the Commander of the Infantry, by threatening action, prevailed on Perdiccas to make Arrhidaes, Philip II's bastard and half-wit, the half-brother of Alexander the Great, joint King. Eurydice, Philip II's legitimate daughter, married Arrhidaes so as to establish her right and that of her offspring as claimants to the throne and the Alexander inheritance.

Under the Regency of Perdiccas, Antipater became governor of Egypt (which in fact he had occupied) and Eumenes governor of Cappadocia. Perdiccas was killed in a battle against Ptolemy, and Antipater, on becoming Regent, appointed Seleucus governor (or satrap, as it was known in the East) of Babylon. Antigonus became governor of Asia. Antipater confirmed Ptolemy in his governorship of Egypt.

In 317 BC Olympias, Alexander's mother, wife of Philip II, caused Philip III to be executed, and a little later Cassander, heir to Antipater who had died, imprisoned Alexander IV and Roxane and then had them killed; Eurydice was made powerless.

A kind of free-for-all now ensued between the several claimants, and the governors now began to refer to themselves as kings. Seleucus was in control in Syria and large areas of Anatolia, Persia, and eastern possessions of Alexander until he lost them to the Indian King Chandragupta. Antigonus now controlled Macedonia, Ptolemy had Egypt and had extended his power into Libya, and included Lydia and Pamphylia in Asia Minor among his possessions. Cappadocia in Central Anatolia was under Attalus, the heir to Eumenus.

By 311 BC five kingdoms existed. Antiochus had succeeded Seleucus in Syria and eastern Anatolia, and Ptolemy had extended his holdings into parts of southern Greece; the Kingdom of Pergamum had become established by the Attalids in Western Anatolia and the Antagonids were in control in Macedonia and the greater part of Greece. There were as well a number of other players such as Lysimachus in Thrace, and the Kings of Epirus and Lyncestis, territories in northern Greece and Macedonia. And by 200 BC the Romans were in occupation of what is now part of Albania.

Antiochus III was also named 'the Great', and he succeeded to the Seleucid throne in 223 BC. As with other successors of Alexander, he too had an ambition to recapture and control the whole of the great King's empire. Not without success in his first campaigns, he gained control of the greater part of Anatolia, and even regained control of territory lost in Iran, east of the Tigris. In turning his attention to Ptolemy, however, he invaded Egypt but lost the battle of Raphia, and was obliged to surrender Palestine, which he had occupied. By 198 BC Antiochus had gained control of Pergamum and Bithynia (Bursa region), and the Greek free cities of Smyrna and Lampsacus. In 203 BC, he made an agreement with Philip V of Macedonia jointly to invade Egypt, whereby Antiochus could avenge his earlier defeat by Ptolemy IV, who had since then died. The Egyptian King Ptolemy V appealed to Rome for assistance, and to the free Greek cities, and again Antiochus failed in Egypt, reaching no further than Gaza, but he did regain Palestine. In 199 BC the Romans declared war on Philip V, ostensibly in support of the anti-Macedonian Greek cities, and they defeated Philip at Cynocephalae in 197 BC, whereby Antiochus lost his ally. However, because he was fired anew by the idea of becoming King of Alexander's country and the true inheritor of the Empire—the previous year he had taken Cania and Cilicia in Anatolia from Egypt—he now occupied Gallipoli and Thrace which was territory belonging to Philip V.

The Roman Proconsul Flaminius arrived in Greece to help settle affairs with the Greek cities following the war with Philip V, and he insisted on Antiochus getting out of Europe, and with a Roman sprat to catch a mackerel, spread a rumour that Ptolemy V of Egypt had died without issue. Antiochus' thoughts now reverted to the idea of the conquest of Egypt, and left Europe, but in fact Ptolemy was not dead.

The great Carthaginian General Hannibal now comes into the story. He had fought successfully against Rome in the Carthaginian Wars, but had been exiled by his own people after they had become subject to Rome. He now became an adviser to Antiochus, and advocated an invasion of Italy. Antiochus began to recruit an army for this purpose, although neither he nor Rome had any real wish for conflict.

In 194 BC, Rome evacuated Greece, but now the Aetolians, who had been Rome's allies against Philip V, believing they had come badly out of the deal, now enlisted the support of Antiochus, offering unbeatable conditions for a victorious campaign against Philip.

Against Hannibal's advice, Antiochus sent an undermanned expedition to Greece in support of the Aetolians, and initially some minor successes were enjoyed; but the Romans now declared in favour of Philip V, an army commanded by the Scipio brothers arrived in Greece and Antiochus was routed at a battle at Thermopylae. He retired in a hurry to Anatolia, while the Aetolians submitted to Rome and Philip.

Antiochus was sure the Romans would not follow up in Anatolia, but then Pergamum, Rhodes and Carthage joined the Roman–Philip V alliance against him, and in 191 BC Roman warships were in the Aegean. The joint naval forces of Antiochus and Hannibal were defeated at a sea battle at Cissas, and Antiochus spent the ensuing winter at Magnesia, a city some 50 miles inland from the Aegean Coast. Then in 190 BC, a Roman army of some 20,000 men under the Scipios moved east. There followed actions by land and sea resulting in successes and defeats for both sides, but the Romans gained and maintained naval control of the Aegean, defeating Hannibal's navy fought by Rome's ally, Rhodes, off the Mediterranean coast at Side in Pamphyllia; and then the combined Roman–Rhodia fleet put paid to Antiochus' fleet off Myonnesus in the Aegean. The King of Bithynia, who was an ally of Antiochus, made a separate peace with Rome, the Roman army crossed the Dardanelles into Asia Minor, and in 190 BC at the Battle of Magnesia Antiochus was defeated, and the Romans were in Anatolia to stay.

Antiochus withdrew to Antioch, and he still had his possessions in the East, but for Europe the Hellenistic age had ended. As an ally of Rome the Pergamum Kingdom of Attalids extended its territory especially at the expense of Bithynia, and it gained the port of Antalya on the Mediterranean, in Pamphyllia. Hannibal at first took service with the King of Armenia, a rising power in Eastern Anatolia, but the Romans and the Carthaginians were after his blood, and rather than submit to captivity and degradation he committed suicide by poisoning.

Mount Sipylus is associated with the mythical Niobe, who was the sister of Pelops and wife of King Amphion of Thebes. On Leto's orders, Niobe's 14 children were killed by Artemis and Apollo, Leto's offspring by Zeus, because Niobe had too proudly denigrated the goddess' comparative infertility. Niobe wept continuously for her children, and in pity Zeus turned her into insensitive stone, though the tears continued. A natural rock formation above Manisa can be said to resemble a mourning woman. At Akpinar, seven kilometres (four miles) southeast, a carved relief, the Tas Suret, is also said to be of Niobe, but this more likely is considered to be a Hittite carving of the Anatolian Mother-goddess Cybele, as the Phrygians called her.

Lying as it did on the Royal Road to Susa, Sardis was a key city for the Hittites and a principal one for the Persians later. The Lydians were indigenous to the region, or they had migrated to it from the east at an early date. Their language is considered to have been a mixture of Semitic and Indo-Aryan. Their principal goddess was Cybele, and their symbol of sovereignty was a double-headed axe. They claimed descent from Atys, son of a Phrygian god, Manes; Omphale, one of their queens, consorted with Heracles and thereby inaugurated the Heraclid Dynasty, which came to an end with Candaules.

Gyges, the Mermnad and a courtier, was Candaules' best friend. The king, wanting to share with him an appreciation of his queen's undressed beauty, persuaded him to hide in her bedchamber. The queen, offended by what she considered an act of indecency, prevailed on Gyges to murder Candaules and marry her.

Under the Mermnad Dynasty, Lydia attained the acme of its power and civilizing influence. The Lydians were probably instrumental in preventing the Greek Ionian colonizers from penetrating too far beyond the coastal areas, and for a substantial time the Lydians later dominated the cities of the coast, except for Miletus. Croesus lost his throne to Cyrus, the Achaemenid Persian, ostensibly because he misinterpreted the response of the Delphic Oracle to a question concerning his invincible power. An inconclusive battle was fought in 546 BC at the Halys River, and Croesus, having got the worst of the encounter, retired to Sardis for the winter to reshape his army. Against the unwritten rules of war of the time, Cyrus followed and took Croesus by surprise. Though Cyrus intended to put the king to death, he changed his mind, and instead Croesus received courteous and generous treatment until his eventual death in exile.

Hellenistic in origin, the Romans reconstructed and enlarged Aphrodisias. An early sanctuary to Cybele—perhaps earlier to the Anatolian Great Mother, with whom the Babylonian goddess Ishtar may have been associated—became one to Aphrodite (Roman Venus). In Byzantine times, in the fifth century AD, it was named Stavropolis and was the seat of a bishop. The Seljuks took it in the 12th century, and again in the 13th after a brief reoccupation under the Byzantine Manuel I (1143–80). After the city's destruction by Timur in the 15th century, the site remained abandoned.

Sights

MANISA

Apart from the Byzantine walls on Manisa's citadel hill, there is little to show for the occupations from pre-Hellenistic through to Ottoman times. In the town, though, are several notable mosques; the oldest is the **Ulu Cami** on Sandik Tepe. Completed during the 1370s, it was built for Isak Celebi, an independent Saruhanoğlu emir, whose tomb is within the complex. Material from an earlier Byzantine structure is incorporated in the surrounding portico. On a main crossroads the **Muradiye** of 1583–86 has been fully restored, and the decoration of the *mihrab* is of interest. In its *medrese* is a small archaeological museum. Nearby, the **Sultan Cami**, dating from 1552, was built for the mother of Suleiman the Magnificent. Close to the *vilayet* (the offices of the *vali*, or governor of the province) on Atatürk Bulvarı is the **Hatuniye Cami** of 1485, built by the wife of Beyazıt II, whose son Murat (later Murat III) served as a governor of this province. The Çeşniger Cami, in the same area, dates from 1475. It is attributed to a slave liberated by Mehmet II, the future sultan, who was a student here.

SARDIS

Some of the Lydian burial mounds on the plain between Manisa and Sardis have been excavated and identified, notably that of Alyattes, Croesus' father, and Gyges, the founder of the Mermnad Dynasty, of which Croesus was the last representative.

The excavations at Sardis separate into three sections. After the road (E5) has crossed the Pactolus River, on the north side is the first group of buildings. In Roman times a large Jewish community lived here, and an impressive synagogue has been excavated and restored by the Sardis Expedition of Harvard University. North of this and adjoining it is a second-century gymnasium and baths, with its

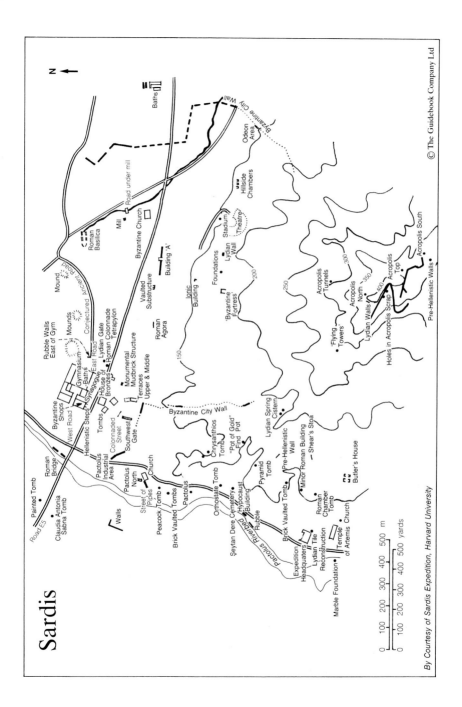

Sardis

N

Baths

© The Guidebook Company Ltd

Road under mill

Mill

Roman
Basilica

Byzantine Church

Building 'A'

Vaulted
Substructure

Byzantine City Wall

Odeon
Area

Hillside
Chambers

Stadium
'Theatre'
Lydian
Wall

Foundations

Ionic
Building

'Byzantine
Fortress'

200

250

300

350

400

Acropolis
Tunnels

Acropolis
North

Lydian Walls

Acropolis
Top

Acropolis South

Pre-Hellenistic Walls

Holes in Acropolis Scarp

'Flying
Towers'

Mound

Mound

Mounds

Conjectured Ancient Road

Rubble Walls
East of Gym

Gymnasium
Baths
Synagogue
House of
Bronzes
Byzantine
Shops
East Road
Lydian Gate
Roman Colonnade
Tetrapylon

Monumental
Mudbrick Structure

Terraces
Upper & Middle

Roman
Agora

150

Hellenistic Steps

West Road

Tombs

Colonnaded
Street

Southwest
Gate

Roman
Bridge

Pactolus
Industrial
Area

Pactolus
North
Church

Pactolus

Painted Tomb

Claudia Antonia
Sabna Tomb

Road E5

Walls

Street
of Pipes

Peacock
Tomb

Brick Vaulted Tombs

Pactolus
River

Şeytan Dere Cemetery

Orthostate Tomb

Chrysanthios
Tomb

"Pot of Gold"
Find Pot

Lydian Spring
Cistern

Pyramid
Tomb

Pre-Hellenistic
Wall

Minor Roman Building

Shear's Stoa

Butler's House

Brick Vaulted Tomb

Hypocaust
Building

Rubble

Roman
Chamber
Tomb

Expedition
Headquaters

Lydian Tile
Reconstruction

Temple
of Artemis
Church

Marble Foundation

0   100   200   300   400   500 m

0   100   200   300   400   500 yards

By Courtesy of Sardis Expedition, Harvard University

elegantly reconstructed nymphaeum. To the west of the synagogue, along the roadside, is a line of shops. Thirty metres (100 feet) east of the synagogue is a **Roman colonnade**, and a little to the east again is a **Lydian gate**.

On the south side of the E5, opposite the above buildings, is a **House of Bronzes**, which may have been a bishop's residence, to the immediate southwest of which are some Hellenistic tombs. South again there is part of a colonnaded street with terraces on its east and west sides, and beyond, on the west, is the **Southwest Gate**. One hundred metres (330 feet) east of the House of Bronzes stands a monumental structure in mudbrick.

Turning south at the E5 crossroads, move down the river from which gold was panned and refined. Refineries have been excavated on the banks, and Lydia may have introduced the minting of coins. The temple is about 1,000 metres (3,300 feet) from the turn, or 150 metres (500 feet) beyond the headquarters and site museum of the expedition. Two columns stand against a jagged sandstone outcrop on top of which the now eroded and serrated acropolis was located. There are sections of Byzantine fortifications on the heights, and excavation on a Lydian-Persian spur in 1985 revealed a Masonic structure, probably the base of a sixth-century Lydian building. Lydian items were also found below a Roman house on this same spur.

The **Temple of Artemis** was begun in 550 BC, built over an earlier one to Athena. As seen from carvings on existing column bases, designs throughout were unusual. During the Ionian Revolt, men from Ephesus set fire to the temple, Sardis being the seat of a Persian satrap. Alexander in his day honoured the citizens of Sardis as non-Greek Hellenes, and as always he encouraged work of reconstruction.

Back at the E5 crossroads, go east 800 metres (2,600 feet) along the road from the synagogue. Off to the north, about 50 metres (165 feet) is a Byzantine cruciform church, and 250 metres (820 feet) northwest of it is another in basilica form. East of these two buildings, 700 metres (2,300 feet), is a baths. To the northeast of the gymnasium are burial mounds. On the south side of the E5, 300 metres (1,000 feet) east of the mudbrick monument, is the area of the Roman agora. East again, 150 metres (500 feet), is a vaulted substructure, then 50 metres (165 feet) to the east is another building that is probably Roman. Southeast from here, 200 metres (660 feet), are the stadium and, further south, the theatre and a Byzantine fortress. East of the stadium, 350 metres (1,150 feet), is an odeon. One important find of 1985 was a child's grave of the tenth century BC.

PAMUKKALE

At the top of the ridge are the ruins of Hierapolis. The minibus stops in an open square not far from a Roman baths of the first century, dating from the reign of

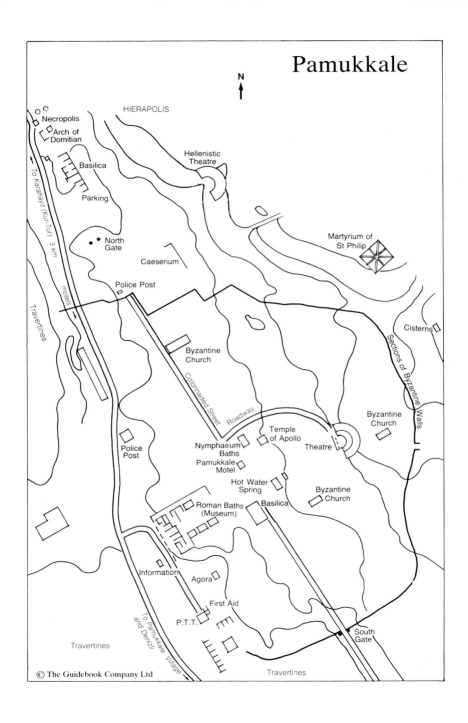

Pamukkale

N

Necropolis
Arch of Domitian
HIERAPOLIS
Basilica
Parking
To Karahayit (Kür-Tür) 3 km
Hellenistic Theatre
Martyrium of St Philip
motels
North Gate
Caeserium
Travertines
Police Post
Cisterns
Byzantine Church
Colonnaded Street
Roadway
Sections of Byzantine Walls
Police Post
Byzantine Church
Temple of Apollo
Nymphaeum Baths
Theatre
Pamukkale Motel
Hot Water Spring
Byzantine Church
Roman Baths (Museum)
Basilica
Information
Agora
First Aid
To Pamukkale Village and Denizli
P.T.T.
South Gate
Travertines
© The Guidebook Company Ltd
Travertines

Tiberius when the city was rebuilt after an earthquake. Now the museum on the grounds features a fine display of statuary and inscribed stelae, among other recovered items. During summer months a mobile bank offering foreign exchange currencies is likely to be standing near the entrance to the museum.

Along the lower, northeastern end of the square are the premises of the Pamukkale Motel, which includes a restaurant, and changing cabins on the right. Behind the motel, on the left, is a nymphaeum, and above this on the hillside is the site of the **Temple to Apollo**. Higher and to the east is the theatre, clearly visible from the square; tour buses drive to the top. Above and to the east of the theatre is a Byzantine church, and above are sections of the city walls.

To the right of the motel is a ruined Byzantine basilica, and above, on a line with the nymphaeum, was the entrance to the plutonium, in which noxious fumes from an underground stream inspired an oracle's prophecies. On the hill above the basilica is the site of the agora, and away to the right of the basilica, continuing in the direction of a colonnaded street, is the **South Gate**.

On the left or northwestern side of the main square, the remains of the colonnaded street lead to the **North Gate** and to the **Necropolis**. Below this, running from the square, a road leads along the ridge to a number of hotels and motels, all of which have their curative water and pools. The road continues for three kilometres (1.9 miles) to the village of Karahayit. At one point it meets and runs parallel with the colonnaded street, where it leads through ruins of former public buildings and private houses, including a basilica, approached by way of the **Arch of Domitian**, a necropolis of many impressive tombs. On the hillside, well above the necropolis, and to the east of it, is the fifth-century **Martyrium of St Philip**, dedicated to the apostle who died here for his faith in AD 80. Philip's two daughters, both reputable as prophetesses, are also buried in the Martyrium.

The Roman agora is behind the museum; nearby are other motels with their pools, and the Ministry of Tourism's information office.

LADIK (LAODICEA)

The church of this ancient city was one of the biblical Seven Churches of Asia. St Paul's stricture on Laodicean Christianity has provided the English language with the epithet 'laodicean', meaning neither positive nor negative, neither hot nor cold. The city is situated below a hill near the village of Eskihisar, with its citadel on the hilltop. The Roman ruins include a stadium, gymnasium, odeon and theatre.

APHRODISIAS

Aphrodisias stands on a low plateau under Baba Dağ, the mountain where the marble for its buildings was quarried. The site is under extensive excavation and reconstruction, with many sections roped off. Nevertheless, there is much of interest to see. From the car park entrance a short roadway leads into a square that was the village of Geyre until this was demolished and the inhabitants transplanted to a new village of Geyre nearby. On the left of the square is a café and a reconstructed timbered building, and on the right, on the northeast corner, is the museum.

Take the path to the left just below the café. A columned structure is next to a Byzantine chapel, along with a number of sarcophagi. There are many of these stone coffins off the approach road to the square, and perhaps the line of the city's walls stood there, with the tombs outside the walls. The pathway skirts the head-quarters and workshops of the archaeological expedition, eventually reaching the theatre. If the area is roped, you may climb the hill to enter the theatre at the level of its uppermost tiers, and look down to the columned façade, dressing rooms, proscenium (stage) and orchestra. In front is a paved court with a stoa and a circular altar, a gymnasium and, on the right-hand side, a columned temple or basilica with an ornamental gateway, and what could be a second agora. This makes for an impressive bird's-eye view.

The area on the right of the theatre, as you descend, has a large and lengthy main agora, under excavation and reconstruction. Go on round to another portico, that of Tiberius, to the area of **Hadrian's Baths**, a complex that includes a gymnasium, a palaestra (exercise ground) and a columned pool or ornamental fountain. The tiled court of the palaestra has a number of tiles with Greek inscriptions.

Continuing northeasterly, past what could be an extension of the main agora, is the **Bishop's Palace**, to the east of which is an odeon (recital hall). North of the palace and odeon is **Aphrodite's Temple**, containing the remains of the Byzantine church that superseded it, making use of the temple's columns and adding an apse.

A considerably large space lies between the palace and odeon and the stadium, situated on the line of the city walls on the north and incorporated as part of them. It is a well-preserved stadium, and it could be of interest to speculate on why theatres and stadiums have on the whole survived in better condition than other structures, and in particular the seating: perhaps it is because the seating is banked, and therefore to an extent reinforced, with only the superstructure liable to damage from earthquake, assault and the erosion of time.

Sections of the city wall are in good condition, particularly to the east of the stadium, near a section with a tower and gateway. A gateway on the left is less obvious but can be clearly seen from the stadium's upper tier.

Following the direction of the walls, again a fair and dusty distance, the tetrapylon (ornamental gateway) has been impressively reconstructed. Much of this area was marshland before it was drained, and between the tetrapylon and the main entrance square there are columned buildings under recovery and reconstruction.

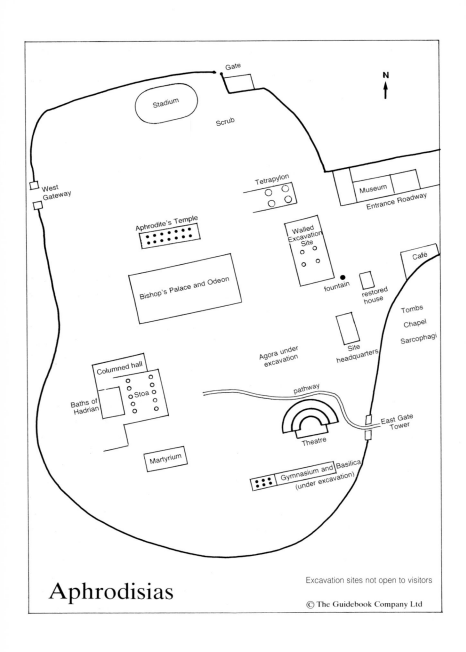

Gate

Stadium

Scrub

N
↑

West
Gateway

Tetrapylon

Museum

Entrance Roadway

Aphrodite's Temple

Walled
Excavation
Site

Café

fountain

restored
house

Bishop's Palace and Odeon

Tombs

Chapel

Sarcophagi

Agora under
excavation

Site
headquarters

Columned hall

Stoa

pathway

Baths of
Hadrian

East Gate
Tower

Theatre

Martyrium

Gymnasium and Basilica
(under excavation)

Aphrodisias

Excavation sites not open to visitors

© The Guidebook Company Ltd

Much statuary and other excavated recoveries of recent excavations are displayed in the museum, though gleanings of earlier excavations are in museums at İzmir and İstanbul, particularly those of the sculpted friezes. Sarcophagi with inscriptions stand along the exterior paths of the museum and in its garden areas.

NYSSA, TRALLES AND MAGNESIA ON THE MAEANDER

Nyssa is situated over a ravine of the Thymbrus, a tributary of the Maeander. Though a Seleucid foundation, the remains of Nyssa are chiefly Roman. As with Aphrodisias, Nyssa seems to have been abandoned in the wake of Timur's devastations. Sections of Byzantine walls remain, and there is a Roman bouleuterion, a library, a theatre, and a constructed tunnel that allowed the river to run under the town.

Tralles was inhabited by Carians when Alexander arrived there in 334 BC. When it was destroyed by an earthquake in 27 BC, Augustus rebuilt it. Anthemius, one of Justinian's architects in the building of St Sophia in Constantinople, came from Tralles. In later history the Byzantines lost it to the Seljuks, Manuel I regained it, then lost it to the independent Emir of the Mentese. The Ottomans took Tralles in 1389, but abandoned it after Beyazıt's defeat by Timur.

Aydın is the chief city of an agricultural province noted particularly for its figs and grapes. Material from Tralles was used in the building of its 1613 **Bey Cami**. The **Cihanzade Cami** of the 1750s is considered a masterpiece of an Ottoman baroque style. Aydın is a centre for camel fighting, the locals maintaining that a camel's bared teeth are much worse than its bite.

In origin Magnesia on the Maeander may have been one of the few inland settlements from the coast settlements of the Ionian Greeks. Themistocles, the Athenian victor over the Persians at Salamis, acquired Magnesia by fief from the Persian Emperor in 460 BC, after he had been exiled from Greece by his fellow Athenians. He is believed to have eventually committed suicide here. In 189 BC, the Romans under Scipio Africanus defeated the Seleucid Great King Antiochus III here, the latter having been supported and advised by the exiled Carthaginian general Hannibal, who committed suicide after that defeat. In 85 BC, Magnesia supported the Romans in their first war against Mithradates VI of Pontus, and the Roman general Sulla, on his victory, declared it a free city. French archaeologists excavated the site of Magnesia in the 1840s and found sections of an Amazonian frieze from the Temple of Artemis. Though there are sections of later Byzantine walls on either side of the E24 main road, the remains of the ancient city—temples in the agora, a theatre, stadium, gymnasium and parts of ancient walls on the hillside—are scant.

South Aegean Coast

In the heyday of Miletus, Lake Bafa was a sizable sea inlet. Fishing is good still, and a few small camping and picnic areas exist on the lake's southwestern shore. The site of Heracleia, beneath Mount Latmos on the northeastern side of the lake, can be reached by boat, and it is also possible to visit the islands in the lake that has Byzantine fortifications. Lat, the eastern Moon Goddess, is said to have had a sanctuary at Heracleia, as did Endymion, the shepherd who became Lat's—or Selene's—lover. Mount Latmos, named after the goddess, has five peaks (or five fingers, as in the Turkish name Beş Parmak). Rising to 1,500 metres (4,920 feet), they add to the impressiveness of the site which, as much as its ruins, will appeal to the adventurous tourist.

There is a Temple to Zeus among the ruins at Euromos, and another can be found at Milas. If possible, allow time for a visit to the mountain Shrine of Zeus at Labranda, the source of more than one sacred spring. Before going on southwesterly to Bodrum, swimmers and sunbathers might like to divert for a while to Güllük, a small port on the coast, with its accompanying beaches. If you decide to go straight from Milas to Bodrum, prepare for a climbing, winding road. Bodrum, its impressive castle dominating the quay, is a thriving international yachting and tourist centre. The hub of the town has narrow streets reminiscent of a Greek island port; the predominating colour is Aegean blue.

Getting There

After visiting Didyma, travellers on foot will have to return to Söke to catch a bus to Bodrum via Milas. Remember that in Söke the minibus *otopark* and the long-distance coach *otogar* are about 600 metres (2,000 feet) apart.

If you are driving, return to the Söke road, back through Akköy, or take the road that joins the 525 from a junction about a kilometre (0.6 miles) south of the Didyma temple. Turn south at the junction along the southwestern shore of Lake Bafa. By boarding a boat at the restaurant here, near the Türgüt Motel, you can cross to Heracleia. Or go there via the shore road, a distance of ten kilometres (six miles).

Back at the southwestern side of Lake Bafa, continue on road 525 to Milas, driving through spiky mountainous country dominated by olive trees. Just off the road on the left, about 20 kilometres (12 miles) after leaving the lakeside and a ruined castle, is **Euromos**. Twelve kilometres (eight miles) further on is Milas, and 15 kilometres (ten miles) to the northeast is Labranda. Güllük is about 20 kilometres (12 miles) from Milas in the opposite direction. It is 66 kilometres (41 miles) from Milas to Bodrum, where there is an international airport.

Historical Background

This was Carian country, and Mausolus, the fourth-century BC king, was, like the Lydian Croesus, greatly influenced by Hellenistic culture. He employed Pytheos, the Greek architect of the Temple to Athena at Priene, to design his temple and many other fine buildings, not only as at Heracleia but elsewhere in his mountainous kingdom. The Romans restored the Carian lakeside city and its walls—probably destroyed in an earthquake—and in Byzantine times it became a Christian centre with monasteries, convents and anchorite cells.

Mylasa (Milas) was the seat of a satrap, or governor, during the Persian occupation of this region. Mausolus was born at Mylasa, or perhaps nearby at what is now Peçin Kale, the acropolis of the ancient city.

Labranda is likely to have been a sacred site from very early times, perhaps for the Dorian colonizers of the tenth century BC, perhaps earlier, though the cult of Zeus Labrayndos seems to have been particular to the Carians.

As Halicarnassus, Bodrum was the birthplace of Herodotus, the fifth-century BC 'Father of History'. In the fourth century BC, the great wonder of the city was the mausoleum built by Artemisia for her husband Mausolus, of which Pytheos may have been the architect. It was decorated with beautiful reliefs, some of battle scenes. In the 19th century a number of the carved metopes from the ruined mausoleum were bought from the sultan by the British Ambassador of the time, Stratford Canning, and are in the British Museum.

Alexander the Great besieged Halicarnassus and almost failed to take it. He may also have offered to marry Artemisia, a widowed queen at the time of his conquests. This Artemisia is not to be confused with an earlier namesake, whose reputation as a mighty warrior was confirmed at the Battle of Salamis, to which she contributed a naval contingent of Carians to fight alongside Xerxes.

Sights

HERACLEIA
Beginning at a stone arch which was the **East Gateway**, there are several Byzantine buildings on a protruding section to the south, including the remains of a fort, a seminary (or perhaps the seat of a bishop) and, down below, rock tombs. To the

west of the gateway is a rock-cut chamber with a columned entrance that was in all likelihood a shrine, either to Endymion or Lat, or perhaps an earlier divinity. To the north of this, close to the village of Kapikiri, is the agora, with its line of shops on the south side. West of the agora are the remains of a temple to Athena. On the edge of Kapikiri is the bouleuterion and, to the north, a Roman baths. East of the baths there is a postern entrance in the towered ancient walls, of which a few imposing sections still stand. You come then to a well-preserved **North Gateway**, in the vicinity of which is another shrine and, west of the gateway, the theatre, cut out of a lower slope of the mountain. The remains of the harbour—remember that the lake was once sea—and **West Gate** lie to the west of the temple.

ON THE WAY TO BODRUM

The second-century **Temple of Zeus** at **Euromos** has 17 of its Corinthian columns upright, supporting substantial portions of architrave. This temple can be a bonus for the traveller by car, set as it is in a small clearing among trees. Fallen column drums, blocks and pedestals, numbered by archaeologists, are ready for restoration and not yet set up. An excavated altar dates from a time earlier than that of the Roman temple. To the north of the temple are sections of the city's Carian walls, and also in the former city's precinct there is part of a columned stoa as part of a Hellenistic agora, and a theatre.

Not far south of Milas at Peçin Kale are the ruins of the ancient city of Mylasa. A Byzantine castle now stands there, along with evidence of a pre-Roman temple and a 13th- or early 14th-century mosque. Modern Milas has an ancient arched gateway, the Baltali Kapı, whose keystone is shaped like a double-headed axe. This is a Hittite symbol, as well as a Minoan one; one theory holds that the Carians may have migrated to Asia Minor from Crete. A **Temple of Zeus** has a single fluted column remaining. Then among the older mosques of Milas, built in the 14th century, under the independent Emirs of Mentese, are the **Ulu Cami** and the **Orhan**, both dating from the early years of that century, and the **Firuz** of 1394.

A paved Sacred Way once ran from Mylasa to Labranda, a roadway that is easily negotiable by car. The site at Labranda is on the Bati Mentese Mountains. The shrine itself, erected by Mausolus, may well have been designed by Pytheos, although this architect was not the only Greek to be artistically employed by the king or by Artemisia, his sister and wife. The ruins lie on several terraces, some Hellenistic in origin but with Roman additions.

Over on the coast to Güllük, having taken a right turn a kilometre (0.6 miles) or so after leaving Euromos, at Kuren is the site of **Iassos** (Kıyıkışlacık), a Carian city with its Minoan memories in excavated houses, Mycenaean murmurs and Hellenistic walls. There are the remains of a theatre among the ruins, a substantial bouleuterion, Roman and Byzantine remains, and some impressive tombs in the necropolis. The legend of a boy's friendship with a dolphin is connected with this site. A principal industry of the city was fishing. Italian archaeologists have excavated the site. The coast can be explored by hiring a boat at Güllük.

BODRUM

Bodrum is situated on a large bay, the castle dominating the eastern arm of the harbour; there is a yacht marina on the west. The site of the mausoleum (see Historical Background) is on Türgüt Reis Caddesi, above the harbour. Contemporary excavators found what they believe to be the base on which the mausoleum stood, its underground foundations having corridors that must have once connected it to the tombs of earlier Carian kings. Above this base, on the panoramic circular road, is the site of the theatre, which must have offered spectators, at least those in the upper tiers, an uncluttered view of the harbour, bay and the off-shore island that partially encloses it.

The Knights of Rhodes built their **Castle of St Peter** on a previous structure, and even this has since undergone several major modifications. The knights have been accused of robbing the mausoleum and making use of material from derelict buildings—a fairly common practice among builders in past ages. Archaeological remains are on display in the grounds, and the museum inside has recoveries from ancient wrecks, salvaged by mid-20th-century divers and archaeologists. The knights are commemorated in a restored chapel, and towers have been reconstructed in Crusader style—English (Plantagenet), medieval French, Italian and German. There is the site of a **Temple of Mars** on a road that runs downhill, off the panoramic highway, to the east of the theatre.

There is bazaar-like interaction on approaches to the harbour. Beach development, however, is away from the town, at Türgüt Reis, Torba, Güllük and other places along the coast, and the many travel agencies offer daily road or sea excursions to one or other of these. A daily service with more than one ferry in operation can take you to the Datça Peninsula to the south. Those sailings take 90 minutes by sea to Gerince, on the northern coast of the peninsula, from where a minibus will take you overland to Datça on the south coast. A traveller going south could make use of this ferry route as an alternative to an overland return to Milas for the journey via Muğla, to Marmaris on the Mediterranean.

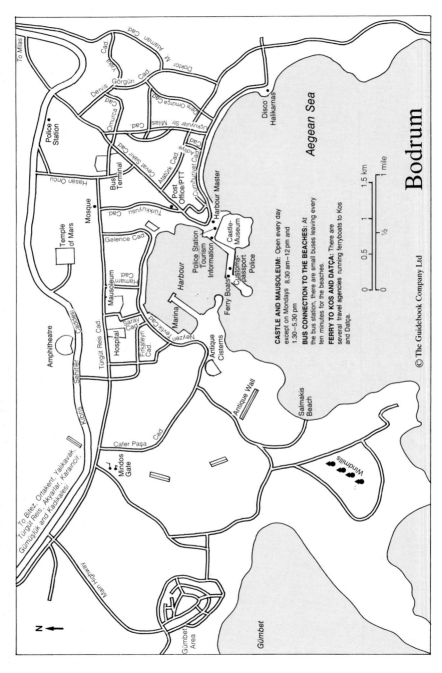

Bodrum

CASTLE AND MAUSOLEUM: Open every day except on Mondays 8.30 am–12 pm and 1.30–5.30 pm

BUS CONNECTION TO THE BEACHES: At the bus station, there are small buses leaving every ten minutes for the beaches.

FERRY TO KOS AND DATÇA: There are several travel agencies running ferryboats to Kos and Datça.

© The Guidebook Company Ltd

Wild flowers and spring poppies of the Aegean region

Aegean Sea

N

To Milas

Police Station

Temple of Mars

Amphitheatre

Mausoleum

Hospital

Mosque

Bus Terminal

Post Office/PTT

Harbour Master

Castle-Museum

Customs-passport Police

Police Station Tourism Information

Ferry Boats

Marina

Harbour

Antique Cisterns

Antique Wall

Salmakis Beach

Disco Halikarnas

Mindos Gate

Cafer Paşa

Windmills

Gümbet Area

Gümbet

Main Highway

To Bitez, Ortakent, Yalıkavak, Turgut Reis, Akyarlar, Karaincir, Gümüşlük and Kadıkalesi

Şenlifer Caddesi

Kıbrıs Cad.

Turgut Reis Cad.

Hamam Cad.

Saray Cad.

Neyzen Tevfik Cad.

Frikateyn Cad.

Gelence Cad.

Türkkuyusu Cad.

Hasan Öncü

Oncu Cad.

Derviş Cad.

Görgün

Yaka Cad.

Doktor M. Alaman Cad.

Dere Omurca Cad.

Üçkuyular Sk. Milas Cad.

Cevat Şakir Cad.

Atatürk Cad.

Cumhuriyet Cad.

Adliye Cad.

Mediterranean Coast

If Bodrum has become internationalized over recent years, Marmaris is super-internationalized. Hotel, motel and holiday complex development has extended round the entire sweep of the bay to the west of the port, a stretch of over ten kilometres (six miles). Its yacht harbour is in three sections and is likely to become the largest in the Aegean and eastern Mediterranean. A Yacht Charter Show is held in here each May.

Datça, to the west, is a holiday centre, having two bays with sandy beaches, plus a harbour and a yacht marina. The visitor might well like to explore the two nearby Dorian sites of Cnidus.

On the way from Marmaris to Fethiye, rock-cut and sculpted tombs, a feature of the coastal cities of this region, can be seen at Caunus, a Carian city whose harbour is now below the marsh. Turkish archaeologists continue to excavate the Carian, Roman and Byzantine remains. You can bathe in hot sulphur springs nearby. The lake here is noted for its fish; the countryside for its wildlife and exotic flora.

Fethiye has developed into a modern town and tourist centre, with yacht marina and harbour, good bathing beaches and accompanying holiday extensions along the shore and on the small islands in the bay.

Xanthus, a principal city of Lycia whose territory this once was, and Tlos, a place of rock tombs, are two of the sites on the road east of Marmaris. At Kalkan, the houses of the town cling like limpets to the base of sheer cliffs that stretch above the sea's edge. With its attractive waterfront and yacht marina, Kalkan is making a fair bid to become an agreeable holiday spot. Kaş, too, has developed as a tourist centre, though on a more modest scale.

The Church of St Nicholas is at Kale (Demre), an unpretentious little town, agreeably Turkish after the internationalized tone of the harbour towns.

Finike, situated on a coastal plain where cotton, citrus and rice are under cultivation, was rebuilt after an earthquake. Unfortunately, little of archaeological interest remains.

Antalya, the principal city of the southwestern coastal region, is set on a creek on an innermost curve of an extensive bay. The modern city stands on a ridge above the ancient town. Many of the wooden houses of the latter have been reconstructed in traditional style and converted into elegant *pensions*. The old harbour has become a yacht marina, while the new harbour is situated some ten kilometres (six miles) to the west, where the mercantile and industrial centre stands.

Alanya is Seljuk, and the resort is dominated by a high rocky promontory, surmounted by a citadel. Beyond Alanya, an arm of the Taurus Mountains makes a dash for the coast and stays there, allowing for only an opening of a coastal plain here and there. Castles are a feature of the landscape in Cilicia. The town of Anamur, midway along the coast, lies about four kilometres (2.5 miles) inland from a long shore, a town backed by a fertile valley and wholly enclosed by mountains.

That arm of the Taurus withdraws again at Silifke to rejoin its parent range, on the edge of the coastal plain. It continues east on a reasonable parallel, a fertile area stretching to the Amanus Mountains and standing at the eastern extremity of the Mediterranean.

At Yümüktepe, near Mersin, there exists evidence of a settlement that is among the earliest yet found in Asia Minor. Taurus, to the east of Mersin, is the birthplace of St Paul. Turkey's fourth-largest city, Adana, further west, is an important centre of the country's cotton industry.

Getting There

To continue to Marmaris from Bodrum by road, return to Milas and take road 330 to Yatagan, 36 kilometres (22 miles), and turn south for Muğla, 24 kilometres (15 miles). From Muğla the road south descends to Gökova at the head of the Gökova Gulf. Continue to the junction (with road 400 that runs east to Dalaman airport and Fethiye) and take the route directly south from the junction, starting on a wide road with an avenue of eucalyptus trees and continuing for 30 kilometres (19 miles) through hilly, wooded country to Marmaris.

Visitors can reach Marmaris and other centres in this southwestern corner of Anatolia by flying into Dalaman airport, near Fethiye, 62 kilometres (39 miles) away, from where the package-tour companies transport their clients by coach to whichever location has been chosen. The *otogar* at Marmaris is on the east of the town, just to the north of the outermost yacht basin.

From Marmaris there is a ferry service to the Greek island of Rhodes, lying just out of sight to the southwest. Turkish lines also operate a service, with sailings at 9am and 5pm each day throughout the holiday months. As with Bodrum and Kuşadası, Marmaris is one of the principal ports visited by the cruise ships of Turkish Maritime Lines (Turk Denizyollari).

Road 400 runs westward from Marmaris along the Cnidus Peninsula for 75 kilometres (47 miles) to Datça which can also be reached by the ferry from Bodrum. The more important of the two ancient Cnidus sites can be reached by a poor, mountainous road, 30 kilometres (19 miles), to the west of Datça.

A minimum of five days should be allowed for a leisurely journey from Marmaris east to Antalya by way of the coastal route, with an extra day if a trip west along the peninsula to Datça and Cnidus Harbour is intended. Wisdom might suggest another day if travelling by coach or minibus.

Heading towards Fethiye from the Gökova junction, take road 400 to the south-east. After 32 kilometres (20 miles), the road bypasses Köycegiz, with its lake and a sea outlet. To the south and east of Köycegiz, after 17 kilometres (11 miles), the Dalaman River forms a delta on which, near the village of Dalyan, is the ancient Carian city of Caunus.

Dalaman airport is 14 kilometres (nine miles) southeast of Ortaca, after which the road alternately ascends and drops through wooded mountain scenery, giving occasional glimpses of peaceful isolated bays at the foot of cliffs, until it skirts the shore of the Gulf of Fethiye. Fethiye, a port of call for Turkish Maritime Lines, is 135 kilometres (84 miles) from Marmaris.

From Fethiye the road runs for 20 kilometres (12 miles) east towards Kemer, but bypasses that town to turn south above the valley of the Xanthus River, the Koca Çay, on the road to Kaş. The valley opens out on to a plain, and the road continues south to Esen, 26 kilometres (16 miles), and then to Kinik, 12 kilometres (eight miles), the stop for Xanthus.

Wooden and stone façades

Lycian rock tombs, Dalyan

Patara, at the southernmost end of the Xanthus valley, is 70 kilometres (44 miles) from Fethiye and ten kilometres (six miles) from Xanthus. Letoon is 55 kilometres (34 miles) from Fethiye and five kilometres (three miles) south and west from Xanthus, near the village of Kumluova.

After leaving Xanthus, rejoin road 400 to continue south, and then southeasterly to Kalkan. A further 26 kilometres (16 miles) along is Kaş, another port of call for the ships of Turk Denizyollari. The road from Kaş to Kale (Demre) is mountainous but then descends into an alluvial plain. The distance to Kale, on the delta of the Demre Çayi, is 47 kilometres (30 miles).

Finike, 29 kilometres (18 miles) east of Kale, is a large port on the western edge of a gulf; the ships of Turkish Maritime Lines call regularly. Limyra is ten kilometres (six miles) from Finike, on the edge of the plain to the north, near the small town of Zengerler. From the *otogar* at Finike you may negotiate with a taxi driver to take you out to ancient Limyra. His charge, when agreed, should include a stay of two hours at the site. From Finike as well, an excursion could be made to Arycanda via the inland road to the north, 35 kilometres (22 miles) on the way to Elmali.

Antalya is accessible by the inland route, by continuing north from Elmali to Korkuteli, which will enable you to visit the mountain site of Termessos. By the coastal route, the road from Finike continues across the coastal plain east of the town, the tourist and holiday accommodations running for a long stretch along the shore.

At Türüncova the road climbs into the mountains, and continues on above the sea for the rest of the journey through pine-forested country. Thus glimpses of the sea below are rare, but the mountainscapes grow more beautiful as the road rounds the Chelidonian Cape, running below the majestic peaks of Phoenix, Solyma and Climax, along the western arm of the Bay of Antalya.

Visits to two coastal sites, Olimpos and Phaselis, are less viable. At Ulupinar there is a turnoff to Olimpos (Olymbos); then three or four kilometres (about 2.5 miles) after passing Tekirova, there is a road to ancient Phaselis.

The road from Finike reaches the coast at Kemer to run along the shoreline. Kemer, 42 kilometres (27 miles) west of Antalya, is an international holiday centre with a yacht marina, motels, hotels, holiday villages and blocks of holiday flats erected by large companies for their employees. This pattern of development is prevalent at most holiday centres on Turkey's Aegean and Mediterranean coasts. Another large one near Antalya is at Beldibi, 25 kilometres (16 miles) west of Antalya.

The bus route we have been on since Finike now reaches the new Antalya harbour west of the city, to run along Akdeniz Bulvarı to Konyaalti Beach. It turns left on a perimeter road and enters the city from the north. The *otogar*, still in its old situation but expanded, is at the north end of Kazim Özalp Caddesi. If you are travelling light, you are within walking distance of the clock tower at the hub of the city.

To reach the site of Termessos from Antalya, go north for six kilometres (four miles) on road 650 to the 350 junction for Korkuteli. At Güllük, 45 kilometres (28 miles), a footpath leads up from beside a café to this 1,050-metre- (3,450-foot-) high city, the mountains folding back in high crests to the north. A half-day excursion out of Antalya, the site of Perge, is 16 kilometres (ten miles) away, or two kilometres (1.25 miles) inland from Aksu. A visit to Perge could take in Aspendos, 26 kilometres (16 miles) east of Aksu, since the principal sight here is the theatre. The turnoff to Aspendos is two kilometres (1.25 miles) after leaving Serik, a town on the main road. The roadway runs north for four kilometres (2.5 miles) to Belkıs. The site of ancient Sillyon, a city of similar date to Perge, signposted four to five kilometres (three miles) beyond the Perge turnoff and eight kilometres (five miles) off the road to the north, could be included in the itinerary as well.

Situated on a squat peninsula with conspicuous seaside development, Side is 32 kilometres (20 miles) east of the Aspendos junction. The road dead ends into a parking area and *otogar*, located beside the ancient theatre. Returning to the main road, you come to the large and newly developed tourist town of Manavgat. Four kilometres (2.5 miles) upstream on the Manavgat River are the Manavgat Falls at Selale; 11 kilometres (seven miles) further east is the *baraj*, or dam. The river is noted for its fine trout.

From Manavgat, Alanya is 59 kilometres (37 miles) east. A spur of the Taurus Mountains approaches the coast here, leaving only a long and narrow plain. From Antalya the road reaches the coast at Kızılcot, 42 kilometres (26 miles) before Alanya, where holiday developments begin. At Okurkalar, there is a section of Byzantine wall; at Alarahan, a Seljuk inn; and at Alara, a fine beach among pines. The road crosses several rivers, and there are holiday villas and hotels at Serapsu, 12 kilometres (eight miles) from Alanya.

Beyond Alanya's long shore towards Gazipaşa, another 46 kilometres (29 miles) along the coast, there are attractive rocky coves that are good for bathing, camping or a picnic. After Gazipaşa the road to Anamur, covering 80 kilometres (50 miles), is reached by way of the most exciting of mountain drives: looking up to high peaks and down sheer heights to remote, rocky and sandy coves, gently washed by sea.

The road from Anamur recommences its mountainous journey, snaking through slopes of tall pine. From the Kosk River the road climbs again to descend to bays at Sipahili, Yanisli and Büyükçekeli, where there is a beach and camping. Silifke is several kilometres inland north of Taşucu. Its *otogar* is on the outskirts of town on a roundabout where all the principal roads converge. Uzuncaburç lies 30 kilometres (19 miles) to the north, in the mountains.

İçel (Mersin) is 84 kilometres (52 miles) from Silifke. Most of the coast has been developed for tourism, to the detriment of at least some of its historical heritage. Holiday camps, motels, hotels and blocks of holiday flats have impinged irrevocably on the rocky coast with its coves and sand beaches.

There are several places where a short stop can be made, particularly when travelling by car. This is more difficult when travelling by bus or coach. The *dolmuş* (minibus) services in Turkey, however, are remarkably flexible, and progress need not be tiresome when travelling for short distances between interesting sites. After you have seen the site, just hail another to carry you to your next chosen destination. The *otogar* in Mersin is some five kilometres (three miles) to the east of the city, with hotels and restaurants located there.

To reach Tarsus, continue 30 kilometres (19 miles) east of İçel (Mersin). Road 750, the E5, which is the main highway from Ankara through to Antakya, passes through the Cilician Gates of the Taurus Mountains at Dulek, north of Tarsus, and reaches the coast five kilometres (three miles) east of Tarsus. Adana is 37 kilometres (23 miles) east of Tarsus, on a dual carriageway that runs from Mersin.

The E5 crosses the Ceyhan River by way of a Byzantine bridge, 25 kilometres (16 miles) east of Adana. On the west bank is the village of Misis. By taking a road

(following pages) Goats pick their way across a valley, gleaning every last blade and root

south from Ceyhan, 24 kilometres (15 miles) after Misis, a journey could include a visit to Yümürtalık.

East of Ceyhan the E5 arrives at Toprakkale, a 12th-century Armenian castle. To the east is the barrier of the Amanus Mountains, and here the E5 turns south down the eastern shore of the Mediterranean. At İskenderun the E5 climbs out by way of the Belen Pass (The Syrian Gates) to Hatay Antakya, 30 kilometres (20 miles) southwest of Antakya. Along the Valley of the Orontes is Samandağ.

Historical Background

Marmaris in ancient times was Physeus, a member of the Rhodian Confederacy. The patron goddess of new Cnidus was Aphrodite. Praxiteles, the most famous Greek sculptor of the time, created Aphrodite in all her beauty and voluptuousness; her nakedness stirred up controversy regarding propriety in a goddess. The statue, it seems, had in fact been commissioned by Kos, whose embarrassed elders subsequently, and prudishly, rejected the completed work of art for a clothed statue. Aphrodite's presence at new Cnidus, though, gave a fillip to that city's economy by encouraging tourism among prurient as well as art-loving visitors from all over the world.

A recumbent lion, once the protector of a tomb near the Cnidus lighthouse, long ago became a resident of the British Museum. When Sir Charles Newton, the 19th-century British archaeologist, dug here, he discovered a fourth-century BC cult image of Demeter in a sacred precinct near a cliff. This goddess may have been patroness of a pre-Dorian site, although multiplicity of gods and goddesses was the order of the day rather than the exception. Demeter, a seated figure, is in the British Museum.

Eudoxus, a fourth-century BC Greek astronomer and geometrician who studied in Egypt, was from Cnidus. A building of new Cnidus, above the houses, has been designated the site of his observatory, from which he studied the star Canopus.

Fethiye, founded in the fourth century BC, was ancient Telmessos of Lycia, standing on a bay within a gulf. A fortified island in the bay was inhabited once by the Snakemen of Telmessos, seers of the Hellenistic world. Earthquakes in 1846 and 1957 destroyed almost all the maritime remains of the ancient city.

At the siege of Troy the Lycians were among King Priam's most faithful allies; their leader was Sarpedon, grandson of Bellerophon, a legendary hero. Bellerophon killed his own brother and another young man in Corinth, and King Proetus sent him to Tiryns. At Tiryns the hero rejected the advances of Anteia, the king's wife, and in anger she lied to her husband over Bellerophon's conduct. Too cowardly to act, the king sent Bellerophon to Iobates at Telmessos, with secret instructions to have him killed. The Lycian king, however, set Bellerophon a number of formidable tasks, one of which was the killing of the dreaded Chimaera. As with Heracles, Bellerophon completed his tasks successfully. After he became king, Bellerophon rode his winged horse Pegasus up to the Olympian Heights where Zeus, angered by this presumption, threw him down and Bellerophon landed in a thorn bush, becoming lame and blind. Zeus kept Pegasus as a pack-horse to carry his thunderbolts.

Given the quantity of the tombs in these Lycian cities, the inhabitants seem to have been preoccupied with death. On one occasion the Xanthians chose to commit mass suicide rather than surrender their freedom: when Harpagus the Persian attacked the city in the sixth century BC, the male Xanthians first killed their families and then went out to their own deaths.

Alexander occupied Xanthus, and after his death it came under Seleucus' control. During the Roman civil wars that followed the assassination of Caesar, Brutus recruited Lycians from Xanthus for his army and levied heavy taxes on the citizens, but later he became so dismayed by the self-destructive tendencies of the Xanthians that he sent ambassadors to plead with them to desist from razing their own city. Under Hadrian (117–38), Lycia prospered and continued to do so throughout Byzantine times and until the Arab conquests of the seventh century.

Kale is Demre, once the Lycian city of Myra that had at one time enjoyed capital status. In Christian times it became a bishopric. Believed to have been born at Patara, St Nicholas—patron saint of children and sailors, whom legend turned into Santa Claus, or Father Christmas—was a bishop here. St Nicholas was martyred during a persecution of Diocletian (284–305) and was buried in his church. In the 11th century his bones were filched by Italian sailors from Bari, an Italian port where an annual festival of St Nicholas is still held. His church at Demre (Myra) was rebuilt by the Byzantines.

Olimpos was a wealthy city in the second century BC. On the heights above the city the Chimaera, the fire-breathing dragon whom Bellerophon mastered, had its lair. Its ghost may still haunt the forest: mariners have sworn, even in recent times, that they have seen its tongues of fire, however diminished in intensity by age.

In origin a seventh-century BC city, Phaselis had three harbours and was famed for its shipbuilding. Its citizens greeted Alexander with a golden crown, unable maybe to fulfil their boast—unlike the men of Xanthus—of being absolute lovers of freedom, willing to fight to the death rather than submit to an alien conqueror.

Attaleia (Antalya) was founded by the Attalids of Pergamum in the third century BC, but became Roman in 133 BC after it had been bequeathed to Rome by Attalus III, the last king of Pergamum. The Byzantines strengthened the walls against the Arab attacks of the seventh and subsequent centuries, and again in the tenth century under Constantine VII Porphyrogenitos, but it fell to the Seljuk

Keyhüsrev in 1207. Taken from an independent emir in 1391, it became the first Ottoman port on the Mediterranean. At the conclusion of World War I, the Italians, under the Treaty of Sèvres, occupied Antalya along with the southwestern region of Anatolia, but relinquished their claim following Atatürk's repudiation of that treaty, and his successful establishment of the present Turkish Republic.

Though Hellenistic by adoption, the Pisidians of Termessos, a tough mountain people, defied Alexander with such determination that he cancelled his intended siege and departed. In early Byzantine times it was the seat of a bishop, but there is mystery later, with little apparent evidence of occupation after the fifth century, certainly not Arabic, Seljuk, emir or Ottoman. Perge was probably founded by immigrants from the Greek mainland and islands during those first early migrations of the first millennium, or perhaps even by Achaeans after the Greek victory of Troy. The period of the city's greatest prosperity seems to have been during the time of the Persian occupation that ended with Alexander's conquests in Pamphylia.

The city's elders agreed to accommodate Alexander upon his arrival at Aspendos. They handed over horses that were intended for Darius, the Persian ruler, with whom they had a contract for the regular rearing and supply of such. After Alexander had gone on his way, though, the elders repudiated their agreement and prepared for a siege by strengthening the walls and by bringing into the city all those citizens living or employed outside it. Characteristically,

(above and opposite) Farming at İncirköy, Fethiye

Alexander was too quick for the schemers and his sudden about-turn found him camped again on the Eurymedon. The elders hardly hesitated over a new capitulation, but this time Alexander took hostages and doubled the amount of levy previously agreed as a contribution to the maintenance of his army. In general, the Aspendians seem to have been thoroughly unneighbourly, as well as perfidious, since Alexander established a court to deal with complaints made by nearby cities, charging that the Aspendians had filched areas of land from them.

The city's founders probably were Ionian, Aeolian or colonists from Cyme on the Aegean coast, who also founded Side further to the east. After the Seleucids (Alexander's successors here), the city along with almost all of Pamphylia became part of the expanding Pergamene kingdom. It eventually became part of the Attalid legacy to Rome, though the Romans would have no doubt conquered it as a matter of course. As Byzantine power weakened in Asia Minor, Aspendos lost its status, as did the other cities along this coast.

With Athena as their protector, people from Aeolian Cyme colonized an already settled city at Side (about 600 BC). Side is the dialect word for pomegranate, and fifth-century BC coins of the region have the helmeted Athena Nike on one side and a pomegranate on the other. Side became a flourishing port, but also a notorious hangout for pirates and a centre of the slave trade. Side stayed prosperous until the arrival of the Seljuk Turks in the 11th century, after which it seems to have lost not only its trade but its inhabitants. In 1895, a new village was established to house Muslim immigrants from Crete.

Alanya was known to the Romans and Byzantines as Coracesium. Antony gave it to Cleopatra. Alaeddin Keykubat (1225), Seljuk Sultan of Konya, chose it as his winter residence and extended and reinforced the Byzantine walls.

A medieval Armenian kingdom existed in Cilicia during the time of the Crusades, and the Armenians were accomplished builders from whom the Crusaders learned much. The knights constructed new castles, and rebuilt or modified existing ones.

In 1130, the German Emperor Frederick Barbarossa, a leader in the Third Crusade, drowned in the Calycadnus River, which flows through Silifke. He fell from his horse in mid-stream, an ominous portent for the success of the Crusade, since his contingent, depleted by sickness and desertions, foundered even before reaching the Holy Land.

The river at Tarsus, the Cydnus, nearly finished off Alexander when he took an impetuous dip: the water had been rendered icy by the melting snows of the Taurus Mountains. Justinian rebuilt the bridge that spans the present stream. Romantic legend says that Cleopatra sailed up the river in her royal barge, but experts claim the river could never have been so navigable. Silting has done its work well here, for stretching away to the south is an extensive forest, where wild boar are hunted in season.

A Hittite inscription from Karatepe, northeast of Adana, identifies Adana as the capitulate of an eighth-century BC Hittite kingdom whose king had suzerainty over other Hittite rulers in Cilicia. Hethoumian kings of the Middle Ages established the Lesser Armenian Kingdom here, with Tarsus, Adana and Mamistra as sister cities. During the Crusades some Frankish leaders chose to stay on in Cilicia rather than pursue their spiritual intention of recovering the Holy Land. In 1919, this region, known as the Hatay, came within the French Mandate for Syria, but was returned to Turkey by agreement in 1938.

Anazarbus succeeded Tarsus as the principal city of the Cilician Plain when caravan trade switched from an east–west to a south–north direction up the line of the Pyramus (Ceyhan) River. Justinian rebuilt it. Centuries later, it became a subject of dispute between the Byzantines and the Armenians, Christian allies against the Saracens, but a compromise solution left it in the hands of the Roupenians. The Armenians supported the Mongol Khan against Baibars, the Mameluke Sultan of Egypt, and when Baibars overran Cilicia after expunging the Latin kingdom at Antioch, he took his revenge by sacking the Cilician cities, putting the men to the sword and taking the women and children into slavery.

If the port of Yümürtalık, south of Adana, was Ayaş—the other Ayaş to the east of İçel (Mersin) seems too distant somehow—it became important after the fall of Antioch to the Muslims. Marco Polo was marooned at Ayaş while a war raged in

Syria, and pirates were active on the seas thereabouts. At one time, merchants of Venice, Genoa and Pisa all had warehouses at Ayaş.

The Plain of Issus is remembered as the site of Alexander's battle with Darius. Some historians claim that the battle was actually fought on the banks of the river at Payas—which also may have been Ayas. The Ottomans revived Payas in the 16th century, as vital to the spice trade. After the battle, Alexander founded the city of Alexandria by Issus at the head of the Gulf of İskenderun. Under the French mandate at the end of World War I, it became Alexandretta but is now İskenderun.

Diocletian built the bridge over the Orontes at Hatay (Antakya or Antioch). This was once the most jovial city in Christendom: the island in the Orontes River was a Coney Island-cum-Las Vegas in its day, with the Roman Empire's most notorious courtesans ensconced in their villas in the hill suburb of Daphne.

Seleucus founded the city, and later Pompey acquired it for Rome, declaring it a free city. The earliest Christian community (or church) is thought to have been started here by Saint Peter. Saint Paul later directed the community when he and Barnabus visited it, and in the early centuries of Christianity its patriarch was a rival to those of Alexandria and Constantinople. In the seventh century Heraclius recaptured Antioch from the Persians, though it fell to the Arabs soon afterwards. It came into Christian hands again with the Latin Crusaders of the 12th century, and remained Christian for 175 years. In 1516, Selim I took Syria and Egypt, and then his Ottomans held Antioch until Turkey's defeat in World War I. When in 1938 the French mandate was relinquished by agreement, Antioch (along with the Hatay region) came under Turkish sovereignty again.

Legend has it that one day, as Seleucus was sacrificing to Zeus on the site under Mount Cassius he had chosen for his city, an eagle swooped down, snatched up the sacrificial animal and dropped it on the northern tip of a wide bay; he interpreted this as a divine sign that he should build his city there. A later successor decided that the site of Antioch was far better for a city; Samandağ (Seleucia) became its port, from which the Latins of Outremer made their escape as Baibars overran them.

Sights

AROUND MARMARIS

As Mobolla, Muğla was the principal residence of the Mentese emirs, their oldest mosque the 14th-century Uç Erenler.

The castle at the centre of Marmaris dates from the time of Suleiman the Magnificent in the 16th century. It has been restored and refurbished, and is now the town museum. The area around it, the old market, is a pedestrian precinct, with restaurants in the bazaar arcades, streets of boutiques—leather and suede goods are a speciality—and narrow walkways with beer houses and discos. The Ministry of Tourism's Information Office is situated close to the old quayside.

Besides climbing the remains of the acropolis situated on a hill north of the town, you may choose to take a boat to the many ancient sites in the area. On the Bözburun peninsula that stretches into the Hisarönü Gulf towards the Greek island of Symi (Sombeki for the Turks) there are sites at **Kumlukübü** and the small port of Bözburun. On the tip of the latter peninsula are the ruins of Loryma, an ancient harbour and castle. Another excursion could start by road to Gökova on the Gökova Gulf to the north, and continue by boat to Sedir Island, known now for some romantic reason as Cleopatra's Island. Here is ancient Cedrai with its walls, theatre and temples.

There are small hotels and a legion of *pensions* in Datça, and *tatil köyü* (holiday villages) along the shore towards Petya on the town's east side, where considerable new development has taken place. In the Petya area, a kilometre (0.6 miles) from the present centre of Datça, is the first of the two Dorian sites of Cnidus; a later settlement is located at present-day Cnidus Harbour on the extreme west of this peninsula.

There is little of old Cnidus left to be seen at Petya, only sections of substantial seawalls and land walls, a few filled-in, experimental archaeological shafts, scattered pottery shards and a lighthouse on a rocky islet.

New Cnidus, at Cnidus Harbour, has more to offer. There is **Aphrodite's Temple**, circular in shape, but the cult image of the goddess has yet to be found. Among other remains is a well-preserved theatre and an odeon. An extensive necropolis of free-standing tombs lies outside the walls and along the approach road to the city. The Ministry of Culture's Information Office in Datça has daily trip to Cnidus Harbour, starting at 9 am and returning at 5pm each day.

FETHIYE

Telmessos, whose ruins from the fourth century BC lie here, has elaborately carved tombs and sarcophagi (massive stone coffins with heavy lids) in the cliff-face at the rear of the town. Take Eski Mezarlik Sokak, a road going inland from the waterfront about one kilometre (0.6 miles) from the Ministry of Tourism's Information Office, leading to Amyntas Yolu, which winds up along the rocky escarpment. Of the tombs, three principal ones have had steps cut to reach them. The inscribed **Amyntas Tomb** is the most impressive, and has an entrance with columns carved in the Ionic order, its gateway, doorways and chamber having been modelled on an earlier timbered Lycian building. Not far from these tombs is a fortress which dates perhaps from the fourth century BC, later occupied by Crusaders and modified.

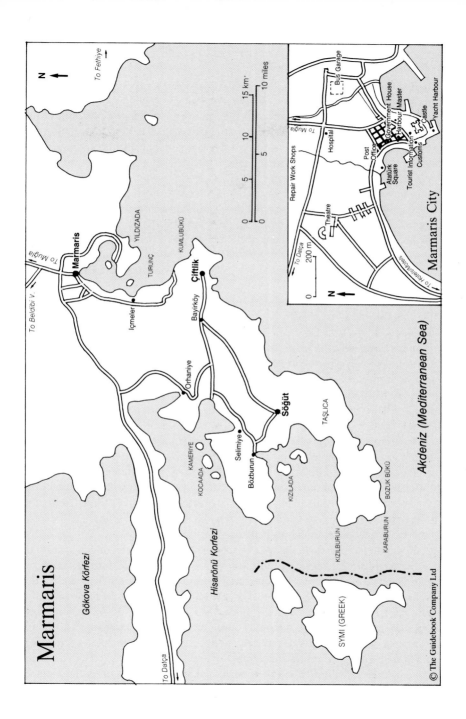

Marmaris

Gökova Körfezi

To Datça

Hisarönü Körfezi

To Beldibi V.

To Muğla

Marmaris

İçmeler

TURUNÇ

YILDIZADA

KUMLUBÜKÜ

Bayırköy

Çiftlik

Orhaniye

KAMERİYE

KOCAADA

Selimiye

Bözburun

Söğüt

TAŞLICA

KIZILADA

BOZUK BÜKÜ

KIZILBURUN

KARABURUN

SYMI (GREEK)

Akdeniz (Mediterranean Sea)

N

To Fethiye

0 5 10 15 km
0 5 10 miles

© The Guidebook Company Ltd

Marmaris City

To Muğla

Bus Garage

Repair Work Shops

Hospital

Theatre

Post Office

Atatürk Square

Tourist Information

Customs

Government House

Harbour Master

Castle

Yacht Harbour

To Datça

To Hisarönü/Kös

N

0 200 m

There are many freestanding column tombs in its neighbourhood. By following the roadway back to the centre, you come to a typical freestanding Lycian tomb in the roadway, and below this the ruins of others and then what may be sections of the town's wall. In the centre of the town are something like 16 sarcophagi, 15 of the Roman period, but near the post office is a Lycian tomb of the fourth century BC, with carvings of city life and battle scenes.

Çalis beach, four kilometres (2.5 miles) to the west, with accommodation, camping facilities and restaurants, and the island of Sovalye opposite are good for bathing. Motorboat transport is available. A mountain road can take you to Belceğiz Bay to the south. En route are mountain guest houses and camping facilities along the bay, with the lagoon-like water of Ölüdeniz a particularly deep azure hue.

With Fethiye as a centre, excursions can be made to the historical sites of Xanthus, 60 kilometres (37 miles) away, Letoon, 55 kilometres (34 miles), and Patara, 70 kilometres (44 miles). The local offices of principal travel agencies arrange daily tours.

XANTHUS AND TLOS

A tomb at Tlos, near the village of Doger beneath Mount Akdağ, 45 kilometres (28 miles) from Fethiye, has a carving of Bellerophon on Pegasus attacking a wild beast, and the tomb is believed to be the hero's. Among the Roman ruins of Tlos, there is an agora, baths and a fort. Tlos gets a mention in Hittite records, and the Hittites might well have been here: the symbol of the moon appears on both Hittite and Lycian coins.

Xanthus' archaeological treasures, the recoveries of an expedition of 1842, are in the British Museum. A French team excavated here in the 1950s, uncovering among other items a number of pillar tombs, a form of burial almost exclusive to this city. The **Harpies Tomb** has elaborate carvings and is so called because of the subject matter of the main relief. On top of another pillar stands a second structure, a hypogea or temple-like building. Plaster reproductions of some of the carved metopes have been set up *in situ*, replacing the originals.

Most pillar tombs are to the west of a Roman theatre of Hadrian's day. North of the theatre is the Roman agora, built over an earlier one. At the northeast corner a pillar or obelisk tomb has a Lycian inscription; the carved frieze from it is in the Archaeological Museum in İstanbul. The acropolis hill, south of the theatre, has the remains of a palace and ruins of a temple, with a cistern below it. At the southwest corner a terrace overlooks the river valley. Many rock-cut tombs exist on the necropolis, outside the city walls to the northeast. West of the burial ground is a Byzantine monastery, and another temple.

The **Nereid Monument**, so-called because of its carvings, stands in the south of

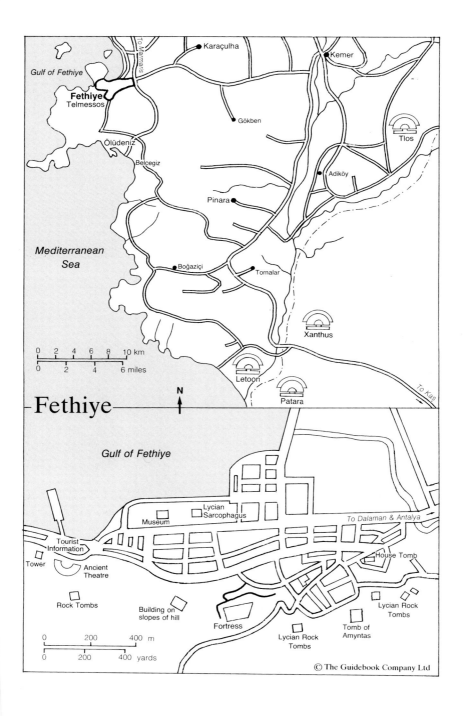

Karaçulha

Kemer

Gulf of Fethiye

Fethiye
Telmessos

Ölüdeniz

Gökben

Tlos

Belcegiz

Adiköy

Pinara

Mediterranean
Sea

Boğaziçi

Tomalar

Xanthus

0   2   4   6   8   10 km
0   2   4   6 miles

Letoon

Patara

To Kaş

Fethiye

N

Gulf of Fethiye

Museum

Lycian
Sarcophagus

To Dalaman & Antalya

Tourist
Information

Tower

Ancient
Theatre

House Tomb

Rock Tombs

Building on
slopes of hill

Lycian Rock
Tombs

Fortress

Tomb of
Amyntas

0   200   400 m

Lycian Rock
Tombs

0   200   400 yards

© The Guidebook Company Ltd

Farming at İncirköy, Fethiye

the city; its sculpted decoration, however, stands in the British Museum. A Roman arch near the **South Gate** has a dedication to Vespasian (69–78). The parking area for the site is located here. Near the theatre, east of the parking area, is a second agora; further east is a Byzantine basilican church.

PATARA AND LETOON

Patara was the port for Xanthus. On the roadway into the site from Övagelmiş is a triple-arched Roman gate and, off to the left, a baths. Further along the track is a basilica-style church and then the **Baths of Vespasian**. West towards the shore is the theatre, and on top of the hill, into which the theatre is built, is a large cistern. North of the theatre, between the trackway and the former harbour, is a Roman temple of Hadrian's time, and alongside the harbour a Roman granary.

Letoon has a **Leto Sanctuary** and temples to Artemis and Apollo, Leto's children. The site is under extensive excavation.

KAŞ

Kaş was Lycian Antiphellus, the harbour of Phellus. It is situated on a bay within a narrow gulf, at the base of a mountain. If you have arrived by bus, go down about 500 metres (1,600 feet) to the waterfront and turn right to follow Hastane Caddesi to where there is a section of the city wall from the Hellenistic period. On the waterfront side there are old houses along the line of the walls that have been converted into *pensions*. Over a kilometre (0.6 miles) along, above the roadway on the right, is a sixth-century BC Greek-style **Theatre of Psellus**. A Lycian structure modified in later Hellenistic and Roman times, it has been partly reconstructed. The site of the agora is alongside the theatre. North of the theatre site is a tomb known as the Doric, due to its style of façade. A passageway surrounds the interior, and there is a carved relief is of maidens dancing.

Turning right on the waterfront, after moving down from the *otogar*, is the harbour, with a Lycian tomb standing on the quayside. There are other rock-cut tombs in the rockface above the harbour. The Greek island of Castelorizo, the most easterly of Greek possessions, lies offshore here. An agency on the waterfront, near the restaurants, runs a one-day excursion to the islands that also includes visits to Patara, the island of Kekova (a sunken city), Letoon and Xanthus, starting at 9.30am and returning at 6.30pm.

Kekova, an elongated island whose sound is a perfect haven for yachtsmen, is just off the coast to the southeast. Its ancient name was Cistene-Dolochiste, and the submerged city of Tersane is a good place for swimming. On the mainland, opposite the town of Kekova, the walled town of Aperlae has a castle, houses and necropolis, all seen to best advantage from the sea.

A RITE OF PASSAGE

*T*he Doric Peninsula widens out to the group of villages and little anchorage of Datcha, where a road, with a daily bus that takes twelve hours, come down from Marmaris, and a steamer stops once a fortnight if asked to do so. Here there was a Kaymakam, a hotel and a new school building, and a feeling of prosperity and security very different from the days of Newton, when pirates hung around and money was smuggled 'as if contraband', and people could only negotiate a bill if a mail steamer called. Yet even now it is a local and a small prosperity, not the old sea-going traffic of the ancient capital—whose walls show at the foot of the sea-hills nearby. A few scattered rowing-boats, like worn-out shoes, lay on the edge of the sands; the life was inland, and the Kaymakam offered to take us to see it in Kinara Koy, a village where the road ends and the westward track begins. A feast, said he, happened that day to be celebrating the circumcision of twelve little boys.

There was an immediate easiness in the landscape when we left the sea. Carob, oleander and almond, the myrtle whose boughs are tied to the tombstones, and Vallonia oak trees with frilly acorns like ruffs—exported for tanning—filled the shallow valleys; the sharp slopes behind were dark with pines. No panthers are here, they say, but bears and wild boars. An ancient temenos stood by the road that leads to Reshidiye, the main centre of the district, a townlet of thirteen hundred souls. Kinara Koy lay to the west, on higher ground. Its up-and-down houses and roofs were crowded with people, and lorry-loads were arriving all the time. Groups of women stood with clean white kerchiefs held over heads and mouths; the young men walked about behind a drum, trumpet and violin; the twelve little boys, the heroes of the day but disregarded, wandered with mixed feelings, and wore embroidered handkerchiefs and tassels stuffed with holy earth to distinguish them from the crowd. Only one of them was rich, spangled with gold coins, but not much happier for that: their moment had not yet come, and we were all intent on feasting.

D B sat with the Elders, and I found a circle in a harim where the food came in a more easy-going way but hotter—flaps of unleavened bread, soup, makarna (macaroni), stew, rissoles, beans, yaourt, and rice, and a sweet sticky paste: we dipped it all up from bowls set on the floor. The houses were as clean as the Swiss, their wooden cupboards and stairs were bare and scrubbed; and the people left their shoes as they came in and wiped their feet on a towel at the stair's foot. They were rough folk and mostly plain to look at, with the excellent manners of the Turkish village, the result of a sure and sound tradition handed down from generation to generation, which breaks into gaiety when ceremony demands it, as an earth-feeding stream breaks into the sun.

There was a bustle now, the doctor had arrived; his razors wrapped in newspapers were laid on a packing-case; the men all crowded into the largest room as audience. A seat in the front row was placed for D B and another for me; the other women remained in their own room, a mother or grandmother stepping out to look round the corner when it was the turn of her child. The rich son of the house, eleven years old, was now seated in the face of all on a chair, frightened but brave; his infantile penis clipped in a sort of pliers; a wipe of disinfectant to the razor, and the moment was over: the child, with a startled look, as if the knowledge that virility has its pains were first breaking upon him, wrung his mouth in his hand to cover his cry, while the men in the room clapped, and someone outside fired a pistol; when the ceremonies were over the child was seated on a bed; visitors as they passed dropped small coins into a handkerchief laid out beside him; and the little creature was out of the harim—a man.

Freya Stark, The Lycian Shore

DEMRE (MYRA)

Walk back from the *otogar* towards the square and take the turning on the left. There are *pensions* in and near the square. Along the street there are several small restaurants, and further on, about 500 metres (1,600 feet), is the **Church of St Nicholas**. Substantial and imposing, it is a Byzantine structure as befits such a renowned and well-remembered saint and benefactor. The precinct is in a good state of preservation, has undergone some rebuilding and may once have been put to use as a *han* (inn).

The ruins of Myra are two kilometres (1.25 miles) away. From the street with the church, turn left in the square and continue on that road. A taxi will take you to Myra and will wait while you visit the site. Take a path beside some tourist boutiques to the theatre, again a remarkably well-preserved building of Roman design, with part of its façade erect and with its arched side entrances to the proscenium. There is a double stairway to the upper gallery, and on a plaque behind the upper tier of seating is a carved figure with an inscription in Greek.

The cliff above the theatre has its quota of burial niches and tombs, and on its summit are the remains of Byzantine fortifications, including a castle wall and, below it, a section of the outer wall. Tombs on another part of the cliff are the **Painted Tomb** and the **Lion Tomb**, notable for their carvings. On the left of the road back to Demre is a vaulted Byzantine structure with arched sections.

If you have decided on a short stay at Demre, there are beaches in the vicinity such as **Sülüklü Plaj**, two kilometres (1.25 miles) away, **Tasdibi**, seven kilometres (four miles) east, **Çayağzi Plaj**, 3.5 kilometres (two miles) south and **Kum İskelesi Plaj**, three kilometres (less than two miles) southeast.

FINIKE AND LIMYRA

The Alakir Cayi flows into the sea at Finike, and if you stroll into town from the *otogar*, going past an interesting mosque, you are almost bound to run into Akil Kildir, an insurance agent and tourist shop proprietor. Akil was helpful to John Marriner, who sailed here over 25 years ago and wrote *Journey Into The Sunrise*, a book about this southwestern region of the Mediterranean coast.

In Limyra, the theatre is off the road to the left as you enter the site area. Dated 141, it is yet another structure in a good state of preservation, with its upper gallery intact. It was built by a wealthy citizen, Opramoas, who made donations to more than one city of this coast. Close to the theatre is the site of a temple. On the escarpment above the theatre was the acropolis, and many Lycian-style tombs on the slopes outside the walls of the acropolis. Two notable tombs of Limyra are those of Çatabura of the fourth century BC, and Tabersele of an earlier date. On the main site is the **Heroon** (shrine) **of Pericleos**, a local ruler, not the famous one of Athens.

The reliefs from this high-walled structure are on display in the Antalya Museum.

Go on beyond the theatre to the main site on the right of the road. A cool stream flows through this site, churning among rushes and areas of fresh grass. On a hot day you may shelter under a shady tree. A German archaeological team is at work excavating and reconstructing a temple in the area of the agora. There are remains of many Byzantine buildings and substantial sections of the city's walls. A Roman baths and another baths here may well be early Ottoman.

Fifth-century BC **Arycanda** is located in forested and mountainous country, and water for its baths came from a nearby waterfall. East of the baths is a gymnasium and, as with all Lycian sites, there are the tombs. Excavations by a Turkish archaeological team from İstanbul are underway.

Olimpos (Olymbos) has a Genoese harbour, a ruined Byzantine bridge and Genoese and Byzantine fortresses. A temple here is dedicated to Haephaestos, the lame blacksmith and armourer god.

ANTALYA

On the ridge are sections of the old city wall still in existence, and Hadrian's Gate, the entry into the old town. The most conspicuous monument within the walls is the **Yıvlı Minaret**, the ribbed or fluted minaret, built by Seljuk Sultan Alaeddin Keykubat (1219–36) when he converted an accompanying church to a mosque. Near this minaret is the **Karatay Medrese**, a theological school of Seljuk construction (1250) with geometrical decoration and a restored doorway in traditional stalactite pattern. This stands above the harbour on a paved terrace with trees, along with the Atatürk Memorial.

In the south of the old town, the **Kesik Minaret** is attached to a fifth-century converted church, which had been built on the site of a Roman temple. This minaret lost its top in a storm in 1851; its crown has since been reconstructed. On the southernmost height of the old town is the **Hidirlik Kulesi**, a tower of an early but unknown date. It may have been originally constructed as a lighthouse.

From the main crossroads just east of the clock tower, a broad avenue, Atatürk Caddesi, with its double line of palm trees on the centre spine, starts off southerly and then curves round to the east. About 50 metres (165 feet) from the crossroads is **Hadrian's Gate** with its towered bastion, one tower on the north side and two on the south. The area about the gate is now a pedestrian enclave. Besides this main entrance to the old town, it can also be entered by taking a downward street on the corner opposite the clock tower, where the **Paşa Cami** is. There are sections of old walls along Atatürk Caddesi, and where the road curves to the east is the main entrance to Mermerli Park, on the west side. Walking down the park's main avenue you reach a southern terrace from where you can obtain an unrestricted view of

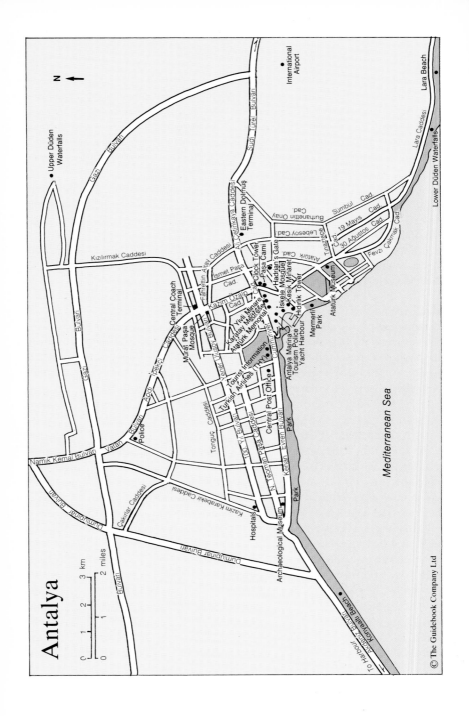

Antalya

3 km
2 miles

N

Upper Düden Waterfalls

International Airport

Lara Beach

Gazi Bulvarı

Suat Türe) Bulvarı

Sümbül Cad.

Lara Caddesi

Lower Düden Waterfalls

Kızılırmak Caddesi

Ali Çetinkaya Caddesi

Eastern Doğmuş Terminal

Burhanettin Onay Cad.

Lebesoy Cad.

30 Ağustos Cad.

19 Mayıs Cad.

Çatknak Cad.

İnazşepe

Fevzi

Ataturk Cad.

Central Coach Terminal

İsmet Paşa Cad.

Clock Tower

Pasa Cami

Hadrian's Gate

Fahıfettin Altay Caddesi

Kazım Özalp Cad.

Yivli Minare

İskele Mosque

Kesik Minaret

Ataturk Museum

Bulvarı

Gazi

Bulvarı

Murat Paşa Mosque

Kaçtay Medrese

Ataturk Memorial

Hıdırlık Tower

Mermerli Park

İpekçi Caddesi

Kenan Evren Bulvarı

Cumhuriyet

Antalya Marina Tourism Police Yacht Harbour

Kenan Unsoy Bulvarı

Police

Vatan

Tourist Information

Turkish Airlines THY

Mediterranean Sea

Namık Kemal Bulvarı

Bulvarı

Tonguç Caddesi

100 Yıl Bulvarı

N Teoman Paşa Caddesi

Central Post Office

Park

Dumlupınar Bulvarı

Çaknar Caddesi

Kazım Karabekir Caddesi

Archaeological Museum

Park

Hospitals

Bulvarı

To Harbour

Konyaaltı Beach

Bakırlıoğlu Bulvarı

Dumlupınar Bulvarı

© The Guidebook Company Ltd

Antalya Bay and—on a clear cool day—the great trio of mountains on the bay's western arm. On the left of the entrance to Mermerli Park is the **Atatürk Museum**.

The **Archeological Museum** is about a kilometre (0.6 miles) away from the Clock Tower, along Kenen Evren Bulvarı, a wide avenue that runs westward from the clock tower at the town's centre and eventually connects with the coastal road, the Akdeniz Bulvarı. The museum has a fine collection of recoveries from sites around this area of the country.

South from the Atatürk Museum, going past the modern stadium, you can make your way out to Lara Beach, a bathing and holiday centre, 12 kilometres (eight miles) out of town. About a quarter of the way there, the Duden Falls spill into the sea; the Upper Duden Falls are 14 kilometres (nine miles) away, to the northeast.

The minibus *otopark* for a journey along the coast to the east is situated near a roundabout at the east end of Cumhuriyet Caddesi (on which the clock tower stands) and the beginning of Ali Çetinkaya Caddesi.

Two mosques of particular interest in Antalya are the 16th-century **Murat Paşa Cami**, located close to the *otogar*, and of an earlier date, the **İskele Cami** on the harbour quay of the old town.

For hotels there is a five-star luxury class Talya and several in lower categories, such as the three-star Büyük Oteli (Grand Hotel) on the terrace just to the east of

(left) A zili made from animal hair (Akkoç village);
(right) Yörük kilim made from wool, Antalya Museum

the Atatürk Memorial. Besides the *pensions* in the old town, there are good if less ostentatious ones south of the *otogar*, such as the White House, in an area of narrow streets on the east side of Kazim Özalp Caddesi. The hotels of the beach complexes are, of course, outside the town.

TERMESSOS

This Pisidian site in the mountains 34 kilometres (20 miles) to the west of Antalya, 1,050 metres (3,450 feet) above sea level, can be visited on a one-day or half-day excursion. Termessos is now a national park.

The climb up the path is a long one, but the views at times are literally breathtaking. In high summer, semi-nomads put their goats out to pasture here. From the remains of the city's outer walls running up and down the slopes, and the Roman gateway, the climb continues a distance to a central agora of the Arcadian aspect. The site's principal buildings—baths, gymnasium, temple and theatre—are signposted and clearly identified, even if the various land levels and entangling undergrowth make the approach difficult. Carved metopes of bird, beast and fish are among the fallen stones in the agora due, one day, to be set up, or removed perhaps to the Antalya Museum.

The Pisidians seem to have been as tomb-conscious as their Lycian neighbours, for the Necropolis has giant sarcophagi, and the almost sheer northern cliff is riddled with burial chambers. A wall encloses the valley at its highest and narrowest point, with the cliff wall to the left a sentry walk.

PERGE

There is a lower town in the plain and a walled acropolis that may once have been a Hittite settlement. On entering the site, the first major building on the west side is a Greek-style theatre set into the flank of a hill. It held 15,000 and served as yet another rendezvous for St Paul, who preached here. The Emperor Trajan (98–117) is given credit for restoring this theatre. A little to the north of the theatre is the stadium, where the vaulted foundations, and a shopping area are in good condition. An arched gallery runs behind the topmost seating.

A long, paved and colonnaded street traverses the site from the south entrance, running through the walls to a Hellenistic gateway between ruined towers and on to the acropolis gateway. This street is crossed at its northern end by another, also paved, on which there were shops. The agora, to the right of the first gateway with the towers, had a columned portico or stoa surrounding it. Just to the left, before this towered gateway, is a baths.

On the approach road, outside the lower line of the walls, is a necropolis, but there are clusters of tombs as well elsewhere in and around the town. The temple site on the acropolis is perhaps a Byzantine church, converted from a Roman Temple to Diana. East of the crossing are sites of a gymnasium and a palaestra, the latter having survived in better shape than the former, and bearing an inscription to the emperor Claudius (41–54), dated AD 50.

The extent of the town in and outside the lower walls suggests that the city enjoyed an appreciable period of peace and security, undergoing heavier fortification only after the passage of Alexander. Excavated recoveries from Perge can be seen in the Antalya Museum.

ASPENDOS

Aspendos is on the banks of the Eurymedon River, which in Alexander's time was navigable as far as the city. The arches of a very fine Seljuk bridge grace the river crossing and account for the stream's name of Bridge River (Köprü Çay). Kimon, the Athenian admiral, won a double victory here, by sea and by land, against Xerxes.

The theatre was constructed by a local architect in the second century and was dedicated to the Roman gods and Marcus Aurelius (161–80). It has survived as the best-preserved theatre of its kind, very nearly intact except for depredations on the proscenium and façade. The building underwent modifications when a Seljuk sultan turned it into a *han* (inn). A festival of drama and music is held here annually.

The theatre backs up to the two hills of the former acropolis, whose steep inclines called only for ramparts, not reinforced walls. Remains on site are few, but include a section of a nymphaeum, a building that housed a sacred spring that was under the protection of nymphs, with niched walls where statues would have been placed. There are also remains of a bouleuterion and behind the **South Gate**, a gymnasium and baths. North of the theatre is the stadium, and north of the town are sections of an aqueduct, constructed to raise the water by reverse gravity to the level of two conduits.

The acropolis at Sillyon, a site inland from Aspendos, was partially destroyed in a 1969 landslide. Its theatre stands at a height comparable to the one in Pergamum. An extensive site, there is a towered gateway, Hellenistic buildings, a Seljuk fort and underground cisterns.

SIDE

Today's ruins are mainly Roman, or rebuildings of Hellenistic structures, or Byzantine additions. The principal streets were colonnaded, and off them there were private houses with mosaic-tiled courtyards, garden ornaments, decorative fountains and frescoed interiors. The Greek-style theatre, erected or restored in the second century BC, is among the largest in Asia Minor; the *cavea* (semi-circle of

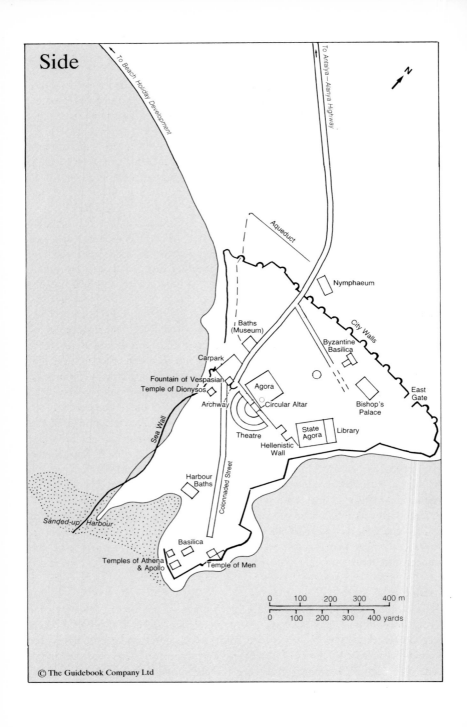

Side

To Beach Holiday Development

To Antalya – Alanya Highway

N

Aqueduct

City Walls

Nymphaeum

Baths
(Museum)

Byzantine
Basilica

Carpark

Fountain of Vespasian
Temple of Dionysos

Agora

Archway

Circular Altar

Bishop's
Palace

East
Gate

Theatre

State
Agora

Library

Hellenistic
Wall

Sea Wall

Harbour
Baths

Colonnaded Street

Sanded-up Harbour

Basilica

Temples of Athena
& Apollo

Temple of Men

| 0 | 100 | 200 | 300 | 400 m |
| 0 | 100 | 200 | 300 | 400 yards |

© The Guidebook Company Ltd

seats) is 120 metres (400 feet) in diameter. The upper tiers and their structural supports were added later and increased seating to 20,000. Entrance was between shops via a portico from the agora, the large rectangular area northeast of the theatre, then through a passageway to an inner arcade, with other passages leading into the orchestra. There are the remains of the stoa that surrounded the agora, and in the southern part the circular foundations of an altar, which may have been a slave market. Off the northern end of the agora, below the *otogar*, a former baths has been restored; it is now a museum. A colonnaded street ran diagonally from the area of the present *otogar* out to the temples on the southeastern tip of the peninsula. Here on the headland was a temple to Athena as well as a **Temple of Apollo** and, east of these, a **Temple of Men** (the Phrygian Moon God) and the remains of a Byzantine basilica.

The roadway into the site has the ruins of private houses on either side as it approaches the agora. There are sections of Roman-built walls, a **Triumphal Arch**, **Fountain of Vespasian** (69–79) and a **Temple of Dionysos** that flanks the theatre on its western side.

The Byzantine walls at the entrance to the site, which incorporate sections of earlier walls, can be followed round to the **East Gate**. Within the line of the walls, to the west, there is a Byzantine basilica in a complex that also includes the **Bishop's Palace**. South and east of the palace is a second agora with, on its east side, an imposing ruin set about a court; this may have been a library, though a statue of Nemesis in one of its niches suggests that the building may have been a law court. Other sculpted figures from this building are now exhibited in the museum. The city's administrative buildings are likely to have been located in this second agora.

ALANYA

The town and beach expansion begins four or five kilometres (three miles) before reaching Alanya's old centre. The main coastal highway continues as Atatürk Caddesi and then for several kilometres becomes Keykubat Caddesi, with countless hotels and motels along its long sandy shore. The *otogar*, on the outskirts, is over a kilometre (0.6 miles) from the Ministry of Tourism's Information Centre opposite the museum, beside Atatürk Park. From here road leads down to the old town and harbour.

From the citadel and its bastions with their towers, the red crenellated walls zigzag down the steep slopes to a gateway of Norman-like durability on the southwest side, while other walls descend on the east to the old town and harbour. The old town, under the east face of the promontory, has an enlarged harbour with a yacht marina, and a wide esplanade and *plaj* (beach) which curves to the east. The

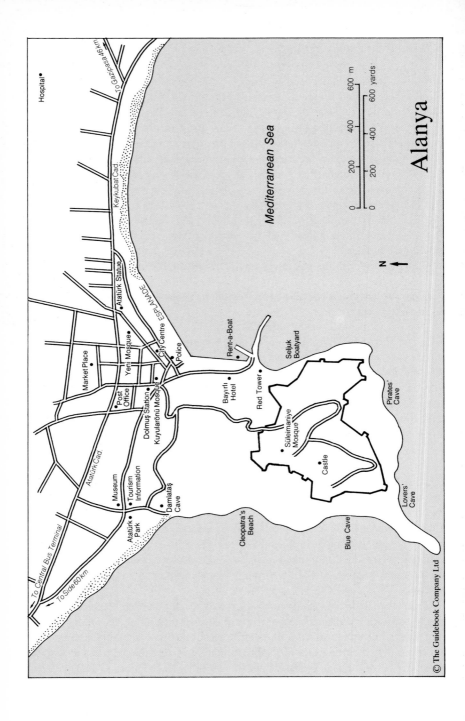

Alanya

Mediterranean Sea

Hospital

To Gazipaşa 46 km

Keykubat Cad.

Atatürk Statue

ESPLANADE

City Centre

Police

Rent-a-Boat

Seljuk
Boatyard

Market Place

Yeni Mosque

Post
Office

Dolmuş Station

Kuyularönü Mosque

Bayırlı
Hotel

Red Tower

Süleimaniye
Mosque

Pirates'
Cave

Castle

Lovers'
Cave

To Central Bus Terminal

Atatürk Cad.

Museum

Tourism
Information

Atatürk
Park

Damlataş
Cave

Cleopatra's
Beach

Blue Cave

To Side 60 km

N

600 m
600 yards

0   200   400   600
0   200   400   600

© The Guidebook Company Ltd

The eight-kilometre wall with three lines of fortifications at Alanya

restored **Kızılkule** (Red Tower) on the quayside is an Alaeddin defence work. Under the rock beyond the southern extent of the harbour are the vaulted galleries of a Seljuk boatyard. This is reached by a roadway from the esplanade running in front of the tower. A pedestrian route up to the citadel heights, signposted to **Kale**, leads off the harbour near the Blue Sky Bayirli Hotel. There is a way up by car, starting opposite the taxi rank at the roundabout, back from the harbour.

On the western side of the promontory is a deep stalactite-stalagmite cave, the **Damlataş Mağara**, widely acclaimed for its ability to cure bronchial and asthmatic disorders. Boats can be taken to other sea caves—the **Pirates'**, the **Lovers'** and the **Phosphorus**—or to **Cleopatra's Beach** in a cove on the most western extent of the rock.

The pedestrian climb to the citadel, 120 metres (400 feet) high, is strenuous but pleasant after you have passed the housing on the lower slopes and reached olive and citrus groves. From the bastions are splendid panoramic views. Among the ruined buildings on the heights is an early mosque, some tombs and a number of cisterns. In the neighbourhood of the towered gateway is the former bazaar and the ruins of a Byzantine church.

For accommodation, the old town has a spate of *pensions* and lower category hotels; the new town has an almost unlimited choice of motels, hotels and *pensions*.

ANAMUR

Bananas and groundnuts are among the principal products of the area, certainly a lush one. Anamur has a few central streets and one or two modest hotels round the main square. The *otogar* is less than a kilometre (0.6 miles) from the square, but there is a local bus service to and from. At the *plaj* are several motels, some *pensions*, restaurants, bars and discos. As well as the bus and taxi service, minibuses run too. Citizens can stroll along a long pier on the *iskele* (harbour) in the evening breeze. There is no marina as yet, and locals proudly claim that their sea is by far the cleanest in the whole Mediterranean basin, of champagne quality.

Anamur's castle—there are several castles in this region of Cilicia—is on the sands at the eastern end of the shore. The walls, towers and turrets of its three wards are in prime condition, its sea wall gently lapped by waves. You can mount by stairway to the battlements.

Anemurium, the ancient city, is on the western extremity of the shore. It is mentioned by Tacitus, but a first-century earthquake destroyed the city; the present ruins date from the third and fourth centuries. The citadel stands on a craggy hill; remains include a baths, a nymphaeum with mosaic decorations, a palaestra, gymnasia, a theatre and a well-preserved odeon. A wall separates the city from its necropolis, situated on the upper slopes, with something like 350 free-standing constructed tombs. Marble and mosaic materials were imported from Cyprus. A lighthouse stands on a headland that is the most southerly point of Anatolia. Though there is evidence of seventh-century occupation of Anemurium, archaeologists believe the city was abandoned shortly after that as a consequence of Arab attacks from the sea.

Ten kilometres (six miles) to the north of Anamur is the **Kusikbukumastim Mağarasi**, the Trofstein Cave. There is a caféteria here.

APPROACHING SILIFKE

The castle of **Softa** stands on its pointed hill on the right of Bozyazi with, further on, some extensive ruins of a habitation the castle must once have controlled. There are bays at Tekeli (Akkaya), at Yenikas—which has an intensive hothouse industry—and at Aydincik, an expanding town from where a road runs north to Gulnar, a distance of 40 kilometres (25 miles). Excavations at Gulnar in 1971 unearthed **Meydancik Kalesi**, a Persian palace of the Achaemenid period (546–334 BC), believed to be such because of the resemblance of carvings recovered there to those at Persepolis.

Ovacık's bay is backed by a coastal plain, and then the road crosses the Yasildam valley to climb again and descend to **Bagsak**, with its bay, beach, holiday facilities, river and castle that keeps guard on a second bay, with its offshore island.

Taşuçu was once a neglected, soporific harbour, but it is now a large and active port catering for ocean-going ships and tankers, albeit with holiday centres on its nearby beaches.

Three kilometres (two miles) before reaching Silifke, a road branches off to Ayatekla. Aghia Tekla is claimed to be the first female saint, converted to Christianity by St Paul. Her angry, rejected, pagan lover had her put to the lions, an ordeal she survived to become an anchorite, or religious recluse. The Emperor Zeno (474–91), a native of the region just to the north, erected a church in her honour; her cave had become a place of pilgrimage. Only an apse of his church remains, but the sacred cave, to be found among the remains of churches and monasteries, is visited still.

SILIFKE

Silifke was Seleucia on the Calycadnus; the site of the ancient city is six kilometres (four miles) distant from the modern, expanding town. The Calycadnus River still flows here, crossed by a fine Roman bridge. The castle, Byzantine with Armenian modifications, stands 200 metres (600 feet) above and away from the town. In 1210, the Armenian king gave the castle to the Knights Hospitallers in exchange for military assistance, and it became known as Camardesium. The horseshoe-shaped towers are a Crusader feature, designed for better observation of an attacking force. The necropolis lies below the castle's walls.

From Silifke, an excursion can be made to Uzuncaburç. This was a city-state under the control of priest-kings. An **Oracle of Zeus Olbius** existed here in the third century BC. The city became Diocaesarea for the Romans and Byzantines.

On a north–south line the city is crossed by a colonnaded street running east–west, and the standing columns of the temple and sanctuary are to the right, before the crossing is reached. The temple was converted to a church by the Byzantines. South of it is a two-storey, second-century building, columned on the upper floor. West of the crossing is a first-century BC temple to Tyche, Goddess of Fortune. At the northern end of the street, above the crossing, is a Roman gateway, to the east of which, along a Sacred Way, is the village of Ura, the site of Olba's residential quarter. As well as the remains of private houses, there are sections of an aqueduct and a nymphaeum. A second-century BC tower stands to the north of the Roman gateway. Gauged by the number of ruins of Byzantine churches, Olba would seem to have been as significant for Christian as it had been for pagan pilgrims. Its necropolis has a number of hypogea, or Roman-style, temple-like tombs.

ON THE ROAD TO İÇEL (MERSIN)

From Silifke, after crossing the plain through Atayurt and Kapisli, the great holiday build-up begins at Susanoğlu, after which Narlıkuyu is the first of the coves along the road. A colourful mosaic known as the Three Graces, lodged in a small museum here, is all that remains of a fourth-century Roman baths.

Twenty-five kilometres (16 miles) from Silifke, two kilometres (1.25 miles) inland—well signposted—are two natural pits known as Çennet and Çehennem (Heaven and Hell). In fact, 'Heaven' is the easier to descend. At the bottom is an 11th-century Armenian chapel, with a spring under an arched rock which is likely to have been a pagan grotto. A descent and ascent of Çennet takes about an hour. Cehennem, believed to have been an acknowledged entrance to the Underworld, is less negotiable without the help of an expert spelaeologist (cave explorer).

Between the mosaic at Narlıkuyu and the two pits are the ruins of Paperon, a Roman–Byzantine city. Inland from the road is a necropolis in which there are tombs modelled out of rock, more than one having an imprint of hands at its entrance; one tomb has the portrait of a lady, and another has the insignia of an Order of Knights. There are underground columned cisterns among Paperon's ruins.

Further along, at Sebaste, the landward side has a low arched bridge near a Byzantine chapel, among ruined buildings. Further inland is a section of an aqueduct.

The road arrives at Corycos with its two maiden castles, one on shore, the other on an island 100 metres (330 feet) out in the bay. The two castles were once con-nected by a sea wall and causeway. In 1361, the last Armenian king of Cilicia gave Corycos to Peter of Cyprus, the last Frankish king in the Near East. Peter's posses-sion was short lived, since Cilicia soon afterwards was overrun by the Mameluke Sultan Baibars. The land castle has the insignia of the Knights of Cyprus over the main gateway. The area is a popular bathing resort with camping and holiday accommodation.

To the east of Corycos is **Ayaş**, whose ruins reveal it to have been a principal city of a Roman province, where Cicero was governor from 52 to 50 BC. Among the ruins is a Byzantine basilica. There are ancient houses on the hillside, and over the hill are many Roman hypogea tombs, one with a sarcophagus on top of it. Many marble sarcophagi with carvings are standing on both sides of what was probably a Sacred Way. Here, too, is a section of aqueduct, another section of which stands at Sebaste. There is contemporary construction among the ruins at Ayaş. There is an organized beach here. Further on at Yemişkumu is a long beach, over-developed with holiday flats.

Kanlıdivane is inland a kilometre (0.6 miles) from the road at Kumkuyu. Here is a large, square-shaped pit, wider and much shallower than either Çennet or Cehennem. On the south wall is a carving of a family group, and on the west side that of a single Roman soldier. North of the pit is an abandoned town with half-buried houses, where semi-nomadic Yuruks spend the winter months, moving to upland pastures in the spring. Yuruk women weave attractive *kilims* for floors, wall hangings or bed covers. Near Kanlıdivane is a section of an aqueduct astride a narrow valley.

After Kanlıdivane and before the main road leaves the shoreline, there are holiday centres at Tirtar, Limanoğlu—the latter has a ruined castle—and Koçahasanli. Beyond a large camping site is the market town of Erdemli. Eighteen kilometres (11 miles) beyond Erdemli, at Mezitli, a right turn leads to Viranşehir, which was **Pompeiopolis**. Here a columned street runs some 500 metres (1,600 feet) to a former harbour, now a sandy beach. Twenty columns with Corinthian capitals stand erect. The city was originally Soli. When Alexander arrived, sick after plunging into the icy waters of the Cydnus at Tarsus, he vented his anger on the citizens by imposing a fine of 200 talents of silver for giving their support to Darius, and he castigated them on their atrocious Greek, hence 'solecism'.

The harbour was an important haven for pirates until Pompey cleared them from the eastern Mediterranean, but then, to compensate them for loss of income and employment, he allocated them accommodation in his new city, whose acropolis mound now has a military post on its summit.

İÇEL (MERSIN)

This modern port, with its large harbour and ancillary services of an oil refinery, storage tanks, grain silos and docks, has developed into a megalopolis. On its coastlines, east and west, are conglomerates of industrial and holiday construction. The old centre of Mersin has a palm-lined esplanade with gardens, hotels and seafood restaurants. From Mersin you may take a boat to Famagusta in Cyprus and destinations further east.

The ancient city is inland several kilometres at Yumuktepe. Thirty-two excavated levels take occupation back to the fifth millennium BC. Walls and fortifications are of several epochs, including Hittite. Many recoveries are in the Archaeological Museum in Adana, and others can be seen at the Hittite museum in Ankara.

TARSUS

St Paul was born here, but there is little now of that Roman period other than an archway known as **St Paul's Gate**. Gözlütepe is ancient Tarsus, an excavated mound on the south side. As at Yumuktepe, the archaeological discoveries go back to the fifth millennium BC. Minoan artefacts, Hittite seals and Mycenaean pottery have been found here, along with Assyrian clay tablets that have revealed a connection with Assyrian kings such as Sennacharib, Sardanapulus and Shalmanazar III.

The reputed Tomb of Sardanapulus, whose claim was that he built Tarsus and Anchialis in one day, is the Donak Taş at Gozlukule, southeast of the town. This monarch abjured those who might read his valedictory to live every moment of life to the full, since personal power was of little more value than a handclap.

Castle lovers should visit **Lampron** at Namrun, by taking the road to Camliyayla, 44 kilometres (27 miles) out of Tarsus. The impressive stronghold was the seat of Hethoumian kings but was later held by the Crusaders.

ADANA

The city stands on the Seyhan River (the Sarus), which is no longer navigable. The river is spanned by a Roman bridge built by Hadrian and rebuilt by Justinian. Of its 23 arches, 14 of the original are still in place. The current bridge was built in the 1960s, just upstream from the old one. The city's **Archaeological Museum** is on the riverside, close to the more recent bridge.

Of the Adana mosques, the 16th-century **Ulu Cami**, behind its high wall, has a Syrian-style minaret with black-tiled courses, a *medrese* and a tomb. It was built by an independent Ramazanoğlu emir. The clock tower in the central market place is an installation of 1882.

Karataş, at the mouth of the Seyhan River (the Pyramus) and busy port in Roman times, is 50 kilometres (31 miles) directly south of Adana. It offers the beaches and bathing facilities closest to the city. For boating and water-skiing, go to the Seyhan Baraji, eight kilometres (five miles) to the north of Adana. The dam is set fjord-like among the Taurus foothills.

A one-day excursion can take in three castles to the northeast of Adana and include the site of **Karatepe**. A short distance east of the Seyhan River a road turns northeast for Kozan, 72 kilometres (45 miles) away. **Tumlu** is the first of the castles, 46 kilometres (29 miles) along the way, standing on a spur in the plain. It has only its walls now—archaic, Roman, Byzantine, Roupenian and Crusader. A line of such strongpoints stretched northwards across the Cilician Plain into the Taurus Mountains, protecting Asia Minor's southern flank. From Tumlu's battlements the citadel of **Anazarbus** can be seen to the north.

Anavarsa, the village next to the ruins of Anazarbus, is separated from them by a Roman three-arched monumental gateway. The citadel is up on an elongated spur, narrowing about the middle where the walls of a keep are thick and the bastions substantial. Beyond the keep, on that section of the spur least accessible, is the burial place of Roupenian kings. There is a chapel here, too, with a frescoed apse.

In the lower town, double walls on the north side are separated by a deep fosse. Byzantine workmanship can be admired in the brickwork of a baths. Along a colonnaded street many column bases are in position, their fallen drums scattered. The theatre and stadium are distant from the public buildings of the agora and the citizen's houses. At the village end of the site you can climb to the spur by a stairway.

Kozan, on the banks of the Pyramus, was Sis, the Roupenian capital. The Byzantine citadel, modified by the Armenians, was constructed on an earlier fort.

In the 13th century the Genoese were granted a permit to reside and trade here. Beyond Kozan the road continues to Vahka in the Taurus foothills, yet another of the line of Cilician strongpoints.

Near Kadirli, which is 36 kilometres (22 miles) to the southeast of Kozan, **Karatepe** is a Hittite site situated among wooded hills. In 1946, bilingual texts in Hittite and Phoenician that were found here aided in the deciphering of Hittite hieroglyphics. Basalt sculptures with inscriptions were also unearthed, including one to Asitawandas, a king and vassal of the Hittite king whose capital was Adana. Though most of the recoveries are in the Hittite Museum in Ankara, a number of carved blocks with inscriptions have been left *in situ*.

MISIS AND YÜMÜRTALIK

Misis was the site of Mopsueste, or Mamistra, one of three Cilician sister cities; with Tarsus and Adana completing the trio. A Roman bridge crossed the river a little way upstream from the present Byzantine one, and its piers are still in place. A colonnaded street ran from this bridge to the city's acropolis. Ruins of buildings stand on either side of the river, with sections of the city walls on the eastern side. In the village is the house that was used as a hostel and workplace by members of an expedition working here, its walls inscribed with their names. Downriver, near Yakapinar, is a carving of a Hittite river god on a rock overhanging the water.

As a separate excursion a visit to Misus could include **Yılankale** (Snake Castle), standing on a high rock above the Seyhan River, a little off the E5, yet seeming to dominate the road. The castle's name is derived from a serpent in the armorial bearing above the double gateway to the inner ward. There are chambers off the courtyard of the outer ward, and a postern gate offers vertiginous command of the countryside.

Like Corycos, Yümürtalık has two castles, the one on land now identifiable by only a few stones alongside the disused harbour, while the castle on the island out in the bay has its walls and gives an impression of being a complete structure. Yümürtalık, a holiday resort for the neighbourhood, could once have been Ayaş, where Marco Polo was marooned for a season.

THE PLAIN OF ISSUS

With its massive walls and rounded towers, **Toprakkale** stands sentinel above a narrow defile that leads into the plain where, in 333 BC, Alexander fought Darius and routed him in the decisive battle of his campaign. The sea has receded here because of silting, and it is difficult to visualize the restricted confines within which the battle must have been fought. A diligent visitor, though, might find arrowheads or other remnants of that conflict.

Beyond Issus, on the marshland to the right of the road, are the ruins of **Epiphania**, with a section of aqueduct prominent. There is a turnoff here to **Payas** where surviving buildings have been attributed to Sinan, but the castle is Venetian.

İSKENDERUN

İskenderun is a modern and developing port situated picturesquely under the Amanus mountains, with an attractive waterfront.

Belen, on the southern pass, is built on twin hills above a deep gorge, and a building of interest is the Ottoman *han* erected under Selim I (1512–20), in which the young Sinan may have had a hand. Down below, on the east, is the Plain of Amik where alongside the Lake of Amik, is the excavated Hittite city of **Alalakh**, with its early Egyptian and Sumerian connections. The **Castle of Bagras** dominates the Belen Pass, the watchdog of Antioch. Saladin however succeeded in storming its formidable defences. Later it came into the possession of the Knights Templar.

HATAY (ANTAKYA)

Byzantine walls exist still on the hills to the east, but the most interesting exhibits of the past are in the museum, close to the bridge. Along with recoveries from Alalakh and elsewhere, and a fine numismatic (coin) section, the museum has the greatest collection of secular mosaics to be found anywhere; a remarkable testimony to the art of the mosaicist.

In the town the **Habibnacar Cami** originated as a Roman Temple to Apollo. Daphne, the fashionable Roman suburb eight kilometres (five miles) out of town, is now the wooded suburb of Harbiye. There is an aqueduct here built by Hadrian, as well as the source of a sacred spring. Apollo lusted after the nymph Daphne, and because she rejected his importunacy, turned her into a laurel bush (*Daphne laureolus*).

SAMANDAĞ

The ruins of the former port are on the northern edge of the wide shore at the mouth of the Orontes River. On the opposite southern edge is sacred Mount Cassius. Still to be seen are the remains of Vespasian's water system that controlled the flow of water in and out of the harbour.

The Crusader **Castle of Cursat** is near the village of Sofular, close to Antakya. **Trapesac** of the Knights Templar is just to the north. **Civlan** is perched 1,000 metres (3,282 feet) high to the northeast, and the renowned **Krak des Chevaliers** is just across the border in Syria. Near the village of İslahiye, on the railway line to Aleppo in northern Syria, is the excavated site of the 14th-century BC Hittite city of **Zincirli**.

Central Anatolia

Ankara, on the central plateau at a height of 855 metres (2,800 feet), is set in a bowl surrounded by hills. It is a city in a desert—though planned cultivation, as elsewhere in western Turkey—is changing the landscape and environment. Climatic temperatures, however, can still be extreme. From Ankara, a two- or three-day trip could include the Hittite sites of Alaca Hüyük, Hattusas and Yazilikaya. A visit to Gordium, the Phrygian capital, can be a day trip from Ankara.

Caesarea (Kayseri) was the capital city of the extensive Roman province of Cappadocia. Though today it is largely modern, Byzantine walls still surround the central medieval city, particularly on the northern section. The monuments are mainly Seljuk, with a Danismend memory or two, and Ottoman touches.

A minimum of three days is recommended for a visit to the rock-hewn churches, monasteries and other sights of this region, the most fascinating monuments of Cappadocia found within the triangle of Nevşehir–Kayseri–Niğde.

Konya's location is strategic, lying as it does on the southern edge of the central plateau and commanding the passes down through the Taurus Mountains into the region of Cilicia. Konya is the centre, too, of a great wheat-growing area of the Konya Plain—explaining, perhaps, the existence of shrines to the Anatolian Great Earth Mother, Phrygian Cybele and, in the time of Hadrian, a sanctuary to Roman Demeter. Southeast of Konya is the site of Catal Hüyük, circa 7000 BC; recoveries can be seen at the Archaeological Museum in Ankara.

Getting There

One long thoroughfare runs from Ulus at the north end of central Ankara to the crown of Cankaya Hill at its southern end, intersecting the main districts of the city. From Ulus Meydani (Ulus Square) with its equestrian statue of Atatürk, the road running south is Atatürk Bulvarı, and it runs through the city's centre at Kızılay to mount the steep hill to the Presidential Palace at the top. At Bakanliklar, a little way up from Kızılay, are the Parliament and government buildings, and on the ascent from there almost all the accredited foreign embassies may be found, except for that of the United States, which is out beyond Kavaklidere, and the Russian, at Maltepe.

To undertake an excursion to the Hittite sites, go out east on the E23 for 120 kilometres (75 miles) through Elmadağ to a road junction six kilometres (four miles) south of Delice. From this junction there is a route along the river, the Delice Ormak, a tributary of the Kızılirmak (the Halys) via Yerköy, 59 kilometres (36 miles), Yozgat, 37 kilometres (23 miles), to Yazilkaya, 40 kilometres (25 miles). Another route from Delice is via Süngürlu, 58 kilometres (36 miles), to Boğazkale (Hattusas), 21 kilometres (13 miles). This latter route is the one to take if you intend first to see the Hittite remains and the museum at Alaca Hüyük, then take from Süngürlu the road to Alaca.

To visit Gordium, go to Polatli, 76 kilometres (47 miles) southwest of Ankara on road E23. Polatli is a kilometre (0.6 mile) off the road to the north, and in the 1960s workmen digging foundations for new houses there, unearthed the top level of a site that subsequently was discovered to go down through many levels, to the Neolithic. Continuing on the E23, 17 kilometres (ten miles) further west, a road turns north for 12 kilometres (eight miles) to Yassihüyük and the site of Gordium.

Turkish Airlines has flights to Kayseri, which is also on the main railway line from Ankara to the east of the country. Key places in Cappadocia can be reached by public transport in combination with the minibus services. As with visits to the Hittite sites and Gordium, there are organized tours to Cappadocia available from established tour agencies in Ankara.

Going south from Ankara on the main E5 highway, turn off some ten kilometres (six miles) past Gölbaşı, at Ogulbey, to join road 66 to Kirşehir, 147 kilometres (91 miles) away. On this route the road crosses the Kızılirmak River over a fine Seljuk bridge. Road 41 forks south 29 kilometres (18 miles) beyond Kirşehir. You can choose either to go southeast to Kayseri, another 137 kilometres (85 miles), and begin your Cappadocian tour from there, or go the 67 kilometres (42 miles) south to Nevşehir where the first 'fairy' cones can be seen and investigated.

From Nevşehir take road 73 eastward. Five kilometres (three miles) along this road is the entrance to the Göreme Valley, the principal visiting centre of the region. At the northern head of the valley, Ürgüp is 21 kilometres (13 miles) east of Nevşehir.

Kaymaklı is 20 kilometres (12 miles) south of Nevşehir on the road to Niğde, and Derinkuyu is ten kilometres (six miles) further. The Soganli valley, east of Derinkuyu, is a rich replica of the Göreme valley, if less accessible. A similar settlement exists at Ozkonak, 20 kilometres (12 miles) northwest of Avanos.

To reach the area of Ihlara, go southwest out of Nevşehir on road 300 to Aksaray, along which are three Seljuk inns, in particular the restored Ağzikara, just before a turnoff running southeast to the Mamazin Dam, or eight kilometres (five miles) before Aksaray. A right fork, 23 kilometres (14 miles) along this turnoff, leads to Ihlara, which is another 11 kilometres (seven miles) further on.

Niğde is 84 kilometres (52 miles) south of Nevşehir. From Niğde to Kayseri, the 128-kilometre (80 mile) road skirts the magnificent Mount Erciyes, 3,916 metres (12,850 feet) high. As Mount Argaeus of antiquity, the mountain peak is perpetually under snow. The site at Kültepe is 20 kilometres (12 miles) northeast of Kayseri on the Sivas road.

For a hurrying traveller, Konya could be a one-day excursion by road from Ankara. The distance by road is 220 kilometres (137 miles) over the wide Konya Plain. There are Turkish Airlines' flights to Konya, and coach and minibus services are as convenient as in most regions of Turkey.

For the traveller along the Mediterranean coast, Konya can be reached from Silifke by bus. The road climbs above the valley of the Goksu River, through the Taurus Mountains, to the plateau by way of Mut and Karaman. This is a recommended journey, to be taken in late afternoon with the light softening mountain peaks and captivating rock formations. After Mut, the feathery green of the Mediterranean pine gives way to the deeper reassuring green of the spruce. Much reforestation is taking place on these mountain slopes, as elsewhere in Turkey's mountain regions. At Konya, the *otogar* is about three kilometres (two miles) northwest of the city centre.

The site of Catal Hüyük lies 34 kilometres (21 miles) southeast of Konya, near the town of Cumra. Twin mounds are located on a track to Kücukköy, ten kilometres (six miles) from the town.

A suggested trip for the motorist is to venture from Konya to Denizli via Isparta. The route takes you west to Beyşehir, to run northwest along the length of the Lake of Beyşehir before diverting through mountainous terrain, and afterwards turning southwest to reach and skirt the eastern shore of Lake Eğridir. The town of Eğridir on the lakeside is an attractive holiday resort, having its quota of *pensions* and hotels, restaurants, a castle and a causeway out to Yeşilköy, or Green Island. After reaching Isparta, the road runs north to Dinar, then turns southwesterly for a longish haul to Denizli, from where Pamukkale and Aphrodisias can be visited.

Historical Background

In 1923, Kemal Atatürk made Ankara the capital of the Turkish Republic that he had founded. The Anatolians of the plateau had supported him in his rejection of the Treaty of Sevres made between the Western Allies and the Turkish sultan at the conclusion of World War I, and they had provided his military strength against the

Greek incursion of 1920–22. Therefore, his preference was for Ankara rather than İstanbul, whose cosmopolitan citizens he had reason to distrust.

The name of the city could derive from Ankuwash of Hittite texts. It became Phrygian when the Phrygians destroyed Hittite power in Central Anatolia. The Persians held it before Alexander arrived in 334 BC. In the third century BC it was in the hands of Galatians, invading tribes who had terrorized western Asia Minor before the Attalids drove them east. By St Paul's day, Ancyra, or Angora, was the capital of the Roman Province of Galatia; the former savage tribes seem to have settled by this time to an urban way of life, with Christian converts, since St Paul addressed an epistle to their church. The Arabs sacked and occupied it in the seventh and eighth centuries and, after the Byzantines had strengthened the defences, again in the tenth. The Seljuk Turks occupied it following their victory at Manzikert, before moving on to make Nikaia (İznik) their capital. Timur (Tamerlane) defeated the Ottoman Sultan Beyazıt I at Ankara in 1401 and might have put an end to Ottoman power had he stayed in the west, but the Mongol Khan returned east and died in 1405. Under later Ottoman sultans, Ankara declined in importance.

Clay tablets in cuneiform script were found at Boğazkale, indicating that in the 18th century BC this city was Hattusas, capital of the Land of Hatti. The Hittites, under their Hattian Indo-Aryan overlords, likely retained a number of their ethnic and social customs. Later, the Hurrians, yet another Indo-Aryan people, moved to the southeast, from the vicinity of Lake Van, and another connected people, the Mitanni moved southeast as far as Babylon. These four peoples seem to have combined to create a Hittite culture.

The early Hittite Kingdom, whose script was in cuneiform, came to an end about the 16th century BC, but this was succeeded by a Hittite Empire, within which the script became hieroglyphic. The empire ended in the 12th century BC when Phrygia became the dominant power in western Anatolia. There was a late flowering of Hittite culture when a number of independent Hittite kingdoms came into being in northern Syria and Cilicia, the last of which, centred on Carchemish on the Euphrates, was overrun by the Assyrians in 724 BC.

The Phrygians are thought to have emigrated to Asia Minor from Thrace, west of the Bosphorus, or even further west from the Rhodope Mountains and the North Aegean. In time they overturned the Hittites in western and central Anatolia and took over as principal power.

Midas is said to have been their king when the Phrygians, in their turn, were overpowered by wild Cimmerian tribes coming across the Black Sea from the Crimea. Midas is said to have committed suicide by drinking bull's blood (as Themistocleos, the fifth-century Greek victor of Salamis, is also said to have ended

The red-tile roofs of old Ankara

his life, after his ostracism by the Athenians and exile in Lampsacus). Midas, though, may well have been an eponymous title for a king, just as Augustus and Caesar had become for Roman emperors.

Gyges, founder of the Lydian Mermnad dynasty at Sardis, fought and expelled the Cimmerians and extended his kingdom and control throughout Phrygia, but by Alexander's time Gordium was no longer a major city, having been reduced in importance under Persian rule following Cyrus' defeat of Croesus.

Prior to his death, Gordios, the patriarchal founder of Gordium, tied the yoke of his wagon-symbol of his peasant origins—to its shaft with an injunction that whoever should untie the knot would make himself master of all Asia. Alexander is said craftily to have cut through the knot with a sword stroke, thereby becoming master of Asia.

Kayseri was probably Mazaca for the Hittites. Under Trajan it became Caeserea, capital of Cappadocia. The Persians occupied it after their defeat of the emperor Valerian (253–60) on the Euphrates. Eusebius (264–340), the historian of early Christianity, was a distinguished bishop here. Influential early Fathers of the Church, born in this city, were Basil of Caesarea, Gregory of Nyssa and the latter's younger brother, Gregory Nazianzus.

In the sixth century Justinian, after extensive reconquests in the east, rebuilt the walls, and for a time it was known as Eusebia. After the Seljuk arrival in Anatolia in the 11th century, Kayseri became the city of a Danismend independent emirate. Afterwards there followed Seljuk reoccupation, Mongol violation, Karamanoğlu possession and Mameluke residence, until Sultan Selim I made it Ottoman in 1513.

Konya is said to have been Kuwanna to the Hittites, Kowania to the Phrygians—the latter believed to have been the only city to survive Noah's flood—Eikonion to the early Greeks, Iconium to the Romans (for a short time Claudiconium) and Ikonion to the Byzantines. St Paul preached to a nascent Christian community at Konya.

From the seventh to the tenth centuries the Byzantine city became a target of the religious and military expansionist aims of the Arabs, but its status changed appreciably when the Seljuks, after losing Nikaia (İznik) to the Knights of the First Crusade, made Konya the capital of their Sultanate of Rum. For the Seljuks it was a sacred city, later to become the centre of the mystical cult of the Mevlana. The Seljuk architectural achievement took place here between the late 11th and the 13th centuries, though almost nothing from the earliest time of that period has survived. Today's monuments date mainly from the time of Sultan Alaeddin Keykubat I (1220–37).

Sights

ANKARA

North of Ulus Meydani, Atatürk Bulvarı becomes Çankiri Caddesi; along this, on
the left, is the site of a third-century Roman baths with a palaestra. To the right of
Ulus Meydani and Çankiri Caddesi is the citadel hill. From the square, take
Hisarparki Caddesi to go up to the Hisar Kapisi (Castle Gate) in the outer wall of
the citadel. Or take Anafartalar Caddesi and mount by way of the narrow market
streets. You then go through the medieval area between the walls. **Parmat Kapisi**
is the gateway through the inner walls, reinforced under the Byzantine emperor
Heraclius in the seventh century. The outer walls and those of the citadel were
strengthened against Arab attacks by the Byzantines in the eighth and ninth centuries, and one of the towers, the **Sark Kulesi**, was refurbished as a strongpoint.
Seljuk defence modifications were added later.

THE ARCHAEOLOGICAL MUSEUM

This occupies a restored *bedesten* (covered bazaar) of the 15th century, along with
a companion *han* of an earlier date. It is situated on a garden terrace down from the
Hisar Kapisi. There are exhibits of early Anatolian civilizations, and from the
Neolithic sites of Catal Hüyük (near Konya, see page 236), Haçılar (near Burdur)
and Yumuktepe (at Mersin), as well as from later Roman, Byzantine and Turkish
periods. The outstanding sections are those containing the Hittite sculptures in
high and low relief, the engraved seals, the worked-iron and bronze medallions and
the jewellery, all an astonishing revelation concerning a people who have become
rediscovered in detail only in the 20th century.

MONUMENTS

Off the right-hand side of Çankiri Caddesi, not far from Ulus Meydani, is a short
street leading to Hukumet Meydani, a square in which there is a **Column of Julian**,
erected for that emperor's visit in 362. In the next square, a little to the northeast,
is the 15th-century **Hacı Bayram Cami**, which has some very attractive tiling.
Along the east side of this square are the remains of a **Temple to Rome and
Augustus**, constructed on the original site of a temple to Cybele; a temple that had
been built over a shrine to Men, the Phrygian Moon God. In the pronaos (body of
a temple) of the present structure, an engraved text recording the achievements of
Augustus has just a few Latin characters remaining. A Byzantine church likely
succeeded this Roman temple.

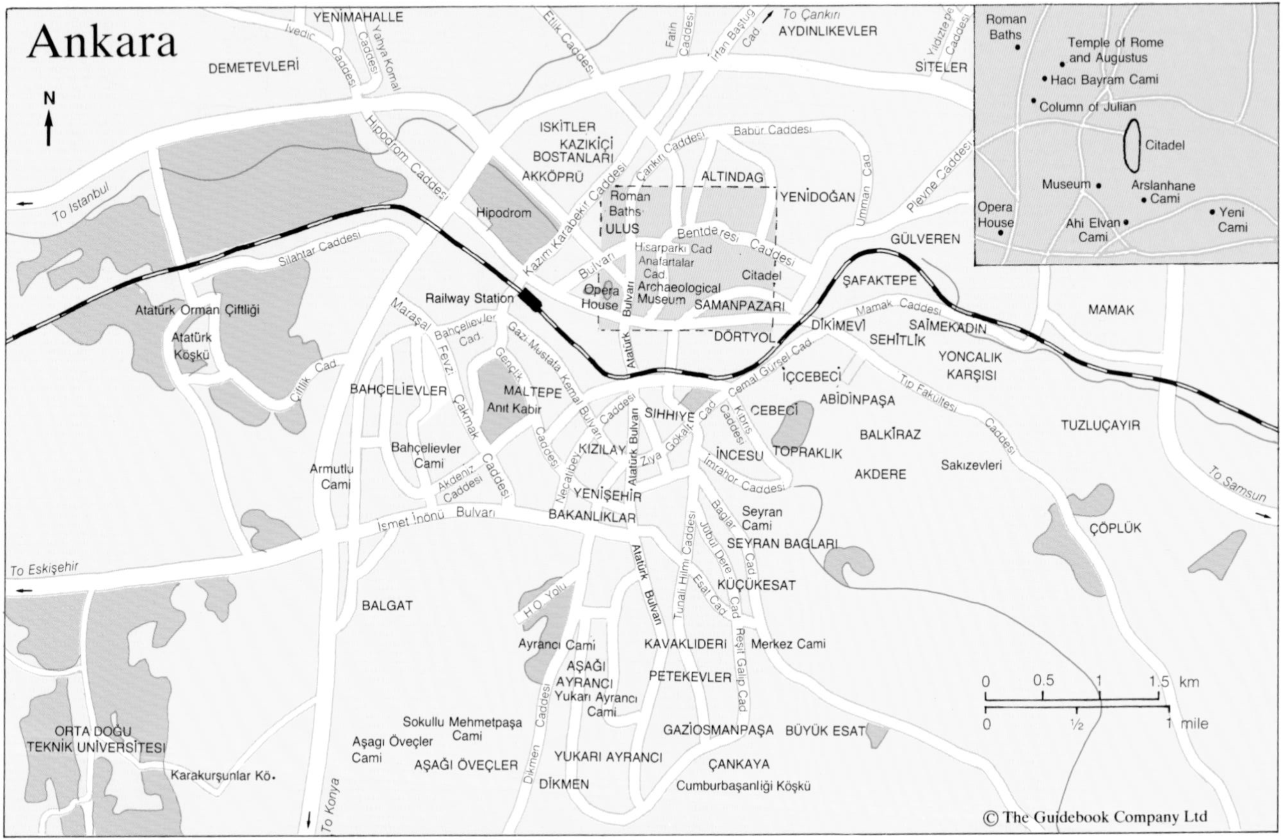

Ankara
N
DEMETEVLERİ
YENİMAHALLE
ISKİTLER
KAZIKİÇİ
BOSTANLARI
AKKÖPRÜ
Hipodrom
ALTINDAG
YENİDOĞAN
AYDINLIKEVLER
SİTELER
Roman Baths
ULUS
Opera House
Archaeological Museum
Citadel
SAMANPAZARI
DÖRTYOL
GÜLVEREN
ŞAFAKTEPE
MAMAK
DİKİMEVİ
SAİMEKADIN
SEHİTLİK
YONCALIK KARŞISI
TUZLUÇAYIR
Railway Station
Atatürk Orman Çiftliği
Atatürk Köşkü
BAHÇELİEVLER
MALTEPE
Anıt Kabir
Bahçelievler Cami
Armutlu Cami
SIHHIYE
KIZILAY
YENİŞEHİR
BAKANLIKLAR
İÇCEBECİ
CEBECİ
ABİDİNPAŞA
BALKİRAZ
TOPRAKLIK
İNCESU
AKDERE
Sakızevleri
ÇÖPLÜK
Seyran Cami
SEYRAN BAGLARI
KÜÇÜKESAT
BALGAT
Ayrancı Cami
AŞAĞI AYRANCI
Yukarı Ayrancı Cami
KAVAKLIDERİ
Merkez Cami
PETEKEVLER
GAZİOSMANPAŞA
BÜYÜK ESAT
ÇANKAYA
Cumburbaşanliği Köşkü
YUKARI AYRANCI
DİKMEN
Sokullu Mehmetpaşa Cami
Aşagı Öveçler Cami
AŞAĞI ÖVEÇLER
ORTA DOĞU TEKNİK ÜNİVERSİTESİ
Karakurşunlar Kö.
To Istanbul
To Eskişehir
To Konya
To Samsun
To Çankırı
Ivedic Caddesi
Yahya Komal Caddesi
Hipodrom Caddesi
Etlik Caddesi
Fatih Caddesi
İrfan Baştuğ Cad
Yıldızte pe Caddesi
Babür Caddesi
Çankırı Caddesi
Ümman Cad
Plevne Caddesi
Kazım Karabekir Caddesi
Bentderesi Caddesi
Hisarparkı Cad
Anafartalar Cad
Bulvarı
Atatürk Bulvarı
Silahtar Caddesi
Mareşal Fevzi Çakmak Caddesi
Bahçelievler Cad
Gazi Mustafa Kemal Bulvarı
Gençlik Caddesi
Çiftlik Cad
Akdeniz Caddesi
İsmet İnönü Bulvarı
Necatibey Caddesi
Ziya Gokalp Cad
Kıbrıs Caddesi
Cemal Gürsel Cad
Mamak Caddesi
Tıp Fakültesi Caddesi
İmrahor Caddesi
Baglar Cad
Jübül Dere Cad
Tunalı Hilmi Caddesi
Esat Cad
Reşit Galip Cad
H.O. Yolu
Dikmen Caddesi
Roman Baths
Temple of Rome and Augustus
Hacı Bayram Cami
Column of Julian
Citadel
Museum
Arslanhane Cami
Opera House
Ahi Elvan Cami
Yeni Cami
0 0.5 1 1.5 km
0 ½ 1 mile
© The Guidebook Company Ltd

MOSQUES

Within the citadel is the Seljuk **Alaettin Cami** (Alaeddin) of 1178. To the south-west of the museum is the **Arslanhane Cami** of the 13th century, so-called because of a stone lion in the forecourt. It has wooden columns, and a *mihrab* in enamelled faience; its carved *minber* is in walnut wood, dated 1290. The late 14th-century **Ahi Elvan Cami** is in a street a little lower down and has Roman columns incorporated in its structure; the *minber* is dated 1413. The **Yeni Cami**, 400 metres (1,300 feet) east of the Arslanhane Cami, was erected in the 16th century in the time of Suleiman the Magnificent.

ANIT KABIR—THE ATATÜRK MAUSOLEUM

This monument is on a hill on the outskirts west of the city. It can be reached by going out on İsmet İnonu Bulvarı from Bakanliklar. An impressive monument to a great man, it is set in landscaped grounds with a marble-paved access roadway. Flanking pavilions have sculptured reliefs, and a wide stairway leads up to the columned mausoleum which houses the marble sarcophagus. Within the complex is a museum containing exhibits of Atatürk's personal belongings.

ATATÜRK ORMAN CIFTLIGI

A legacy of Atatürk, to the north of Anıt Kabir, is a memorial to his far-sightedness; the Atatürk Orman Ciftligi is a model farm he pioneered. Its dairy products can be sampled at a restaurant there. In the grounds are two constructed lakes, an aquarium and a small zoo.

NATIONAL THEATRE AND OPERA HOUSE

Ankara's National Theatre and Opera House is on Atatürk Bulvarı, between Ulus Meydani and Kızılay. Behind the Opera House is the Youth Park (Gençlik Parki) where there is a boating lake, restaurants, cafés and fun-fair pavilions.

FISHING, BOATING AND WINTER SPORTS

The Çübük Dam, out on the airport road, is good for a picnic, for fishing and boating, as is Gölbaşı Lake, 22 kilometres (14 miles) south of the city. Elmadağ, the mountain range to the east of Ankara, is a popular centre for winter sports.

AN EXCURSION TO THE HITTITE SITES

Hattusas, at Boğazkale (or Boğazköy) stands on an irregular outcrop cut by deep ravines, buttressed by spurs. Its walls—especially the bastions on the south and east—are still remarkably strong.

Mounting a pathway from the plain, you pass the ruined palace in which,

Sorting the wool, old Ankara

among other buildings, are the archives where the bilingual clay tablets were found. Here too are the kilns in which they were fired; evidence suggests that the entire building was ultimately destroyed by fire.

Moving round the spur you reach the **King's Gate**. A sculpture of a Warrior God found here is in the Ankara Museum. He has a beaked nose and is wearing a kilt-like skirt with a heavy belt and a helmet with ear guards. His weapons are an axe, a sword and a belted dagger and, as with most Hittite figures, he appears to be on the march. Within the walls of the city are the sites of four temples. A tunnel still leads down to a postern gate in the outer wall. The next entry along the line of the walls is the **Gate of the Sphinxes**. One of the sphinxes is in the İstanbul Archaeological Museum, another in Berlin. A third entry, the **Lion Gate**, has a rampant lion on each jamb of the main portal.

Below the spur on its north side, a principal temple stands on an elevated shelf of land in the plain, its court paved in black basalt. The peristyle has a double tier of massive, square-shaped columns in a double tier, the inner sanctum perhaps even less accessible than Apollo's at Didyma. The deity of Hattusas would have been the Great Mother of Anatolia, the Sun Goddess, seated in that formal austerity of Egyptian deities: her appeasement may have called for the human sacrifice of a prisoner of war, disgraced soldier or runaway slave. The city's administrative offices were probably within the temple complex, with the marketplace adjoining it. A **Sacred Way** led from the gate in the lower city's walls to the temple's entrance, and here a large stone receptacle no doubt served for ritual ablutions. Boğazköy, the village, is outside the gate, and the quarters of the Assyrian merchants may well have been located there.

Entrance to nearby **Yazilkaya** is through a fissure in a rock outcrop. On the walls on either side of a lower chamber is a line of carved deities converging on a panel on the end wall. On the panel, a marriage is depicted between Arinna, the Mother Goddess, and Sharma, the Weather God. A gryphon guards the short stairway to an upper chamber. The main relief here is of Sharma in an attitude of genuflection, with a smaller figure of a standing king between his knees, as though under the god's protection. The god's symbol of divinity is a high conical-shaped hat. The carving has been assigned to the reign of Tudhaliyas IV, 1250 BC. Another carving in this chamber is of a Sword God, and there is also a panel of 12 figures who appear to be hurrying, each carrying a sickle-shaped object.

Alaca Hüyük is 30 kilometres (19 miles) to the northeast of Boğazköy and Yazilkaya, situated outside the town of Alaca. Sections of the outer walls remain, as well as a gateway with sphinx carvings on either jamb, in which two creatures are leaning or projecting out of the stone. On another block is a double-headed eagle holding a hare in its talons, a goddess over its head. There are other less definable carvings along this wall. Among the widespread excavations is a palace, and an early oval-shaped altar. Tombs of kings, some dating back to Hittite times, have yielded weapons, bronze standards and pottery. Many recoveries are housed in the museum in Alaca, alongside the headquarters and hostel of the Turkish archaeological team. Exhibits include a selection of decorated pottery of several periods, weapons, artefacts and reconstructed tombs and burial urns. The garden has a Hittite lion, along with examples of Byzantine carved sarcophagi and inscribed stelae.

GORDIUM

Among the excavated buildings is a palace dating from about 700 BC. Phrygian pottery is colourful, highly decorated and often amusing. At Gordium too, huge metallic-tinted amphorae (two-handled narrow-necked jars) were found, at least one bearing an inscription in Lydian. As at Polatli, the excavated shafts descend through many formerly occupied layers. Although most recoveries have gone to the museum at Ankara and elsewhere, there is a display in the workshops of the American expedition that formerly dug here. Phrygia had a reputation for its ivory artefacts, faience beads, gold filigree and items in terracotta.

Away from the excavated city is the **Burial Place of the Kings** whose funerary mounds have been opened. A corridor—ingeniously concealed—leads down through the mound to a hardwood-panelled burial chamber. Finely carved wooden screens surrounded the tomb. Because this country had been heavily forested, the Phrygians used timber extensively in construction. A model for houses of a later age, a typical Phrygian house was a half-timbered structure on two floors, with an upper wooden balcony and balustrade overlooking a central courtyard.

The Sakarya River flows on the eastern side of the site excavations. Here the Greek Expeditionary Force was halted in its 1920–22 conflict with Turkey, and from here it retreated. The lines of former trenches of that struggle are discernible along the banks of the river.

CAPPADOCIA

On the route to Nevşehir, a stop can be made at **Hacıbektaş** where a neat complex includes a monastery, a library, a small museum and the **Tomb of Hacı Bektaş**, who founded an Order of Dervishes, the Bektasi, whose precepts incorporated Shia, Sunni and Christian tenets. Members of this order were appointed teachers in İstanbul to boys recruited or abducted into the Corps of Janissaries. The grounds of the monastery complex are well tended and offer a favourable place in which to pause.

Nevşehir is at the base of a hill that is honeycombed with caves and crowned by an **Ottoman citadel**. The first cones can be seen on the right of the road as you approach the city, and you can get into some cones to explore them, as you might a cave.

HITTITE THEOLOGY

Professor John Garstang, who excavated Yumuktepe at Mersin and worked elsewhere in Turkey, is a fascinating interpreter of Hittite theology. He believes that the gods and goddesses of the peoples who contributed to Hittite culture were brought together at Yazilkaya to witness a marriage that would synthesize the various conflicting religious beliefs; quantity had led to duplications of the divine services for which each deity was responsible. At Yazılıkaya, too, there was the attempt to establish protocol among the higher echelon of divinity, as well as in the lower echelon, such as the deities in procession on either wall of the lower chamber.

In the Wedding Panel, the principal gods and goddesses of the Hittite and Hurrian pantheons are represented. Arinna is the Sun Goddess, and in origin this shrine may have been hers. Sharma, the Weather God of Anatolia, is her son and consort. In the Hurrian or Hurrite pantheon, the Queen of Heaven was Hebat, her son and consort was Teshub. On the panel, Hepatu is depicted as the Mother Goddess, with Teshub as her consort, while Sharma, a figure smaller in size than Teshub, is standing on the back of a lion to the rear of Hepatu. It should be remembered, though, that in such a wall carving, size could denote distance or elevation rather than importance. Sharma carries a double-headed axe, which is a Hittite symbol, while Teshub stands astride the shoulders of Namni and Hazzi, who were either minor deities or superseded or demoted gods. Elsewhere in Hittite depictions, Namni and Hazzi are personalized mountains, and in others they represent Night and Day. In yet other carvings, Teshub as the Weather God is depicted in a chariot drawn by two bulls, Sari and Hurri, and again in others the Bull Gods seem also to represent Night and Day. In the Wedding Panel, each bull is a separate entity; one is associated with Teshub, the other with Hepatu.

To the rear of Hepatu and Sharma, two goddesses share a two-headed eagle which holds a lyre between its claws. These two goddesses are the daughter and the granddaughter of Arinna. At the back of Teshub is Telepinu, a god of vegetation, and third in line in the hierarchy of Young Gods. A Young God such as Teshub—as with such gods in other religions, for example Adonis, Tammuz, Osiris, Baal—is the god who must die, be sacrificed or be hidden away during the summer drought, later to be reborn, revived or found again in the spring through the agency of the Mother Goddess, and he becomes her consort. In some Hittite texts, Telepinu is the Young God, and he, as with Teshub in others, is the protagonist in a fight with the dragon Illuyankas in which, at first, the dragon gets the upper hand but is finally killed by the Hero God through the favourable intervention of the Mother Goddess or one of her agents.

Professor Garstang believes that an annual ceremony was conducted at Yazılıkaya in which a marriage was enacted and consummated between the reigning king in the role of Teshub and a priestess of the sanctuary in that of the Mother Goddess.

THE GÖREME VALLEY

More than 350 Rupestrian churches have been carved out of the volcanic tuff in the valley. Most have finely carved architectural features, and many are decorated with geometric or pictorial frescoes. A local publication on sale at the entrance provides detailed information. There are also guides for hire.

Of particular interest are the restored frescoes of **Elmalı Kilise**, opposite a monastery on the left as you move from the site's main entrance. The monastery rooms are on more than one level and include a chapel, refectory and kitchen area. The **Karanlık Kilise**, **Yilanli** and the **Tokatli** churches should be visited. A number of the churches are signposted for the convenience of visitors, but personal exploration is possible and recommended.

Ortahisar, built around a pinnacle of hardened sandstone, Cappadocia

ÜRGÜP

This town has developed into a tourist centre with hotels, *pensions*, boutiques and restaurants—and the wine of the district is most potable. Many of the cones in the vicinity are fitted out as well-appointed dwellings. **Avcilar**, too, has its cones and converted rock dwellings. **Uç Hisar** has a carved edifice consisting of three castles, and **Ortahisar's castle** dominates a needle-pointed mass of carved-out dwellings, with churches and monasteries in its neighbourhood. **Cavuş In** is a village at the base of a semi-circular cliff that harbours a legion of caves—note here the **Church of St John Prodromos** (John the Baptist). At **Avanos**, on the north bank of the Kızılirmak River, the potteries make use of the district's red earth; objects in onyx are also manufactured. Nearby **Zelve** has the entrance to yet another valley of conic shapes and concealed ecclesiastical structures. **Sarı Han**, near Avanos, has a Seljuk *han* with a fine gateway and courtyard.

KAYMAKLİ AND DERINKUYU

Entry to these two many-storeyed underground cities is by tunnel. Chimney-style shafts or ducts supplied air to the thousands of villagers and town-dwellers who took refuge in them from the frequent and anarchic depredations of marauding armies from the seventh to the 15th centuries.

In the neighbouring valley of **Çemil**, among other structures is the **Monastery of the Archangelos**, a feature of which is the large arcaded refectory. At Girgoli the **Aghiasma of St Luke** is on the site of an ancient sacred spring, amid several accompanying chapels. Near it, at Sinasos, is a **Chapel of the Virgin Mary**. Damsa, another village close by, has a Seljuk mosque.

NIĞDE

Niğde has a claim to Hittite origin, but its standing monuments are mainly Seljuk. A ruined castle, probably Byzantine, stands on the hill above the town. The Seljuk citadel, with its polygonal keep, dates from the 11th century. It was restored under the Ottomans in the 15th century, when a wall with bastions was built round the citadel's mound. South of the citadel is a triple-domed mosque of 1203, later restored by Sultan Ala et Tin and bearing his name. Below the mosque is a long, arched covered market. The Mongol 14th-century mosque opposite the market is the **Süngür Bey Cami**. By a town gate in the citadel walls is the **Eskiciler Çeşmesi**, a fountain of 1421, behind which is the **Şah Mescit**, a small mosque of the 15th century with Byzantine columns incorporated in its structure. Near the Süngür Bey Cami, the **Ak Medrese** (theological school) has a modest archaeological museum. The building is a Karamanoğlu one of 1402 (the Karamanoğlu became the heirs of the Sultanate of Rum following its disintegration). The **Dış Cami** is Ottoman of the

16th century. The largest of three tombs, the **Hüdavent Türbesi** of 1312, is that of a princess; the two other tombs are of a later date.

IHLARA AND THE PERISTREMA GORGE

With extra time, a visit could be made to the Peristrema Gorge in the foothills to the west and south of Nevşehir. In the Ihlara valley, churches and monasteries are as legion as at Göreme, except that here there are constructed buildings carved out of the tufa. In the gorge itself, the crossing of the Melendez River is made by foot-bridges or, if the river is not in spate, by fording. Churches to be seen for their colourful and dramatic frescoes are the **Egri Taş Kilise**, the **Kokar** and the **Purenli Seki**; there is abstract decor in the **Ağacili Kilise**, which has steps up to it formed from tree trunks.

KAYSERI

The Byzantine fort within the citadel was strengthened by the Seljuks in 1224 and again under the Osmanlis. The latter reinforced the walls and the Citadel's 19 square or rectangular defence towers. The Seljuk lions at the gate keep watch on the covered bazaar over the way. The gateway is double, and there is an inscription over the inner gate relating to Mehmet II, the Conqueror, who added the small mosque and fountain within the walls. Stairways lead up to the accessible sentry walk.

The Ulu Cami near the bazaar is a Danismend twin-domed structure begun in 1135, but completed later under the Seljuk reoccupation. The **Huant Hatun Cami** dates from 1237. Huant Hatun was the Georgian wife of Sultan Alaeddin Keykubat; her octagonal-shaped tomb is in the mosque complex. There is also a *medrese*, now the Ethnological Museum.

Behind the park, a double building of 1205, the **Çifte Medrese**, has a fine entrance. It was founded by Sultan Keyhusrev. Another building, the **Giyasiye**, was designed as a medical school, one of the first of its kind; the other, the **Sifahiy**, was a hospital. The **Sahibiye Medrese** dates from 1267, and this also has a fine entrance. The restored interior houses a collection of Seljuk stone carvings. The **Hacı Kiliç Cami and Medrese** on Cumhuriyet Bulvarı is of 1249 origin. The **Güllük Cami**, dating from 1210, was rebuilt about a century later by the Seljuk Gulluk Samseddin; it has a fine *mihrab* of floral tiles and a carved cornice. An Ottoman mosque in the park, the restored **Kurşunlu**, is said to have been designed by Sinan in 1518.

A *kumbet* is a mausoleum, and there are several outstanding ones in the city. The **Döner Kumbet** (Revolving Mausoleum), an ornate Seljuk construction of 1275, is decorated with leaf-patterned carvings, arabesques and feline creatures. Its

(left) Homes carved from pinnacles
of sandstone, Uç Hisar;
(above) Frescoed rock-cut church,
Göreme, Cappadocia

tower is cylinder-shaped on a square foundation and topped by a conical roof.
Close by is the **Sırcalı Kumbet** (Faience Tower) though here much of the tiling that
gave it its name has gone.

The **Archaeological Museum** on Atatürk Bulvarı includes Hittite finds from the
site at Kültepe.

KÜLTEPE

The clay tablets in cuneiform that record the transactions of Assyrian merchants
were found at Kültepe, the Hittite city of Kanesh, and were key elements in the
deciphering of Hittite texts. Assyrians, who traded throughout Anatolia, lived in
established quarters outside a major city, forming a *karum*, or bazaar, a group of
traders, merchants and artisans, such as metalsmiths. As well as Hittite recoveries,
the site revealed evidence of Akkadian occupation under Sargon (c. 2500 BC) and
of a later Anatolian coalition that was formed against Naram Singh, Sargon's grandson. Pre-Hittite pottery known as Cappadocian ware, decorated with geometrical
and symbolic motifs, seems to have originated at Kanesh. Levels of two Phrygian
cities of the ninth and fifth centuries BC have also been also identified.

KONYA

Most of Konya's present-day urban development has happened west of the old city.
Nearly all the monuments of Konya are situated on or near an east–west axis, running for about 1.5 kilometres (one mile) between the square where the Mevlana
Monastery is situated and the central park, with the Alaeddin Mosque on its hill.
The Seljuk citadel was erected on the ancient mound that has provided excavators
with information on the site's earlier, as well as earliest, occupiers, and is now
incorporated in Alaeddin Park, at the western extremity of the central axis.

From the crossroads and roundabout near the *otogar*, take a minibus indicating
its destination as Uçler, or ask to be let off at Mevlana. If you arrive after dark, you
will have no difficulty recognizing your stop: floodlighting illuminates the
monastery with its unusual green cone; Selimiye Mosque is not far off.

Starting at the **Mevlana Tekke**, or monastery, now a museum, you enter a
fountained court. Entrances to the principal rooms lead off one side, with the cells
of dervishes, or monks, off to the other three sides. On the left of the main entrance
into the complex, two cells have been reconstructed and fitted out; one as if
occupied by a dervish and the other by the head dervish, or abbot. In the arcade is
a display of fine prayer rugs.

One of the principal rooms of the complex has the coffins of the abbots,
including the fine marble sarcophagus of Mevlana. The walls of this section are
hung with fine drapery, and Mevlana's tomb is covered by a brocade which was

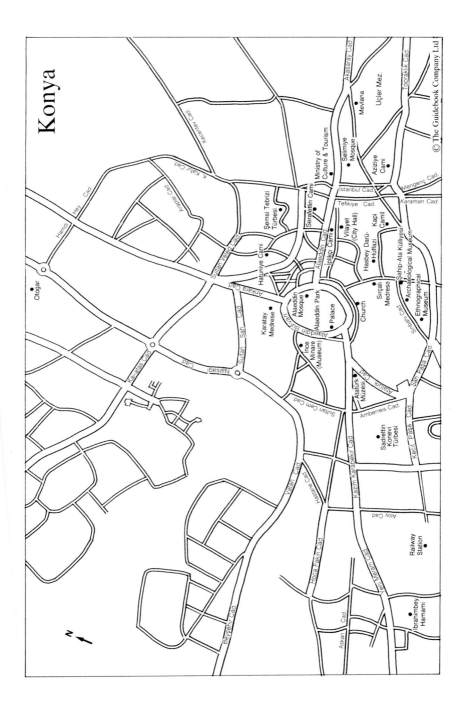

Konya

Otogar

HTey Cad.

Hamdi Cad.

Keçeler Cad.

K. Kalur Cad.

Arpalar Cad.

Sultan Veled Cad.

Hatuniye Cami

Şemsi Tebrizi Türbesi

Karatay Medrese

Alaeddin Mosque

Alaeddin Park

Alaeddin Bulvari

Palace

İnce Minare (Museum)

Serafettin Cami

Ministry of Culture & Tourism

Akasaray Cad.

Topraklık Cad.

Üçler Mez.

Mevlana

Selimiye Mosque

Aziziye Cami

Mengenc Cad.

İstanbul Cad.

Karaman Cad.

Tefikiye Cad.

İplikçi Cami

Alaeddin Cad.

Vilayet (City Hall)

Kapi Cami

Hasbey Daru-Huffazi

Şahip-Ata Külliyesi

Sırçalı Medrese

Church

Archäological Museum

Ethnographical Museum

Sircan Cad.

Şah Paşa Cad.

Atatürk Bulvari

Ankara Cad.

Sultan Şah Cad.

Naljəgj

Karaaslan Cad.

Sultan Cem Cad.

Atatürk Müzesi

Amberreis Cad.

Sadrettin Konevi Türbesi

Keçi Paşa Cad.

Kazım Karabekir Cad.

Aloy Cad.

Railway Station

Hoca Fakih Cad.

Hasene Cad.

Vatan Cad.

Beyşehir Cad.

İbrahimbey Hamami

Yeni Meram Cad.

Askan Cad.

N

© The Guidebook Company Ltd

(left) The Ince Minare (Slender Minaret Mosque), Konya;
(above) The astonishing façade was built in 1258

donated by Sultan Abdul Hamit II in the 19th century. A newel post at the head of each coffin has the turban of the occupant wound about it; the number of turns of the cloth, it has been said, indicates the degree of sanctity attained by the tomb's occupant. At the rear of this chamber is the chapel. A second principal room is the one in which the ritual dance of the Order took place. In it there is a display of fine manuscripts, including a Koran and the works of Celaleddin Rumi Mevlana (1207–73), the Order's founder. Other cases hold exquisitely woven prayer rugs, while another contains musical instruments used in a ritual dance.

Outside, the green conical dome of the monastery rises above a wide-ribbed drum of glazed turquoise tiles, the top of the drum encircled by a blue Kufic-scripted band. This section of the complex is Seljuk of the 13th century; the other external structure is 16th-century Ottoman, with a single minaret.

The **Selimiye Mosque**, next door, was begun in 1558 by Selim II while he was governor of Konya, but it was not completed until he became sultan in 1566. Sinan is said to have had a hand in the construction. Substantial columns rise to a high dome; windows round the base of the dome let light into the open interior.

Moving west along Alaeddin Caddesi, the Ministry of Tourism's Information Office is on the right. Further on, in an opening to the right, is the **Serafettin Cami**, an open-style mosque with side chapels and a central domed area. A Seljuk building modified in Ottoman times, it was ultimately restored in the 19th century after being damaged in a fire.

Some distance down, past the local bus stops and a small garden area, you eventually reach the large, circular **Alaeddin Tepesi** (Alaeddin Hill or Park). The **Alaeddin Mosque**, the central monument on the park's mound or hill, has undergone recent restoration. Within a walled section of the complex, which has a Seljuk façade built over a Byzantine structure, are the tombs of Mesul I (1156), Kilic Arslan II (1192), Rukneddin Suleiman II (1204), Giyaseddin Keyhusrev II (1246), Kilic Arslan IV (1266) and Giyhaseddin Keyhusrev III (1283), as well as those of royal sons and other princes.

Walking clockwise on Alaeddin Bulvarı—the road that encircles the park—start from Alaeddin Caddesi, opposite a *cay bahce* (tea garden), with Ordu Evi (barracks) inside the park. On the left is the **Ince Minare and Medrese** with its decorated entrance and turquoise-ribbed minaret which, struck by lightning once, is minus its top. The *medrese* is now a **Museum of Stone and Wood Carvings**. Further round and on the same side is the **Karatay Medrese** of 1251, with a dome decorated in blue tiles with gold embellishments. The tall entrance has a carved stalactite pattern and an entwined-rope motif. A calligraphic frieze, incorporating the names of the first four caliphs, runs round the base of the dome. The *medrese* now houses a **Tile Museum**. Going further round, inside the park, are the remains of a **Seljuk palace**, which may have been built over a Byzantine one, protected by an arched concrete structure.

By taking a street running south from the park, you come to the **Sircali Medrese** of 1242, now a **Museum of Carved Tombstones**. In a street running east from just below the Sircali Medrese is the **Hasbey Darul-Huffazi** of 1421, a School of Koranic Studies founded under the Karamanoğlu. A little further south of the Sircali Medrese, and to the right, is the **Sahip-Ata Kulliyesi** with its mosque and **Tomb of Fahrettin Ali**. Fahrettin Ali was a grand vizier who held office from 1269, in the reign of Giraseddin Keyhusrev III, until 1288 in the reign of the latter's successor. Near the tomb are the **Archaeological Museum** and, slightly to its west, the **Ethnographical Museum**.

Returning then along Alaeddin Caddesi, before reaching the area of Serafettin Cami, you approach the imposing stone building of the **Vilayet**, or offices of the governor of the province. Near it is the **İplikci Cami**, built in the late 12th century and since restored. Back towards the Mevlana Square, on a street leading to a market area, is the **Azızıye Cami**. This is a baroque mosque of 1641 with a very high decorated marble doorway and a columned portico. It has interesting twin minarets, each with an ornamented cupola. In an area to the north of Alaeddin Caddesi is the site of the **Hatuniye Cami** of 1213, which, alas, has only its minaret left standing on an octagonal base. West of it in another street is the **Semsi Tebrizi Türbesi**, a minaret of the tutor and spiritual guide of Mevlana.

As a community, Konya is proud to be the repository of the fundamentals of Islamic faith, although a general aspect of austerity has become modified in recent years. If women as yet have little chance of spiritual elevation, their presence in the city has become less veiled. Perhaps this is due to the influence of Western backpackers with their less conventional gear. However, modesty is required of all female visitors at Muslim shrines, and cotton skirts are on loan at the Mevlana.

ÇATAL HÜYÜK

The site of Çatal Hüyük southeast of Konya was excavated in the 1960s by James Melkaart of the British Archaeological Institute in Ankara. The finds are Neolithic, c. 7000 BC, and the artefacts unearthed are of a level of culture beyond anything that could have been expected of such a period. Wall paintings are on plaster, not on the bare rock. Recoveries are in the Ankara Museum and include a reconstruction of a Neolithic settlement based on the excavator's findings.

THE MEVLEVI—
THE WHIRLING DERVISHES

At the completion of a series of spiritual exercises, the novitiates of this Order of Dervishes attained their ultimate state of mystical perception in a formal dance. Revolving to the accompaniment of drum, flute and stringed instruments, the novices wore a white, flared, ankle-length robe and white jacket. As the dancer rotated, right arm held up in prayer, the left downwards, the skirt spun out in a whorl. A white conical-shaped hat resembling a high-crowned fez was worn. Symbolically, the hat represented a tombstone, while the jacket and skirt represented the tomb and shroud respectively. The white jacket would be removed at the beginning of the dance, thereby implying that earthly connections had been discarded.

Celaleddin Rumi Mevlana was a Persian citizen born in 1207 at Balkh in what is now Afghanistan. His father was a distinguished theologian, and the family, displaced by Mongolian rampaging, was eventually invited to Konya by the Seljuk Sultan Alaeddin Keykubat. Celaleddin was a lyrical poet; his spiritual mentor, Sems, was a mystic Persian philosopher and unorthodox teacher, whose death Celaleddin mourned in a sequence of poems. Celaleddin was an Islamic counterpart of a St John of the Cross, and his religious philosophy, based on universal and non-sectarian divine love, combined Islamic, Christian and Zoroastrian precepts. He was also an exponent of religious tolerance. His poetry earned him the title of Mevlana, the equivalent of a British Order of Merit, and he was appointed court advisor on religious questions. Subsequent abbots of the Order served in this capacity with later Seljuk and Ottoman sultans. The Rumi in Mevlana's title refers to the Seljuk name Rum, for Rome. His poetry, beliefs and teachings have come to be associated with Sufism.

Atatürk's reforms at the time of the establishment of the Turkish Republic included closing of religious houses and Islamic schools. His intention seems to have been to end what he considered to be the narrow, anachronistic influence of the imams (Muslim leaders) on the daily lives of the ordinary people in towns and villages; and the wearing in public of all forms of religious garb was banned.

The Mevlana monastery was closed, and its rituals ended. Today, however, a festival of the Mevlana is held on each anniversary of Celaleddin's death, 17 December 1273, during which a performance of the dance is given. The exemplars are recruited not only from within Turkey but also from volunteers, young men who consider themselves converts to and exponents of Sufism, from other countries. Authorized performances have also been given outside Konya at folklore festivals in other parts of the country, and abroad.

Southeastern Anatolia

Among the inhabitants in Gaziantep are minorities of Christian Turks, Arabs and Kurds, among others. This population is more or less reflective of the population of the towns of southeastern Turkey, near the border with Iran and Iraq.

Called Antep by the citizens, Gaziantep was awarded the prefix 'Gazi' (the title for a distinguished general) after the city's stubborn resistance to occupation by the French during Atatürk's War of Independence. Today Gaziantep is known for its pre-eminent copperwork and the profitable cultivation of pistachio nuts, with large orchards extending to the south and southeast from the city. With a day to spare, a diversion to Nemrut Dağ to the northeast of Gaziantep can be taken, to the mountain-top tomb of Antiochus I.

The Hittite site of Carchemish can be seen by diverting to the south for an hour or two from Nizip, south of Gaziantep. After crossing the Euphrates River at Birecik on the way to Şanlıurfa, you are in Mesopotamia, between the Euphrates and the Tigris. At Edessa, Şanlıurfa was the capital of a Latin county during the time of the Crusades. Another important site, Harran, can be reached by diverting again to the south. Harran stands alongside a village of beehive-style houses, a form of domestic construction common in northern Mesopotamia.

The frontier route from Şanlıurfa to Mardin runs through the Plain of the Jezireh. This region is dotted with mounds that indicate the extent to which it was once populated, before 13th-century Mongol invaders destroyed the dikes that controlled the man-made waterways of Mesopotamia. The Plain of the Jezireh is believed to be the location of the biblical Garden of Eden.

Diyarbakır stands above the Tigris. This ancient city's black basalt walls and towers stand, still impressive from whichever direction you approach them. The river flows round the base of the hill on which the city stands, and out through a ravine on the east side. In the early part of this century the Tigris was navigable by raft from here to Baghdad, but this is no longer possible.

Getting There

Travel into the southeastern region of Turkey could start at Adana or Antakya. The E5 turns south at Toprakkale, but the E24 continues east through the Amanus Mountains to Gaziantep, 136 kilometres (85 miles) away.

To visit Nemrut Dağ from Gaziantep, take the Kahraman Maras road, 53 kilometres (33 miles), to Narlı, then go northeast to Gölbaşı, 73 kilometres (45 miles). Gölbaşı is along the railway line from Gaziantep, Kahraman Maras or Narlı. From Gölbaşı take the Adiyaman road, and after 12 kilometres (eight miles) turn southeast onto a road to Besni, from where the really strenuous part of the trip begins. Go east for 45 kilometres (28 miles) to Eski Kahta on the Kahta Cayi (Nymphaeon River), after which it is a climb of several hours on foot, though a minibus service is available.

To visit Carchemish (Karkamis), turn off the E24 at Nizip, 36 kilometres (22 miles) from Gaziantep. Take a road running south 30 kilometres (19 miles) to Barak. This is the frontier with Syria and you should ask at the military barracks for permission to proceed a kilometre (0.6 miles) further, on to the site. Near the site a railway bridge crosses the Euphrates, carrying the line to Aleppo in Syria.

Back on the road, 15 kilometres (nine miles) east of Nizip, you cross the Euphrates by a long bridge at Birecik, a pleasant-looking town that mounts from the river's bank to a citadel. In Seljuk times there had been a bridge of boats here. Şanliurfa (Edessa) is 83 kilometres (52 miles) from Birecik.

As with Carchemish, Harran is along the Turkish-Syrian frontier. Go out of Şanliurfa south on road 885 to Akcakale, and after 32 kilometres (20 miles) take a turning for Altinbasak, 12 kilometres (eight miles) east. The site is beside the village.

The distance from Şanliurfa to Mardin is 185 kilometres (115 miles). There are ruins on the outskirts of Viranşehir, which a truly inquisitive traveller might find time to explore. At Kızıltepe, the high mountain barrier to the north moves dramatically closer; stretching up from the plain to where Mardin stands perched high on the edge of the plateau. One kilometre (0.6 miles) beyond Kızıltepe, turn left and after 11 kilometres (seven miles) begin the climb to Mardin, a further nine kilometres (six miles).

Leaving Mardin on the east side, road 955 descends southeasterly to join the E24 on the Jezireh Plain again. At Nusaybin, 30 kilometres (19 miles) east of the road junction, is a main frontier crossing into Syria and the last Turkish station on the railway to Baghdad. From the 955 road junction with the E24, the main road continues to Cizre, 131 kilometres (81 miles) east, where the E26 runs southeasterly through Silopi to the frontier and crosses 46 kilometres (29 miles) into Iraq.

Going northwest from Mardin through mountain and wooded country, the journey then becomes pastoral and riverine. About two kilometres (1.25 miles) southeast of Diyarbakır, a Roman bridge with ten irregular arches spans the river. Diyarbakır can be reached as well from Şanliurfa, a distance of 186 kilometres (116 miles), although the more felicitous approach is from Mardin.

Historical Background

At the time of the First Crusade, Gaziantep, along with Maras, 82 kilometres (51 miles) to its northeast, became part of the Latin County of Edessa. As Gurgun, Maras was the centre of a 12th-century-BC Hittite kingdom that used hieroglyphic script; it was referred to in Assyrian texts as Markasi.

In the first century Gaziantep was Roman Germanicea. The Arabs took it from the Byzantines in the early seventh century, and from then until its occupation by the Seljuks in the 11th century, it changed hands between Arabs and Byzantines as the fortunes of war favoured this empire or that one, until the Crusaders arrived. For a period after that it became part of the Christian Kingdom of Cilicia until over-run by Baibars. Selim I (1512–20) took it for the Ottoman Empire; its citadel, as it exists now, is as the Ottomans rebuilt it.

Mithridates Callinicus founded his kingdom of Commagene in the first century BC; it stretched north from Gaziantep to Adiyaman, a distance of 150 kilometres (93 miles). In later alliance with Rome, the country became a buffer state between Rome and Persia. Antiochus I claimed to be related to Alexander through his mother Olympias and father Darius. Though his ambition was great, his achievements were few. His tomb, nevertheless, is spectacular.

Şanliurfa dates back to the 16th century BC, when Egypt controlled it but allowed the Phoenician-Syrian occupants a degree of independence. Later there was Hurrite-Mitanni (Hittite) occupation that spread throughout northern Mesopotamia. Alexander's Macedonians named it Edessa after his birthplace. At one time Edessa was governed by 11 successive Aramaic rulers, the Abgars, who held power for 400 years from the second century BC. One Abgar prince claimed to own a cloth—the Mandillion—bearing the imprint of Christ's face and given to him by Jesus himself. John Curcuas, a successful Byzantine general under the Emperor Romanus Lecapenus, took the Mandillion back to Constantinople after his tenth-century victory over the Arabs. Yet another Byzantine general, George Maniaces, reoccupying Edessa, took back to Constantinople another sacred relic, a letter purported to have been written by Jesus to that Abgar prince to whom the Mandillion had been given. Another Abgar prince (179–214) was the inspirer and promoter of Christian-Aramaic literature. Edessa became Ottoman in 1536, though its territory was not incorporated into the empire until 1637.

The site at Harran was Roman Carrhae, important as a stronghold on the military road from the Mediterranean to the Upper Tigris. Here in AD 53, more than 20,000 Romans were killed and another 10,000 taken prisoner, including the Roman general Crassus, who surrendered the Imperial Eagles to the Parthian King,

Unique to Harran, these dry-stone beehive huts are used for grain storage. The Bible records that Abraham lived in Harran

Oroder I. In 1104, Bohemond and Tancred, the Norman-Franks of Sicily, lost a battle to the Saracens, thereby ending their hope of extending their territory as far as Mosul, and putting a seal on the fate of the Latin County of Edessa. Tradition has it that Abraham spent several years at Harran on his journey to Canaan.

Sadly, a 19th-century Ottoman sultan settled numbers of dispossessed Circassians on land below Mardin, but though they worked with a will they were unable to discard the habits or the clothing of their Caucasian homeland, and many succumbed to physical exhaustion while others were decimated in an outbreak of cholera.

Mardin was Marde when Justinian and Chosroes the Persian fought for its possession. In the continuous struggle between those two empires, Mardin, along with other towns of the region, changed hands frequently as this side or that gained ascendancy. In the 12th century, Mardin fell to an Ortokid emir and, with only a minor temporary change or two, has stayed Muslim ever since. Saladin failed to take the city. A Mongol horde also besieged Mardin for eight months without success. One story holds that at a critical time during the siege, the defenders made yoghurt out of dog's milk and sent some to the besiegers. This gift convinced the Mongol commander that ample supplies remained still in the city, so he relented the siege and departed.

Excavations within the inner walls of Diyarbakır have identified what is believed to have been in origin a Mitanni settlement, then a city of the Urartu, then Assyrian. As heirs of Alexander, the Seleucids occupied it, and because it commanded so strategic a crossing of the Upper Tigris it became an object of perennial conflict between the Romans and the Persians, then Byzantines against Persians. Under Justinian one siege lasted so long even the supply of rats ran out, and a group of hags took to cannibalism, murdering lonely victims at night, but were caught and brought to justice eventually because of the infernal smell of their charnel pots.

Arabs captured the city in 639. In 660 it became part of the Omayyid Caliphate and in 750, that of their Abbasid successors. In 974, the Byzantines under John Tsimiskis succeeded in recapturing Diyarbakır, but for only a brief occupation, as the Persians later did for a limited period in the 16th century under Sah Ismail. It became Ottoman in 1515.

Sights

GAZIANTEP

In this modern city is evidence of Seljuk occupation after the 11th century in the fortress at the city's centre and in the *medrese* in Karagoz Caddesi. Excavations at an ancient mound on the edge of the city, on the road going east to Nizip, however, uncovered evidence of occupations that go back to the fourth millennium BC. Among exhibits in the **Archaeological Museum** is a collection of Hittite recoveries.

At 2,000 metres (6,560 feet) on the summit of **Nemrut Dağ**, the great pyramidal tomb of Antiochus I is 150 metres (500 feet) wide and 50 metres (164 feet) high. There are reliefs of both Alexander and Darius and of eagles and lions. The entrance is on the north side, with terraces on the other three. Headless Greek and Persian deities sit on a bench as though in heavenly judgement, and on the slope below are their giant heads, looking like characters in a Becket play, buried up to their necks.

On the way up, **Eski Kale**, a castle at Eski Kahta, has an inscribed relief, dated 50 BC, of Antiochus clasping the hand of Heracles. Here a Roman bridge crosses the Cendere River, a tributary of the Euphrates. At Karakus there are standing columns of a mausoleum of Commagene queens.

CARCHEMISH

This was the capital of one of the last of the southern Hittite kingdoms which fell to the Assyrian, Sargon II, in 717 BC. From the top of the citadel mound there is a fine view of the Euphrates as it executes a series of loops and throws off several subsidiary streams. On the riverside below the mound are the remains of a water gate. The ruins of a palace and other buildings of an extensive city lie at the citadel's base, with carved black basalt pedestals and spread-eagled column drums. There is a Sacred Way within the inner city, as well as two gates in the sections of wall still standing. Parts of the site, though, are in a restricted military area. T E Lawrence worked under Sir Leonard Woolley on the excavations here, and Gertrude Bell was also a member of an expedition that included D G Hogarth.

ŞANLIURFA

The citadel is still substantially walled and towered, with a deep fosse on two sides. It stands on a high elongated spur in the north of the city; climb by way of a path to a postern gateway. Inside the gate a plinth with two standing Corinthian columns is known as the **Seat** (or Throne) **of Nimrud**. In its vicinity are several ruined Byzantine buildings. On the unwalled section of the spur are caves that were the nurseries of suckling gods. These became the shrines of saints, and on the ridge above is a Muslim burial ground with domed tombs of Seljuk and Arab princes.

Below the spur are several connecting pools that may have been created by Justinian's engineers, who built Edessa's fortifications. The pools are fed from a sacred spring, Calirrhoe, and contain a large shoal of carp that are deemed to be sacred. The citizens feed the carp and do not filch them. Abraham is said to have camped by this spring on his journey from Ur into Canaan. Alongside the longest

(following pages) West Terrace, Nemrut Dağ

of the pools is the arched wall of the 17th-century **Abder Rahman Medrese**, in the grounds of which is a small mosque. On the quay at the end of this pool there is a 13th-century oratory (a place for private prayer), the **Malkim el Halil**.

In the centre of the old city, near the spur, is the **Seljuk Ulu Cami** of the 11th century, a building influenced by Persian architectural styles. Its minaret is hexagonal, and, for the fact-finder, its circumference equals its height. A church opposite this mosque is Nestorian. A Nestorian theological school existed here in early Christian times and continued even after that doctrine had been anathematized. When the Emperor Zeno closed it in 479, the expelled teachers continued as missionaries throughout Persia, Central Asia, India and China—the legendary Prester John is believed by some to have been a Nestorian priest.

The site of **Harran** has revealed Hittite, Assyrian, Persian and Roman occupation, and in Assyrian times there was a sanctuary here of the Moon Goddess Sin. There are a number of Byzantine ruins, an Islamic fortress and an eighth-century Omayyid mosque with a tall square minaret.

MARDIN

The citadel is on a ledge above the town and is Roman in origin but much modified over succeeding centuries. Among the buildings inside the citadel walls are the castle and the ruins of two mosques. Off the main square in the town below is the **Sultan Isa Medrese** of 1385, built on two levels, each section having it own portico. The 11th-century **Ulu Cami** has a high-walled court, but the mosque was restored in the 14th century, again in the 15th and more recently in the 19th century. The **Latifiye Mosque** dates from 1371, but its minaret is of 19th-century origin. The **Sehidiye Cami** and the restored **Reyhanli Cami** are both 14th-century buildings, and the **Kasım Paşa Medrese** dates from the 15th century.

Mardin had 1,200 Christian families at the turn of the 20th century, though a majority has since then emigrated, mostly to America. It is the seat of a metropolitan Bishop of the Jacobite Monophysite Church. Like the Nestorian, the Monophysite doctrine of Jacob Baradaeus was anathematized by the early church, though the doctrine is subscribed to still by Syrian Christians. There is a Jacobite monastery in a valley a little to the east of Mardin. The main structure dates from the sixth century, and the monastery is active in that its chapel is used by Mardin's remaining Christians. A boarding school may still exist on the premises for orphan boys, their teacher appointed from Aleppo. Destitute elderly persons are also given accommodation in the former monastery cells. From the top of one of the craggy peaks that rise above the monastery and its almond groves, the prophet Elijah is said to have ascended to Heaven in the chariot of fire.

East of Mardin is Nusaybin, Assyrian Nisibis in the first millennium BC. As an important junction much fought over by armies from the West and the Middle East, Nusaybin has little to show for its perpetual martyrdom other than a Roman arch, an early Christian church and a Muslim tomb.

DIYARBAKIR

Diyarbakır was Amida to the Romans, who built the walls that enclose an inner city situated on an artificial mound. These interior walls have three gateways, including one in the main wall, which lead to the outer city. There are four gates in the outer, black basalt walls, which are four metres (13 feet) wide and ten metres (33 feet) high, with a postern and 70 towers.

Of the four gates, the northern one, **Harput Gate**, has semi-circular flanking towers. On the towers are Roman and Arabic carvings in relief; one carving shows a bird with outstretched wings. The columns and arch of the gate are Byzantine, and an inscription refers to an inn or a guesthouse that had to be demolished to make way for the gate. Another inscription in Greek is a record of the arrival of an emissary sent by Justinian, while a Latin one includes the names of Gratianus, Valens and Valentinian. Arabic inscriptions refer to building operations.

The **Mardin Gate** (Bab el Tel, Hill Gate) is the southern one; the Bab el Rum or **Urfa Gate** and the Bab el Dicle or **Yeni Gate** (or New Gate, Tigris Gate or Water Gate) are on the western and eastern sides respectively. Between the Mardin and Urfa gates, the walls and bastions form a salient known as the Yedi Kardes (Seven Brothers). A main street, running between the Harput and the Mardin gates, is crossed by another which fades out near the Urfa Gate. Outside the Urfa Gate the **Sarı Saduk Türbe's** exterior has attractive tilework.

The finest of the city's buildings is the **Ulu Cami** of 1091, built by the Seljuk Malik Shah, son and successor of Alp Arslan, the victor of Manzikert. Restored in 1155, it has a large rectangular court with two fountains. Reliefs of lions and bulls decorate a main entrance, and on the right as you enter are the columns of a Roman building, their bases almost a column-depth below the present level of the paving. Two-tiered colonnades grace either end of the court. The entrance to the prayer hall is on the left, and the minaret, square in structure and with courses of black tiles, stands apart from the main building. The superstructure is Ottoman. The **Archaeological Museum**, to the west of the Ulu Cami, is in the **Zincirli Medrese**, a late 12th-century Ortokid emirate foundation.

Opposite the Ulu Cami, on the edge of a large square, the 16th-century **Hasan Paşa Han** has a fountain in its courtyard and shops on the ground floor under the colonnade and on the balcony. The entrance to the court has calligraphic decoration. Another 16th-century *han*, the **Dellfiller** at the Mardin Gate, stands alongside the **Husrev Paşa Cami**, constructed 1522–28 by the Ottomans.

In the market area near the crossroads of the two main roads, the **Behram Paşa Cami** of 1573, with its ribbed minaret, is the largest in the city. The church to the south of this mosque is a Monophysite one. Other Ottoman mosques are the **Fatih Paşa** of 1522, the **İskender** of 1551, with its fine porch and pleasant garden, and the **Kasım Padishah** of 1512, situated in an alleyway approaching the Mardin Gate. The **Nebi Cami** (Peygamber or Mosque of the Prophet) dates from 1524 but has undergone frequent restoration.

Although the towers on the inner city walls are Byzantine in origin, most probably of the sixth century, they were reconstructed by an Ortokid emir in the 12th century and again in the 16th century by Suleiman the Magnificent. The mosque within the citadel walls is a 12th-century Ortokid construction, as is the palace. Inside, too, is the Byzantine **Church of St George**. The modern development of the city is extensive outside the walls to the northwest of the city, where the railway station and the long-distance coach station are. The airport is to the south of the city.

Locals in Şanliurfa, in the far east of Turkey, appear more Arab than Turk. Shown here are two visitors leaning over the parapet of the sacred pools at Şanliurfa

ROUGH JUSTICE

'*I* am sorry,' said the Pasha, 'that they hung the Koord before your windows. I told them not to hang him before the house of the Persian Plenipotentiary, where there is a gibbet; but to take him to any place where the Koords resorted, and as there are many coffee-houses near you, that is the reason probably why they hung him there. His story is a curious one: I have been looking after him for the last three years; he has robbed and murdered many people, though he was so young a man, but he had always escaped my agents. At last, a few days ago, he stole a horse, in a valley near here, from a man who was travelling, and whom he beat about the head and left for dead. He brought the horse to Erzeroom and offered it for sale, when the owner, who had recovered, saw him selling the horse, and gave him up to the guard. He was brought up for judgment before me, when I said to him, "Who are you?" After a silence, the man said, "There is fate in this, it cannot be denied. I am **** whom you have been searching for these three years. My fate brought me to Erzeroom, and now I am taken up for stealing one poor horse. I felt when I took that horse that I was fated to die for it. My time is come. It is fate." And he went to be hung without any complaint.' I said he deserved it, and hoped others would take warning by his death.

The Koord above mentioned was hanged in so original a manner that I must shortly describe it, as it took place immediately under my windows. What we called at school a cat-gallows was erected close to a bridge over the little stream which ran down the horsemarket, between my house and the bottom of the hill of the citadel. The culprit stood under this; the crossbeam was not two feet above his head; a kawass, having tied a rope to one end of the beam, passed a slip-knot round the neck of the Koord, a young and very handsome man, with long black hair; he then drew the rope over the other end of the beam, and pulled away till the poor man's feet were just off the ground, when he tied the rope in a knot, leaving the dead body hanging, supported by two ropes in the form of the letter V. Hardly anyone was looking on, and in the afternoon the body was taken down and buried.

Robert Curzon, Armenia, 1854

Black Sea Coast

The forested mountain ranges along the whole length of the Black Sea coast supply a tranquil backdrop to sandy beaches and a sea that frequently is more animated than either the Mediterranean or the Aegean. A motorway, however, now adds noise, fumes and concrete uniformity to the area's former unpretentiousness.

Sinop marks the boundary between the western and eastern sections of the Black Sea coast. Assyrians exploited the mineral resources in the region. As well as gold, Jason's Argonauts may have been in search of minerals: even in our industrial age villagers are said to lay sheepskins in the streams to collect gold dust, thereby transforming the legend of the Golden Fleece into fact.

East of Sinop, the Kızılirmak River finds its way to the sea through Bafra, an important centre of Turkey's tobacco industry. Samsun is Turkey's largest Black Sea port. The Pontic Mountains descend abruptly in wooded slopes, and in many villages boat-building is a traditional craft. Along the coastal stretch near Ordu, and to the east of it, hazelnuts are under intense cultivation.

Under the Ottomans, Trabzon retained its profitability until overland trading routes were revived, to the port's disadvantage. The coming of the railways in the 19th century also contributed to its diminishing importance. Today, trade and international tourism have, to a great extent, helped to revive Trabzon's prosperity. Turkish Maritime Lines has regular sailings from İstanbul, calling at Amasra and Sinop and other ports on the way to Trabzon; an expanded harbour also caters for larger cruise ships. There is a yacht marina here.

Getting There

From İstanbul, visits to resorts on the western section of the Black Sea coast can be made on a daily basis. There is Kilyos on the western side of the Bosphorus, or Şile on the eastern side. Akçakoça, 140 kilometres (87 miles) east of Şile, is best reached from Adapazari or Duzce on the E5 from İstanbul to Ankara.

From Akçakoça, the coastal road runs to Ereğli (Heracleia Pontica), 32 kilometres (20 miles) northeast, and the large industrial port of Zonguldak, a total of 90 kilometres (56 miles).

Beyond Zonguldak, Amasra (ancient Sesamos), the next major destination, has bathing facilities set off by a Byzantine fortress that was restored by the Genoese in the 14th century. There are several holiday resorts between Amasra and Sinop, 250 kilometres (155 miles) to its east. A coastal journey to the east of Sinop is perhaps better arranged from Ankara, from where the 795 road to Samsun, 362 kilometres (226 miles), passes through Hittite territory, and visits to Boğaskale, Alaca Hüyük and Yazilkaya could be included in an itinerary for visiting the Black Sea coast on its eastern section.

After Samsun, Terme is one of a number of small resorts. Ünye, an attractive port, is 27 kilometres (17 miles) further east. Beyond Fatsa, continue to Ordu, 75 kilometres (47 miles), then Giresun, another 51 kilometres (32 miles) along. Tirebolü is 48 kilometres (30 miles) east of Giresun, and from Tirebolü it is another 40 kilometres (25 miles) to Trabzon.

Historical Background

Ereğli, or Heraclea Pontica, was named after Heracles (Hercules) who sailed with Jason's Argonauts, at least for part of the journey, tackling one or more of his prodigious labours en route.

Called Sinope by the Milesians of the seventh century BC after they arrived to colonize it, Sinop was the birthplace of Diogenis (Diogenes), the cynic philosopher. Hercules went down into the Underworld here to fetch up Cerberus. Hittites settled here. It is Amazon country, and maybe the skirt-like kilt worn by a Hittite warrior became the source of that Amazon legend.

In 88 BC, Mithridates VI, King of Pontus (120–63 BC), raised a coalition of neighbouring states to drive the Romans out of Asia Minor. Several thousand Romans were massacred without this being achieved. After three Pontic Wars, the Romans took Sinop in 66 BC, extending Roman rule throughout Asia Minor. In 1261, after the Byzantines had returned to Constantinople, the Genoese, in rivalry with the Venetians, made an agreement with Michael VIII (1261–82), whereby they established trading posts along the Black Sea and elsewhere. Later they negotiated similar agreements with the Seljuks, as well as with independent Muslim emirs, who were building castles or modifying existing ones. The Ottoman Mehmet II took Sinop in 1458.

Samsun was ancient Amisus, another Milesian colony. The 12th-century Seljuks preferred Samsun as their major port to Sinop, and of course the Genoese were influential in trade here, even under the later Mongol occupants, who seem to have made more effective use of their opportunities here than elsewhere. After the Mongols, the Emirs of Kastamonu made it part of their independent fief until the Ottomans eventually took it.

Atatürk landed in Samsun on 19 May 1919 and, though carrying the authority

(following pages) This sacred pool lies at the centre of a complex of mosques and medreses (Koranic Colleges) in Şanliurfa

of the sultan, set about organizing resistance to the sultan's threatened capitulation to the Western Allies. Atatürk then worked towards the establishment of a republic.

Terme is on a river that was probably the Thermodon, at whose mouth stood Themiskyra, a city of the legendary Amazons. Ünye was Oenoe, designated as a place where Xenophon and his Greeks may have arrived at the coast after first glimpsing the sea from the mountains above Trabzon. They trekked and fought their way here from Cunaxa in Persia where they had served as a mercenary contingent in the defeated army of Cyrus the Younger in his revolt against his imperial brother.

Fatsa was the Milesian port of Polemon. Perşembe, on the cape to the north of Ordu, was Cotyora, from where Xenophon and the Greek survivors are said by some accounts to have boarded ship for Heracleia. It may be that separated contingents of Xenophon's army made use of various means and routes to get themselves home.

Giresun was founded by Milesians from Sinope. Identified as Kerasus, it provided the Greeks with their name for the cherry. Lucullus, the ultimate Roman victor against Mithridates, is said to have taken local cuttings of the cherry back to Italy.

Trabzon, in the territory of the former Byzantine Empire of Trebizond, as Trapezus was the capital that survived the fall of Constantinople by eight years. Originally Trapezus had been colonized by men from Sinope, but reinforcements later came from Arcadia in the Greek Peloponessus. Trapezus stayed neutral throughout the Pontic Wars. Some two centuries later Hadrian added a number of buildings, and in the sixth century, Justinian reinforced the city's defences. In the seventh and eighth centuries Arab aggression in Anatolia restricted overland transport; the port of Trapezus gained by the consequent increase in sea traffic. When the Seljuk Keykavus took Sinope, the Comneni Emperor of Trebizond was able still to maintain his independence by signing judicious treaties and entering into alliances with both the Seljuks and the Palaeologi Emperors of Constantinople. The princesses of Trebizond were reputed for their beauty, and this attribute came to be used as a valuable diplomatic pawn, though it was alleged in some quarters that too lavish a use of cosmetics not infrequently mitigated against a princess's natural advantages.

Suleiman the Magnificent was born at Trabzon, and Selim I set out from here to extend Ottoman power throughout the whole of Anatolia, a process begun by his predecessor, Beyazıt II.

Sights

Ereğli has the remains of Byzantine and Ottoman walls, and a castle restored by the Genoese. An equestrian statue honours Atatürk's stay at **Samsun**, and there is an **Atatürk Museum**, as well as an archaeological one. The site of the city's original foundation is on Karasamsun, to the northwest of the city overlooking the harbour. The **Pazar Cami** is a Mongol mosque of the 14th century.

Unye's *belediye* building is an 18th-century structure. The town's beach is at Camlik, and beyond this are the Fok Fok Margaralarya, sea caves that are a breeding haven for seals.

Giresun Ada (Aretia), an island off the harbour at **Giresun**, offers good bathing, as well as the ruins of a Byzantine monastery. A **Temple to Ares** here is likely to be of pre-Milesian date. A Byzantine fortress and remnants of city walls stand above the town itself. In the mountain villages above Giresun, 'bird villagers' are said to be able to communicate over long distances by a system of whistling.

More than one castle exists in the bay at **Tirebolü**, which was the ancient port of Tripolis, and a Byzantine tower here may have been built as a lighthouse. Further on is **Gorele**, with its monastery and a ruined castle.

TRABZON

Houses and buildings of the modern town climb the slopes, which rise gently on the west side and rather steeply on the south of the centre. The ancient acropolis is on high ground, a kilometre (0.6 miles) or more west of the harbour, with a gorge on either side. A connecting bridge stretches over the eastern gorge, where sections of old walls and the remains of towers stand.

For the visitor, an essential stop is at **Ayasofya**, the Church of St Sophia, a kilometre (0.6 miles) distant on the coastal road to the west. In origin the church was the domed basilica of a 13th-century monastery, later converted to a mosque. It became desanctified under Atatürk and declared a museum. In the mid-20th century, David Talbot Rice and his team meticulously and patiently uncovered the magnificent wall paintings and decoration from under centuries of plaster and whitewash. As well as the murals, there are sculpted reliefs in the south porch that depict the Temptation of Christ.

From the *belediye* in Park Square—the Turkish Airlines terminal is here—go alongside the park and turn left, then right, to reach the Tabukhane Deresi gorge. Before crossing the bridge, turn right to the **Church of St Ann**, the oldest in the city, which dates from the eighth century but was restored in the ninth. Nearby is the former site of the **Church of St Basil**, of similar date, in use for a long time as a

Trabzon tea plantation

warehouse. Higher up is the **Church of St Eugenius**, converted to a mosque as the **Yeni Cuma** or New Friday Mosque, with its tall slender minaret a landmark. Damaged by fire in 1340, the present cupola and porch were added later and the nave enlarged.

On the other side of the bridge is the **Orta Hisar Cami**, or the **Fatih Mosque**, in origin the **Church of the Panaghia Chrysokephalos** (the Golden-headed Virgin), which probably dates from the tenth century but has been considerably modified. It was so named from the gilded copper of the cupola. Going on past the **Orta Hisar**, out to the edge of what was the old town and over another bridge, you will find the **Hatuniye Cami**, built in 1514 for Gulbahar Hatun, the mother of Selim I, and her tomb is alongside.

Back at the terminal, go past the Atatürk memorial and turn left on Maras Caddesi. Beyond Cumhuriyet Caddesi, on the south side, are the *bedesten* and the former tenth- or 11th-century **Church of St Gregory**, now in use neither as a church nor mosque. The **Pazar Kapi Cami** is in this area, as is the **Iskender Paşa Cami**, both buildings of the early 16th century. On Boztepe, a hill south of the harbour, is the cave **Church of the Panaghia Theoskepastos**, which had originated as a **Shrine to Apollo**. Nearby is the 13th-century **Church of St Philip**, now a mosque.

TURKEY AND THE EU

Gary Mead

Turks introduced coffee to Europe; they gave Amsterdam its tulips. Where would homes throughout Europe be during the Christmas festivities without Santa Claus? St Nicholas—also known as Santa Claus—was born in Demre, on Turkey's Mediterranean coast. Turkey is European, of that there can be little doubt. Yet İstanbul is the only city in the world which is built on two continents—Europe and Asia. Turkey is also a nation which, inevitably, looks in two directions.

In some respects Turkey is already closely interwoven with European institutions. It is a member of the Council of Europe, a purely inter-governmental organization, separate from the EU and bearing a strong resemblance to the United Nations. Turkey also has Associate Member status of the Western European Union, which was founded in 1954 as a defence alliance between the UK, France, Belgium, Luxembourg, Italy, Germany and the Netherlands.

In recent years, however, Turkish political leaders of almost all hues—including some of the more moderate Islamist groups—have sought to strengthen ties with Europe, primarily by seeking membership of the European Union. Turkey applied for membership of the EU on 14 April 1987, but this application has so far been blocked on two occasions, much to the annoyance of many Turkish politicians and the many thousands of influential Turkish sympathizers within the EU.

Who has been behind the campaign to prevent Turkish accession to the EU? And on what grounds? After all, Greece, Turkey's old rival and, in recent times, bitter opponent over the division of Cyprus, was accepted into this particular club long ago.

There has been strong opposition to Turkish membership of the EU from Germany. In March 1998 Wolfgang Schauble, parliamentary party leader of the CDU (Christian Democrats), told a conference on

German–US relations in Berlin that he opposed Turkey's entry into the EU because it could 'endanger the identity and political workability of the EU', a view which is hard to comprehend given that the EU is preparing itself for an enlargement to include several central and east European states, whose economic and political compatibility with the EU's founding members is far from obvious. But with the removal of Chancellor Helmut Kohl's CDU from power, and the formation of the SDP-Green alliance to govern Germany, there may be some hope of a less intransigent attitude.

If Poland, Hungary, the Czech Republic, Slovenia and Estonia are to be admitted to the EU by 2005—with Bulgaria, Latvia, Lithuania, Romania and Slovakia lining up behind them—then any continued opposition to early Turkish entry not only becomes meaningless; it borders on the insulting.

The thorn in the side of Turkey's relations with the EU is, of course, Cyprus, a land divided between pro-Greek and pro-Turkish communities since 1974. For many Turks (and other observers) it was inexplicable for the EU to admit Greece to its ranks in the late 1970s, following the partition of Cyprus. Today the Cypriot government—composed exclusively of Greek Cypriots, and which controls 60 per cent of the island—is internationally recognized by all except Turkey. In early 1998 the Cypriots started negotiations on application for membership of the EU. That Cyprus has received warmer encouragement in its application than Turkey has profoundly irritated Turkish political and business leaders, and with good reason.

An exasperated Mesut Yilmaz, prime minister and head of Turkey's coalition government, acknowledged in March 1998 that Turkey's record on human rights and its economic problems (with inflation running at almost 100 per cent annually) do not assist it in its wish for EU membership. But he added, with justification, that there have been notable reforms—the abolition of the death penalty, relaxation of the anti-terrorist powers of the state, and amnesties for opposition voices—and that in his view the opposition to Turkish EU membership has deeper and more sinister roots: 'We believe their opposition to our membership does not stem from humanistic, democratic concerns, but only from cultural and religious bias.... If Europe is courageous enough for a multi-cultural and multi-religious future, it is a must that Turkey should be included.'

This problem needs to be resolved, and rapidly. There have already been understandable threats from senior Turkish figures that if the EU does not want Turkey then it will find trade and political alliances elsewhere. Some Turkish politicians have suggested that the country's Customs Union agreement with the EU, in existence since 1996, should be torn up, as it serves only to open the domestic Turkish market to EU exports, and is of no real benefit to the Turkish economy.

As we head into the new millennium, the failure to absorb Turkey fully into the ranks of the leading European institution looks like a huge strategic mistake. Leaders of the EU lecture Turkey on the need for improvements to its human rights record, wag their fingers at it over Cyprus, but do nothing at all to encourage Turkey and offer nothing concrete in exchange for concessions in either of these two fraught areas. In September 1997 Mesut Yilmaz made a tremendous conciliatory gesture towards the EU, saying: 'We know our short-comings and we are determined to solve them.' At the same time he accepted that Turkey's ambition of immediate membership was unrealistic.

But the extended hand was spurned, and increasingly Turkey may decide to look east. This, say pro-European Turks, can only encourage extremist political movements, greater social disruption, and a slide towards precisely those negative values to which the EU says it wants to put an end.

Çifte Minare Medrese. In the background are the Bingol Mountains

Detail of a magnificent portal at the Işak Paşa Palace, Doğubayazıt. The palace was begun in 1685 by Colak Abdi Paşa and completed by his son İşak, a Kurdish chieftain, in 1784. The palace mosque is still in use

Eastern Anatolia

East of Trabzon, Rize is at the centre of Turkey's tea-growing country, a town of wooded hills and terraces. Not surprisingly, wood-carving is a local trade. For the walker and mountaineer there is the hinterland with its lovely valleys and manifold high peaks, and there are trout streams for the angler.

Travelling out of Trabzon, a visit to the **Sumela Monastery** can be either a part-day excursion from Trabzon, or a stop on a projected journey to Erzurum and Turkey's southeast region. Until the exchange of populations between Greece and Turkey after their 1920–22 War, the Greek-speaking population was high in the Trabzon area, and several Orthodox monasteries here were active.

Erzurum is a staging point for coach services from Ankara to Tabriz and Teheran, and for services through to Georgia and Armenia. Erzurum is on the railway line from Ankara to Van and beyond. Board the ferry at Tatvan to cross the lake. This journey takes about four hours and is most congenial at sunset.

As you approach the town of Doğubayazıt, Mount Ararat (Ağrı Dağı) becomes the focus of attention in a somewhat arid panorama. The reputed final resting place of Noah's Ark, the mountain is best viewed from the Iranian border. The striking İşak Paşa Sarayi, built by a Kurdish prince, stands above a rocky valley outside Doğubayazıt.

Getting There

From Trabzon, the traveller may want to continue east 74 kilometres (46 miles) on the coastal road to Rize. Hopa, 118 kilometres (74 miles) east of Rize, is the last Turkish coastal town before the Georgian border.

Sumela Monastery is situated in the mountains 46 kilometres (29 miles) south of Trabzon. You leave the city on the main E390 road to Maçka, 28 kilometres (18 miles) away. This is the route the majority of travellers are likely to take if they intend to make a journey to Lake Van or to go further east into Iran. From Maçka a road leads off to the monastery—Meryemane—17 kilometres (11 miles) southeast.

The E390 continues south by way of the grandiose Zigana Pass, 2,010 metres (6,600 feet) high, and at Torul, 88 kilometres (55 miles) from Maçka, turns southeastward in its mountain journey to Gumushane and Bayburt, then down to the plateau at Askale, 179 kilometres (112 miles) from Torul, to join the E23 leading the 53 kilometres (33 miles) east to Erzurum.

From Erzurum the E23 continues east through Pasinler, Horasan and Eleskurt to Ağrı, a total of 177 kilometres (110 miles). The next town is Doğubayazıt, 95 kilometres (59 miles) away, from where it is another 35 kilometres (22 miles) to the Iran border crossing at Gurbulak.

Go back to Ağrı, from where road 985 runs southward 81 kilometres (50 miles) to Patnos. Malazgirt, where the historic Battle of Manzikert was fought, is 40 kilometres (25 miles) southwest from here. From Patnos it is 46 kilometres (29 miles) eastwards on road 280 to Ercis at the northern end of Lake Van. Continue east for 26 kilometres (16 miles) to meet the 975 road going south to Van, a further 63 kilometres (39 miles). The harbour and railway station on the lakeside are two kilometres (1.25 miles) from the centre of town.

Train passengers from Ankara board the ferry at Tatvan on the lake's southwestern end and cross to Van, a distance of 88 kilometres (55 miles). Both Erzurum and Van have airports.

From Van the road leads 30 kilometres (19 miles) south to Gevas, a pleasant market town with a stream tumbling through its central square. A bus destined for Tatvan can take you round the south side of the lake. Six kilometres (four miles) west of Gevas is a landing stage for the ferry to and from the lake island of Akdamar.

Historical Background

The Battle of Manzikert was fought in 1071 southwest of Ağrı near the town of Malazgirt. Alp Arslan defeated the Emperor, Romanus IV, and thereby opened up western Anatolia to the Seljuks, and later to the Turkoman tribes harassed by the Mongols.

A kingdom of the Urartu existed at Van, c. 1000–700 BC. Though indigenous to the region, the gods of the Urartu seem to have had an affinity with those of the Hurrians, as did the language, and through the Hurrians a Hittite association. Skill at metalworking was among this people's accomplishments.

Queen Semiramis of Assyria, after falling in love with a local Urartian prince, built a palace at Van. Following devastation brought by the Cimmerian tribes, and then occupation by Scythians from the South Russian steppes and the Crimea, Armenians settled in the region.

By the first century BC, Tigranes had established an Armenian kingdom around Lake Van, which spread over what is now the border with the Republic of Armenia. Proselytizing Christians converted Tiridates, the Armenian king who consequently declared his state Christian, some 20 years prior to Constantine I's declaration of the Roman Christian Empire.

At the conclusion of a period notable for Christian schism and heresies, the Armenian church emerged as Monophysite and thereby alienated from both Constantinople and Rome.

Sights

THE SUMELA MONASTERY
Founded in the fifth century and dedicated to the Virgin Mary, the monastery is set precipitously at a height of 250 metres (820 feet) above the level of the roadway. The premises were restored under Alexius III of Trebizond (1330–90), who was crowned here. The entrance stairway has 93 steps. Inside, a stairway descends into the main courtyard off which are the principal buildings, including a church constructed under a rock. The frescoes of the church have been restored.

ERZURUM
Although the history of Erzurum—Theodosiopolis for the Romans, named after Theodosius II (408–50)—is a long one, evidence of the city's past dates mainly from Seljuk times. The castle, which has endured many changes of ownership and undergone numerous rebuildings, is not open to the public.

The most interesting building is the 13th-century Seljuk **Çifte Minare Medrese** with its arched doorway in stalactite design and its fluted twin minarets—which gave their name to the *medrese*—with their carved bases. The central court has porticoes whose arcades are decorated in arabesques and geometric patterns.

The spacious **Ulu Cami** nearby dates from the 12th century, and behind it are a number of tombs, all with the distinctive cone-shaped dome on a circular drum that distinguishes the Mevlana Tekke at Konya.

MOUNT ARARAT
Despite its arid surroundings, the mountain's magnificence can be altered dramatically by weather, its top frequently shrouded in cloud, while snow invariably

Built by King Gagil, the tenth-century Church of the Holy Cross (Akdamar Kilesi) features wonderfully varied exterior relief carvings. Situated on an island in Lake Van, the church is one of the most beautiful examples of Armenian architecture

decorates its lower peaks. Ararat rises to 5,156 metres (16,922 feet) above the valley of the Aras River. While frequent expeditions search diligently for conclusive proof of Noah's Ark, at least one Turkish pilot has claimed to have seen a ship's timbers up there.

For climbers, the best approach to the mountain is from Iğdir, 51 kilometres (32 miles) north of Doğubayazıt, or from Aralik on the Turkish–Armenian border, 15 kilometres (nine miles) northwest of the border crossing.

Doğubayazıt, a town of frontier inconsequence, has at least one fantasy to offer in the 18th-century **İşak Paşa Sarayi**, a palace and mosque, which stands over a valley some six kilometres (four miles) southeast of the town. The walled enclosure, built by a Kurdish prince, is a mix of architectural styles. There are ruins of a settlement nearby, dating back to the Urartu.

VAN AND THE LAKE

On the lakeside, midway between the centre of town and the harbour and railway station, is an 80-metre-(263-foot-) high ridge. It is 2,800 metres (9,200 feet) long and 120 metres (400 feet) wide, surmounted by a citadel with towered walls. Urartian texts in cuneiform were found in a funerary chamber here. The town's museum includes a display of Urartian artefacts and inscriptions.

The ancient city itself is below the ridge on the side nearest the lake, and here as well are the ruins of two Armenian churches and three Seljuk mosques, the **Ulu Cami**, **Kurşunlu Cami** and **Husrev Paşa Cami**. Five kilometres (three miles) east of the town, at the site of **Toprakkale**, is the mound of what is likely to have been the capital of the Urartian kingdom: recoveries from a temple are in the British Museum, along with inscriptions in cuneiform, and items in bronze and ivory. A concealed stairway within the mound leads up to a chamber that could have been part of the palace. King Menuas was a canal builder who brought water from the Hosap River to the city. At Hosap (or Güzelsu), 58 kilometres (36 miles) southeast, there is another castle on a spur that has a polygonal keep and a barbican with heraldic lions.

Lying at an altitude of 1,750 metres (5,750 feet), with an area of 3,737 square kilometres (1,442 square miles), Lake Van is Turkey's largest lake, nearly seven times the size of Lake Geneva. Surrounded by mountains, the lake is dominated on its northwestern shore by Mount Suphan, at a height of 4,434 metres (14,552 feet). At the western end of the lake Nemrut Dağı, 3,050 metres (10,010 feet) high, has its own two volcanic lakes lying 700 metres (2,300 feet) below its wide crater, with hot springs on the west side and ice-cold ones on the east. The wild boar is hunted in season in the woods of Nemrut Dağı, and wild geese frequent its lakes.

Lake Van is too sodium-slaked to encourage fish or wildlife except at the mouths of the rivers emptying into it, nor is swimming here particularly refreshing. Besides gulls and cormorants, the occasional pelican can be seen.

There are several islands in Lake Van, including Kuç, Carpanak, Adu and, the most interesting, Akdamar, with its tenth-century Armenian church and monastery. The external carvings on the church are of pleasing dramatic interest: besides saints and biblical personalities, parables are depicted, including one of Jonah and the whale. The interior decoration has colourful frescoes. Of the monastery buildings little is left now but the grounds, which are maintained by gardeners.

Southeast of Lake Van are the rugged yet inviting Hakkâri Mountains that extend across frontiers into Iran and Iraq, with the Turkish town of Hakkâri lying at 1,748 metres (5,740 feet). In trekking to Hakkâri, an adventurous hiker might well find himself in company with an equally adventurous bear.

Practical Information

Accommodation

Hotel classifications are set by the Turkish Ministry of Culture and Information. A complete list of hotels is available, on sale in bookshops. There is a shorter listing in the Ministry's *Turkey Travel Guide* on complimentary issue at its Information Offices, though some numbers may have changed. The telephone numbers listed below were correct at the time of publication. The room rates given are an indication only of likely charges. The market is a free one; rates are not set by the Ministry and can vary between hotels of a similar category. In some areas of the country though, hotel licences are issued by local authority, and rates are set by categories, in which case the information should be posted in each room. In holiday centres, where anticipated tourism may not have reached the desired level, or in off-peak seasons, a more favourable price than the one asked can be negotiated.

Casual travellers are unlikely to be on the lookout for four- and five-star hotels, and the choice is ample in the lower categories, particularly with the increasing number of *pensions*. These range from hostels and family-style to club-like sophistication. Hotel rates outside İstanbul and Ankara are likely to be lower than the ones indicated for the major cities.

Among new hotels is the **Bosphorus** at Beşiktaş, hugging the shoreline. For the moderate cost-conscious traveller, who seeks calm of mind along with an appreciation of tasteful architecture, there is the **Kariye Hotel**, a converted timbered mansion in the pedestrian-only area that now surrounds the Church of St Saviour in Chora, the Kariye Cami Museum, with its beautiful 14th-century mosaics and frescoes. Another choice is the **Hotel Richmond** pleasantly situated near Tünel in the totally pedestrian İstiklâl Caddesi. A more cost-conscious visitor might go for the **Vezir Han**, a thrifty conversion at Sultanahmet, close to the **Sublime Porte** where former Grand Viziers gave audience to the world's ambassadors. A truly economic traveller might try the **Hotel Lodge** at Tepebaşi (near the revered Pera Palace Hotel, rendezvous of T S Eliot's Smyrna merchant). Other possibilities are the **Hotel Büyük Hamit** and the **Soğut Oteli** behind the Municipal Offices, the Belediye of Greater İstanbul, close to the Aqueduct of Valens, and neighbouring Sinan's **Sehzade Cami**, within whose walled grounds is an inscribed stone marking the centre not only of the city, but of the former East Roman World.

For gambling addicts, or those who merely enjoy an occasional flutter, most five-star hotels run a casino. There is a fixed entry charge, which includes a buffet dinner, mitigating to an extent any losses sustained while playing the tables. This activity may soon be unavailable to the hopeful, successful or suicidal since there is a bill in the Turkish Parliament the intention of which is to close the public casinos.

As inflation drives hotel rates higher, the traveller has a better chance of negotiating prices at the reception desk, particularly at hotels below the five-star category.

In its most recent hotels brochure, the Ministry of Tourism quotes the following range for the cost of accommodation in Turkey:

Five-star	Single room US$52–400	Double room US$70–600
Four-star	Single room US$28–250	Double room US$37–345
Three-star	Single room US$13–180	Double room US$16–250
Two-star	Single room US$9–144	Double room US$16–238
One-star	Single room US$7–100	Double room US$10–130

Cities

İSTANBUL

FIVE-STAR

The Bosphorus Bayıldım Caddesi 2, Taslik Maçka, Beşiktaş. Tel 259 0101; fax 259 0105. Air conditioning, 14 restaurants and bars, 24-hour room service, Swiss Butler Floors, conference rooms, health club, direct dial, radio, television, laundry service, doctor.

Conrad Hotel Yildiz Caddesi, Beşiktaş. Tel 227 3000; fax 259 6667. 1317 beds, 627 rooms.

Divan Hotel Cumhuriyet Caddesi 2, Taksim. Tel 231 4100/11; fax 248 8527. 191 beds, 96 rooms, suites. Air conditioning, outdoor parking, restaurant, coffee shop, bar, conference rooms with translation services, room telephone, radio, television, refrigerator, laundry service, barber and hairdresser, nursery, rent-a-car. Breakfast included in room price.

Hilton Hotel Cumhuriyet Caddesi, Harbiye. Tel 231 4646; fax 240 4165. 770 beds, 410 rooms, 13 suites. Air conditioning, outdoor parking, central heating, restaurants, coffee shop, conference rooms, Turkish bath, swimming pool, motor-boat hire, tennis courts, room telephone, radio, television, refrigerator, laundry service, barber and hairdresser, reduced rate for children, casino, car rental, helicopter service. The Hilton is isolated in its large hillside precinct off the main boulevard. The lounge and rooms on the Bosphorus side have uninterrupted views of the waterway, as does the rooftop restaurant. The arcade off the entrance lobby boasts fashion shops and jewellery vendors. At the Cumhuriyet entrance are a THY booking office, bookshop and some travel agencies. The swimming pool and tennis courts stand in a large, cultivated garden area.

Hyatt Regency İstanbul Taşkışla Caddesi, Taksim. Tel 225 7000; fax 225 7007. 360 deluxe rooms. Air conditioning, central heating, restaurants, choice of lounges, Turkish bath, sauna, health club, swimming pool, tennis courts, golf, room telephone, radio, television, in-room safe, laundry service, valet. In the heart of the business district, with shopping and entertainment nearby. Just 13 miles from the International Airport.

The Marmara Taksim Meydani, 80090 Taksim. Tel 251 4696 (30 lines); fax 244 0509. 704 beds, 424 rooms, suites. Air conditioning, indoor parking, central heating, restaurant, bar, cocktail lounges, nightclub, disco, conference rooms with translation services, banquet facilities, Turkish bath, sauna, swimming pool, telephone, radio, television, refrigerator in room, barber and beauty parlour, reduced rate for children, casino, slot machines, car rental, helicopter service. At the hub of city activity in Beyoğlu, the Marmara's rooftop restaurant offers panoramic views with Turkish and European cuisine. Its shopping arcade includes a baker, patisserie, watchmaker and jewellers.

FOUR-STAR

Dilson Sıraselviler Caddesi 49, Taksim. Tel 252 9600; fax 249 7077. 180 beds, 90 rooms. Air conditioning, outdoor parking, central heating, restaurant, conference facilities, room telephone, radio, television, refrigerator, laundry service, nurse, reduced rate for children, motor-boat hire, sailing. Breakfast included in room price.

Kalyon Hotel Sahil Yolu, Sultanahmet. Tel 517 4400; fax 638 1111. 76 beds, 38 rooms, suites. Air conditioning, central heating, restaurant, conference rooms, beach, room telephone, radio, television, refrigerator, laundry service, nurse, reduced rate for children. Breakfast included in room price.

Pullman Etap İstanbul Meşrutiyet Caddesi, Tepebaşi. Tel 251 4646/63; fax 249 8033. 370 beds, 200 rooms, suites. Air conditioning, restaurant, bar, disco, conference rooms, swimming pool, room telephone, radio, television, refrigerator, laundry service, barber and hairdresser, nursery, reduced rate for children, rent-a-car service.

Richmond Hotel İstiklâl Caddesi 445, Beyoğlu. Tel 252 5460; fax 252 9707. Radio, television, air conditioning, conference rooms, ballroom, restaurant, streetside café, bar, rooftop restaurant.

THREE-STAR
Grand Star Sıraselviler Caddesi 29, Taksim. Tel 252 7070; fax 251 7822. 143 beds, 79 rooms, suites. Outdoor parking, central heating, restaurant, conference rooms, room telephone, radio, refrigerator, laundry service, nurse, reduced rate for children.
Harem Ambar Sokak 1, Selimiye, Üsküdar. Tel 310 6800; fax 334 7730. 204 beds, 100 rooms, suites. Outdoor parking, central heating, restaurant, conference facilities, Turkish bath, sauna, swimming pool, room telephone, laundry service.
Pera Palas Meşrutiyet Caddesi 98/100, Tepebaşi. Tel 251 4560/71; fax 251 4089. 200 beds, 116 rooms, suites. Air conditioning, outdoor parking, restaurant, bar, room telephone-television, laundry service, reduced rate for children. Breakfast included in room price. Worth at least one night's visit to experience a fast fading Edwardian elegance and expansiveness. Many of the rooms overlook the Golden Horn.

TWO-STAR
Bern Murat Paşa Sokak 16, Aksaray. Tel 523 2462; fax 521 5394. 104 beds, 46 rooms, suites. Air conditioning, outdoor parking, central heating, room telephone-radio, laundry service, reduced rate for children, slot machines. Breakfast included in room price.
Büyük Londra Meşrutiyet Caddesi 117, Galatasaray. Tel 393 1619; fax 245 0671. 70 beds, 42 rooms, suites. Central heating, room telephone, radio, television, refrigerator, laundry service, reduced rate for children. Breakfast included in room price.
Keçik Fethi Bey Caddesi 18, Lâleli. Tel 511 2310; fax 538 1400. 140 beds, 72 rooms, outdoor parking, central heating, restaurant, conference rooms, Turkish bath, sauna, room telephone-radio, laundry service, barber and hairdresser, reduced rate for children, half-pension rate. Breakfast included in room price.

ONE-STAR
Bristol Meşrutiyet Caddesi 235, Tepebaşi. Tel 251 3835; fax 252 5929. 90 beds, 54 rooms. Breakfast included in room price.
Dakar-Italya Sefer Bostan Sokak 2–4, Beyoğlu. Tel 252 1128; fax 244 6825.
Gecit Lâleli Caddesi 5, Aksaray. Tel 518 6765; fax 518 6765.
Karatay Sait Efendi Sokak 42, Lâleli. Tel 518 5554; fax 518 5291.

ANKARA
FIVE-STAR
Büyük Ankara Atatürk Bulvarı 183, Karaklidere. Tel 425 6655; fax 425 5070.
Büyük Surmeli Çihan Sokak 6. Tel 231 7660; fax 229 5176.
Hilton Hotel Tahran Caddesi 12. Tel 468 2888; fax 468 0909.
Sheraton Ankara Hotel Noktali Sokak Kavaklidere. Tel 468 5454; fax 467 1136.

FOUR-STAR
Aldino Kavaklidere. Tel 468 6510; fax 465 6517.
Best Atatürk Bulvarı 195. Tel 467 0880; fax 467 0885. 108 beds, 48 rooms, suites.
Conference rooms, sauna, nightclub.
Dedeman Buklum Sokak 1. Tel 417 6200; fax 417 6214. 455 beds, 252 rooms,
suites. Swimming pool, nightclub, barber and hairdresser.
Içkale Gazi Mustafa Kemal Bulvarı 189, Maltepe. Tel 231 7710; fax 230 6133.

THREE-STAR
Apaydin Bayındır Sokak 8. Tel 435 4950; fax 433 4005.
Elit Olgunlar Sokak 10, Bakanliklar. Tel 417 4695; fax 417 4697.
Metropol Olgunnlar Sokak 5, Bakanliklar. Tel 417 3060; fax 417 6990. 68 beds, 32
rooms.
Tunali Tunali Hilmi Caddesi 419. Tel 467 4440; fax 427 4082. 96 beds, 54 rooms.

TWO-STAR
Akman Ulus. Tel 418 9875; fax 417 4943.
Ercan Dennizçiler Caddesi 36. Tel 309 2722; fax 311 7170.
Ersan Meşrutiyet Caddesi 13. Tel 418 0875; fax 417 4943.

İZMIR
FIVE-STAR
Grand Efes Hotel Gaziosmanpaşa Bulvarı 1. Tel 484 4300; fax 441 5695. 585 beds,
296 rooms.
İzmir Hilton Gaziosmanpaşa Bulvarı 7. Tel 441 6060; fax 441 2277.
Princess Zeytin Sokak, Narlidere. Tel 238 5151; fax 239 0939.

FOUR-STAR
Ege Palace Cumhuriyet Bulvarı 210. Tel 463 9090; fax 463 8100.
Pullman Etap İzmir Mithatpaşa Caddesi 138. Tel 489 4090; fax 489 4089.
Pullman Etap Konak Mithatpaşa Caddesi 128. Tel 489 1500; fax 489 1709.
Sevranoğlu Tur Mihtat Paşa Caddesi 128. Tel 489 1500; fax 489 1709.

THREE-STAR
Anba Cumhuriyet Bulvarı, 124. Tel 484 4380; fax 484 4383. 296 beds, 148 rooms.
İzmir Palas Vafi Cinar Bulvarı 2, Alsancak. Tel 421 5583; fax 422 6870. 296 beds,
148 rooms.
Kilim Kaşim Dirik Caddesi. Tel 484 5340; fax 489 5070. 164 beds, 88 rooms.
Kismet 1377 Sokak 9, Alsancak. Tel 633 2595; fax 633 5346. 114 beds, 64 rooms.

TWO-STAR
Katipoğlu Fevzipaşa Caddesi 41/2. Tel 441 5171; fax 441 5171. 82 beds, 41 rooms.
Kaya Gaziosmanpaşa Bulvarı 45, Cankaya. Tel 483 9771; fax 483 9773. 100 beds, 50 rooms.

ONE-STAR
Babadan Gaziosmanpaşa Bulvarı 50. Tel 712 7081; fax 712 7331.

Coastal Resorts

ANTALYA
FIVE-STAR
Antalya Dedeman Lara Yolu. Tel 321 7910; fax 321 3873.
Club Hotel Sera P O Box 444 Lara, 07003 Antalya. Tel 323 1170; fax 323 1179.
Hotel Ofo-Antalya Ucyol Mevkii Lara, Antalya. Tel 323 1000/01; fax 323 1016.
Sheraton Voyager Antalya Hotel 100 Yil Bulvarı. Tel 243 2432; fax 243 2462.

FOUR-STAR
Antalya Hotel Lara Caddesi. Tel 323 3380; fax 323 0497.
Voyager Konyaalti Mevkii. Tel 243 2432; fax 243 2462.

THREE-STAR
Atan Tel 321 7855; fax 321 7558.
Bay Murat Demirçikara Mah. Tel 323 3061; fax 323 2809.
Kislahan Kazim Ozalp Caddesi. Tel 248 3870; fax 248 4297.
Lara Guzelova. Tel 349 2930; fax 349 2936.

TWO-STAR
Bigehan Sarampol Caddesi, Lara. Tel 248 3950; fax 248 7956.
Yalcin Lara. Tel 241 8932; fax 241 8934.

BODRUM
FIVE-STAR
Munamar Vista Tel 455 3360; fax 455 3359.
Otel Karia-Princess Tel 316 8971; fax 316 8979.
Sea Garden Tel 368 9015; fax 368 9048.

FOUR-STAR
Ambrosia Tel 343 1816; fax 343 1879.
Colossus Tel 316 3419; fax 316 5140.

THREE-STAR
Gokçe Club Armonia. Tel 393 6315; fax 393 6318.
Tutun 21 Sokak. Tel 414 5067; fax 414 5069.

FETHIYE
THREE-STAR
Malhun Seytalli Mevkii. Tel 613 1131; fax 613 1132.
Mara Keal Caddesi. Tel 614 9307; fax 614 8039.
Ölüdeniz Belcegiz Mevkii. Tel 616 6525; fax 616 6055.

TWO-STAR
Mortabelle Hisarönü Koyu. Tel 616 6901; fax 616 6847.
Prenses Fevzi Çakmak. Tel 614 1305; fax 614 4479.
Sesel Barbaros Sokak. Tel 613 1454; fax 613 1132.

KAŞ
THREE-STAR
Aqua Çukurbağ Yarimadas. Tel 836 1896; fax 836 2021.
Ekici Arison Sokak. Tel 836 1825; fax 836 1823.
Mimoza Elimali Caddesi. Tel 836 1272; fax 836 1368.

TWO-STAR
Kekova Milli Guvenlik. Tel 836 1950; fax 836 1952.
Pirat Koyici Mevkii. Tel 844 3178; fax 844 3183.

KUŞADASI
FIVE-STAR
Fantasia Oteli Ilica Mah. Tel 614 8600; fax 614 2765.
Onura Hali Feyzullah Mah. Tel 614 8305; fax 614 3727.

FOUR-STAR
Imbat Kadinlar Deniz Mevkii. Tel 614 2000; fax 614 4960. April-September. 278 beds, 140 rooms.

THREE-STAR
Club Deniz Karaova Mevkii. Tel 633 1320; fax 633 1327. March-November. 818 beds, 409 rooms.
Kismet Akyar Mevkii. Tel 614 2005; fax 614 4914. April-October.
Ozcelik Atatürk Bulvarı, Yat Limani, Karşısı. Tel 614 1781; fax 614 8763. All year. 140 beds, 70 rooms.

TWO-STAR
Akman İstiklâl Caddesi 13. Tel 614 1501; fax 614 2351. April-October.
Aydin Inönü Bulvarı. Tel 614 4034; fax 614 4035. All year.

MARMARIS
FIVE-STAR
Elegance Kemeralti Mah. Tel 412 8101; fax 412 2005.
Grand Azur Kenen Evren Bulvarı. Tel 412 8201; fax 412 3530.
Mares Içmeler Koyu Mah. Tel 455 2200; fax 455 2201.

FOUR-STAR
Aqua Sahil Sokak. Tel 455 3633; fax 455 3650.
Laguna Içmeler Koyu. Tel 455 3710; fax 455 3622.

THREE-STAR
Platan Bakirkoyu. Tel 485 7031; fax 485 7030.
Sunrise Kenan Evran Bulvarı. Tel 412 3371; fax 412 5279.

TWO-STAR
Angora Boynuzbuku Mevkii. Tel 412 1175; fax 412 5274.
Halic Oteli Tel 412 1683; fax 412 9200.
Ideal Tel 412 2483; fax 412 1102.

SELÇUK
THREE-STAR
Selçuk Pinar Oteli Atatürk Mah. Tel 892 2507; fax 892 3033.

TWO-STAR
Ak Ugur Mumçu Sevgi Yolu. Tel 892 2161; fax 892 3142.
Kalehan Isabey Mah. Tel 892 6154; fax 892 2169.
Victoria Isabey Mah. Tel 812 3203; fax 812 3204.

Cappadocia

NEVŞEHIR

FOUR-STAR
Altinoz Kayşerı Caddesi. Tel 213 5305; fax 213 3817.

THREE-STAR
Kavas Ürgüp Yolu. Tel 213 2170; fax 213 9966.
Kapadokya Tel 213 5329; fax 213 4223.

ONE-STAR
Viva Kayşerı Caddesi 45. Tel 213 1326; fax 213 1642.

ÜRGÜP

FIVE-STAR
Dedeman Tel 213 9900; fax 213 2158.

FOUR-STAR
Büyük Almira Tel 341 8990; fax 341 8990.
Mustafa Tuzyolu. Tel 341 3970; fax 341 2288.
Perissia Tel 341 2930; fax 341 4524.

THREE-STAR
Arkadas Tel 341 2395; fax 341 2648.
Burcu Kaya Tel 343 3200; fax 343 3500.

TWO-STAR
Sarnic Tel 341 2340; fax 343 2344
Tassarah Tel 341 2344; fax 341 2444.

The East

DIYARBAKIR

THREE-STAR
Demir Izzet Paşa Caddesi 8. Tel 228 0848; fax 222 4300. All year.
Turistik Ziya Gokalp Bulvarı. Tel 224 7550; fax 228 6460. All year.

TWO-STAR
Diyarbakır Büyük Inönü Caddesi 4. Tel 228 1295; fax 221 2444.
Kristalim Satu Sok. Tel 224 0297; fax 224 0187.

ŞANLIURFA
THREE-STAR
Harran Atatürk Bulvarı. Tel 313 2860; fax 313 4918. All year.

TWO-STAR
Ferit Karahan Inönü Bulvarı. Tel 552 0520; fax 552 0521.
Koran Ipek Yolu Caddesi. Tel 313 1809; fax 312 1737.

TRABZON
THREE-STAR
Aksular Uzunkum Mevkii. Tel 230 1130; fax 229 4759.
Besikduzu Sahil Caddesi. Tel 871 3544; fax 871 1816.

TWO-STAR
Kosk Inönü Caddesi. Tel 228 3196; fax 228 1292.
Ozgur Taksim Caddesi. Tel 326 4703; fax 321 3952.
Sumela Inönü Caddesi. Tel 228 4067; fax 228 2105.

ONE-STAR
Horon Sira Magazlari 125, Trabzon. Tel 326 6455; fax 321 6628. All year.

VAN
THREE-STAR
Büyük Urartu Itastane Sokak, Van. Tel 212 0660; fax 212 1610. All year. 150 beds, 75 rooms.
Yakut Tel 212 2832; fax 216 1610.

TWO-STAR
Bes Kardes Cami Caddesi. Tel 216 1116; fax 216 6460.
Büyük Asur Cumhuriyet Caddesi. Tel 216 8792; fax 216 6968.
Gorbulak PTT Karşısı. Tel 312 7295; fax 312 7644.

ONE-STAR
Caldiran Sihke Caddesi. Tel 216 2718.
Guzel Paris Cumhuriyet Caddesi. Tel 216 3739; fax 216 6968.

Restaurants

İSTANBUL

BEYOĞLU

Ciftnal Samanyolu Sakak, Osmanbey. Tel 240 12 80.

The China Restaurant Lamartin Caddesi, Taksim. Tel 250 84 34, 250 62 63. Medium priced.

Four Season (Dort Mevsim) İstiklâl Caddesi 509, Tünel. Tel 245 89 41.

Galata Tower at the top of the tower, Kuledibi. Tel 245 11 60.

Garden '74 Bestekar Sevki Bey Sokak 74, Balmumçu. Tel 266 09 77.

Green House at Hilton Hotel Cumhuriyet Caddesi, Elmadağ. Tel 246 70 50 (ext. 8973).

Gunay Cumhuriyet Caddesi 349/1, Harbiye. Tel 240 83 95.

Haci Baba İstiklâl Caddesi 49. Tel 245 43 77.

Haci Salih 3 İstiklâl Caddesi, Anadolu Han 201/1. Tel 243 45 28.

Hasir Kalyonçuküllügü Caddesi 94/1, Tarlabaşi. Tel 250 05 57, also known as the Greek Taverna.

International Press Club Kennedy Caddesi, Sarayburnu.

Japanese Restaurant Ismet Inonnu Caddesi, Taksim. Several hotels now have Japanese restaurants.

Kulis Core (George) İstiklâl Caddesi 209A, Beyoğlu. Tel 243 20 46. International cuisine with specialities. Open 12 noon–12 midnight. Medium cost.

Liman Rihtim Caddesi, on the third floor of Karakoy Boat Terminal. Tel 244 10 33.

Mazgal Nispetiye Caddesi 12, Etiler. Tel 263 35 50.

Otag 85 Steak House, Yenni Tarlabaşi Caddesi 7, Taksim, and 3 Taksim Square. Tel 245 42 51.

Orient Express at the Marmara Hotel Taksim Square.

Pera Palas at the hotel, Meşrutiyet Caddesi, Tepebaşi.

Pronto Valikonagi Caddesi, Suleiman Nazif Sokak 3/A, Nisantasi. Tel 248 77 26.

Rejans Olivo Cikmazi 15, Galatasaray. Tel 244 16 10.

Ristorante Italiano Cumhuriyet Caddesi 6B, Elmadağ. Tel 247 86 40.

Swiss Cumhuriyet Caddesi 14/1, Elmadağ. Tel 240 46 18.

ON THE BOSPHORUS

Abdullah Emirgan Koru Caddesi 11. Tel 163 63 06. Turkish/French. Good but expensive.

Ali Baba Kirecburnu Caddesi 20, Sariyer.

Balikci Karatutuk Caddesi 172, Yenimahalle, Sariyer.

Bosfor   Cayirbaşi Caddesi 312, Büyükdere. Tel 142 03 64. Fish restaurant. Recommended. Medium price range.

China Palace (Huang Kung), Kirechurnu Caddesi 19, Tarabya. Tel 162 26 57. Chinese cuisine. Overlooking water. Expensive.

Erol Kilyos Yolu, Nalbantçeşme, Sariyer.

Feliz Kefeliköy Caddesi 168, Tarabaya. Tel 162 01 52. Fish restaurant. Superior dishes, moderate prices.

Han Yahya Kemal Caddesi 4, Rumeli Hisar. Tel 165 28 68. Fish restaurant. Good food, moderate prices.

Huzur 1 Caddesi 23, Arnavutkoy. Tel 163 42 19. Fish restaurant. Moderate prices.

Kiyi Kefeliköy Caddesi 126, Tarabaya. Tel 162 00 02. Fish restaurant. Medium prices.

Kosem   Kefeliköy Caddesi 90/92, Tarabya. Tel 162 01 58. Fish restaurant. Consistent quality and service. Moderate prices.

Marti   Karakutuk Caddesi 2, Yenimahalle. Tel 142 06 64. Fish restaurant. Consistent and unpretentious. Moderate prices.

Nese Büyükayama 29, Arnavutkoy. Tel 165 10 93. Turkish cuisine. In the hills (downhill from Etiler). Very moderate.

Yeni Bebek   Cevdet Paşa Caddesi 122, Bebek. Tel 163 34 47 . Turkish and French fish dishes. High standard of food and service. Medium price range.

OLD CITY

Asitane Restaurant Kariye Hote, Edirne Kapi. Tel 534 84 14.

Borsa Yali Köşkü Caddesi, Yali Köşkü Hani 60/62, Sirkeci. Tel 522 41 73. Turkish cuisine. Food is recommended more than decor. Open midday only. Moderately priced.

Cemal Balik Capariz Sokak 27, Kumkapi. Tel 527 22 88.

Cinaralti Capariz Sokak 12, Kumkapi.

N.B. The choice of restaurants at Kumkapi, a fisherman's paradise and pedestrian complex, is manifold and competitive, the ambience festive.

Kapri İstanbul Caddesi 44, Yeniköy. Tel 573 44 84. Turkish and international cuisine. Expensive.

Marmit İstanbul Caddesi 64, Yeşilköy. Tel 573 85 81. French/Turkish cuisine. Game dishes. Three-course set menu with wine. Evenings 6pm–12 midnight. Reservations. Expensive.

Pandeli Mişir Carsisi 1, Eminönü. In the Egyptian or Spice Bazaar, on an upper floor. Tel 522 5534, 527 3909. An İstanbul institution that should be attended at least once. Book in advance. Midday only. Medium cost.

Büyükçekmece and **Küçükçekmece**, by a lake out of town to the west via the E25, are places where those in the know go to eat meat. There are several restaurants set among fine bridges built by Sinan.

BURSA

Anatolia Cekirge Meydani. Tel 36 71 10/18.
Öz Kent Kültür Parkiçi. Tel 36 76 66.
Selçuk Kültür Parkiçi. Tel 36 76 58.
Serman Atatürk Caddesi, Oba Ishan, first floor. Tel 21 61 93.

İZMIR

Bakus Etap İzmir Hotel, Cumhuriyet Bulvarı, Alsancak. Tel 14 42 90/99.
China Town 1379 Sokak, Efes Is Hani 57A, Alsancak. Tel 25 73 57/58.
Efes Büyük Efes Hotel, Cumhuriyet Meydani, Alsancak. Tel 14 43 00 (ext. 849).
Golden Atatürk Caddesi 314/A, Alsancak. Tel 22 03 41.
Ikizlar Fevzi Çakmak Caddesi 314/A, Alsancak. Tel 22 03 41.
Palet Yali Caddesi 294/I, Karsiyaka. Tel 11 84 36.
Park Kültür Park. Tel 13 96 20.
Yengeç Cumhuriyet Bulvarı 236, Alsancak. Tel 21 73 68.

ANKARA

China Town Köröğlü Sokak 19, Gaziosmanpaşa. Tel 127 70.
Hulya Hösdere Caddesi 199/A, Cankaya. Tel 138 2961.
Karadeniz Karanfil Sokak 11, Kizilay.
Kazan Ahmet Ağaoğlu Caddesi 26, Cankaya.
Liman İzmir Caddesi 11/15, Yenişehir.
RV Tahran Caddesi 13, Kavaklidere. Tel 127 0376.
Yahha Hemseri Sokak 28, Gaziosmanpaşa Tel 137 8348.
Yakamoz Köröğlü Caddesi 38, Gaziosmanpaşa. Tel 134 3746.
Washington Bayındır Sokak 28A, Kizilay. Tel 131 2218.

Turkish Information Offices

AUSTRALIA
Suite 101
280 George Street
Sydney NSW 2000
Tel (612) 9223 3055
Fax (612) 9223 3204

AUSTRIA
Singer Strasse 2/8
1010 Vienna
Tel (431) 512 2128/9
Fax (431) 513 8326

BELGIUM
Rue Montoyer 4
1040 Brussels
Tel (322) 513 8230
Fax (322) 511 7951

CANADA
Suite 801
Constitution Square
360 Albert Street
Ottawa Ontario K1R 7X7
Tel (613) 230 8654
Fax (613) 230 3683

DENMARK
Vesterbrogade II A
1620 Copenhagen V
Tel (4531) 22 3100
Fax (4531) 22 9068

FINLAND
Mikonkatu 6 C 18
00100 Helsinki
Tel (3580) 66 6044
Fax (3580) 66 6061

FRANCE
102 Avenue des Champs-Elysèes
75008 Paris
Tel (331) 4562 7868
Fax (331) 4563 8105

GERMANY
Tauentzien Str. 7
10789 Berlin
Tel (4930) 214 3752
Fax (4930) 214 3952

GERMANY (continued)
Baseler Strasse 37
60329 Frankfurt-Main
Tel (4969) 23 3081/2
Fax (4969) 23 2751

Karlsplatz 3/1
80335 Munich
Tel (4989) 59 4902
Fax (4989) 550 4138

GREAT BRITAIN
First Floor
170-173 Picadilly
London W1V 9DD
Tel (44171) 629 7771
Fax (44171) 491 0773
E-mail eb25@cityscape.co.uk

ISRAEL
1 Ben Yehuda St
63801 Tel-Aviv
Tel (9723) 517 6157
Fax (9723) 517 6303

ITALY
Piazza Della Repubblica 56
00185 Rome
Tel (396) 487 1190
Fax (396) 488 2425

JAPAN
233-6 Jingumae
Shibuya-Ku
Tokyo
Tel (813) 3470 6380
Fax (813) 3470 6037

KUWAIT
P.O. Box 15518
De'eyah
35456 Kuwait
Tel (965) 242 4248
Fax (965) 242 4298

NETHERLANDS
Herengracht 451
1017 BS Amsterdam
Tel (3120) 626 6810
Fax (3120) 622 2283

RUSSIA
Chistyprudny Blv. No. 5/10
Moscow
Tel (7095) 929 0572
Fax (7095) 929 0573

SINGAPORE
20-B Nassim Road
Singapore 1025
Tel (65) 732 9702
Fax (65) 732 8032

SPAIN
Plaza de España
Torre de Madrid 13-3
Madrid
Tel (341) 559 7014
Fax (341) 547 6287

SWEDEN
Kungsgatan 3 S-111
43 Stockholm
Tel (468) 679 8320/1
Fax (468) 611 3828

SWITZERLAND
Talstrasse 74
8001 Zurich
Tel (411) 221 0810/2
Fax (411) 212 1749

USA
821 United Nations Plaza
New York NY 10017
Tel (1212) 687 2194/5
Fax (1212) 599 7568
Home page
http://www.turkey.org/turkey

1717 Massachusetts Avenue NW
Suite 306
Washington DC 20036
Tel (1202) 429 9844
Fax (1202) 429 5649

Chronology

3000–1200 BC	Early Bronze Age; Hittite
1000 BC	Ionian, Aeolian and Carian settlements
340 BC	Alexander crosses to Anatolia, defeats Persians on the Granicus River
333 BC	Alexander defeats Darius at Battle of Issus
323 BC	Death of Alexander
323–138 BC	Wars between the successors of Alexander; the intercession of Rome; Roman inheritance of the kingdom of Pergamum; Asia Minor becomes a Roman province
34–23 BC	Octavius Caesar defeats Antony and Cleopatra. Rome gains Egypt
AD 44–50	St Paul's mission. First Christian churches at Antioch (Antalya)
284–304	Diocletian reigns. He separates the Empire, and rules in the Eastern part from Nicomedia
306–337	Reign of Constantine I
324	Constantine sole Emperor
330	Constantine builds 'New Rome' on site of Byzantion, declaring it Christian
392	Theodosias I outlaws Paganism; its temples are destroyed
470–474	Romulus last Emperor in the West
527–565	Reign of Justinian. He codifies the law, and in addition to Latin, Greek becomes an official language of the Empire
632	Death of Mohammed in Medina
636	Arab invasions in Asia Minor and elsewhere
717–718	Arabs besiege Constantinople
813	Bulgarians besiege Constantinople
1096	The First Crusade
1230–1240	Ertogrul established on the Karasu, northwest of Kutahya
1259	Osman born at Sugut
1289	Death of Ertogrul
1290–1299	Osman creates an Emirate

1301	Osman defeats a Byzantine force at Nicomedia
1317	Osmanlis besiege Bursa
1326	Bursa surrenders to Orkhan, son of Osman. Death of Osman
1329	Nicaea surrenders to Orkhan
1338	Nicomedia surrenders. Osmanlis arrive at Haydar Pusha in Bosphorus
1345	Orkhan fights as ally of Cantacuzeno, Byzantine claimant to the throne in Europe
1346	Orkhan marries the daughter of the Bulgarian Czar
1349	Ottomans fight for Cantacuzenos to save Thessaloniki from falling to the Serbs
1353	Ottomans help Cantacuzenos recapture Adrianople in Thrace
1354	Orkhan captures Gallipoli
1359	Death of Orkhan
1360–1361	Murad I conquers Thrace
1362	The Imperial Corps of the Janissaries formed, mainly of Christian boys
1363	Byzantine Emperor Cantacuzenos recognizes Ottoman Conquest of Thrace, and allies with Murad against the Emirs
1365	The Republic of Ragusa signs a commercial treaty with the Ottoman Sublime Porte
1366	Adrianople (Edirne) first capital of the Ottoman Empire
1373	Byzantine Emperor becomes an Ottoman vassal
1378	Schism between Roman Church and that of Constantinople
1379	City of Philadelphia, the last Byzantine possession in Asia Minor, surrenders to the Sultan
1385	Ottoman invasion of Albania, occupation of Sofia
1387	Genoa concludes commercial treaty with Murad
1388	Venice concludes commercial treaty with Murad; first Ottoman entry into Greece at invitation of Theodore Palaeologer to fight with him against the Franks
1389	Serbians defeated at Kosovo; Murad assassinated on battlefield
1390	First Ottoman naval strike against Chios, Eubeia and Attica Ottomans raid Hungary

1391	First failed siege of Constantinople by Beyazıt, this Sultan captures Adalia (Antalaya) the first Ottoman port on the Mediterranean
1396	Crusade led by Sigismund of Hungary defeated at Nicopolis in Bulgaria
1397	Ottoman invasion of Greece. Argos taken. Theodore becomes an Ottoman vassal
1392–1399	Movement of Muslims from Anatolia into the Balkan Peninsula
1402	Timur defeats Beyazıt, and occupies Bursa. He takes Smyrna from the Christian Knights of St John. Ottoman emigrants expelled from Constantinople by the Emperor Venetiani and Genoese assist Osmanlis to cross into Europe in their flight from Timur
1413–1421	Reign of Mehmet I, Sultan in Bursa
1421–1451	Reign of Murat II, Sultan in Adrianople
1451–1482	Reign of Mehmet II Conqueror of Constantinople
1453	Mehmet II enters Constantinople
1481–1512	Reign of Beyazıt II
1512–1520	Reign of Selim I
1520–1566	Reign of Suleiman the Magnificent
1566–1574	Reign of Selim II
1571	Battle of Lepanto, defeat of Ottoman navy
1653	Unsuccessful siege of Vienna
1789–1801	Education becomes obligatory under Selim III
1808–1830	Reign of Mahmut II. He abolishes the Janissaries
1821	Greeks revolt. Ottomans lose much of mainland Greece
1839–1876	Sultan introduces the Tanzimat, a reform plan for Westernization
1856	Treaty of Paris. Ottoman Empire accepted as a European state
1877–1905	Autocracy of Abdulhamit II
1881	Mustafa Kemal (Atatürk) born in Thessalonika
1908	Young Turks prevail on Abdul Hamit to restore Parliament
1912–1913	The Balkan wars. Turks lose Macedonia and parts of Thrace

1914–1918	Turkey a World War I ally of Germany
1915	Kemal Atatürk successful at Gallipoli
1918	Turkish surrender to Allies
1919	War of independence
1919	Sivas conference at which Atatürk becomes leader of the Nationalists
1920	Treaty of Sevres; the Ottoman Empire in dissolution; Grand National Assembly formed; Greeks arrive at Anatolia
1922	Greek defeat and expulsion
1923	Treaty of Lausanne. Exchange of nationals between Greece and Turkey
1923–1938	Atatürk reforms and creation of Turkey as a modern western republic
1938	Death of Atatürk

Glossary

acropolis	the highest part of a city built on a hill or prominence
acroterium	carved figures at the corners of a pediment
adyton	the innermost sanctuary of a temple
agora	the market place; centre for official offices
amphitheatre	a circular stadium
amphora	a large pottery jar with handles and a narrow neck
apse	church recess, usually vaulted and semi-circular
aqueduct	a high structure built as a conduit for water
architrave	a large beam above and opening, or columns
atrium	a courtyard at the centre of a building, unroofed except above a surrounding colonnade
basilica	a large oblong building; the nave of a church
bas-relief	a light carving in stone
bouleuterion	a council chamber
capital	the decorated head of a column
cavea	the auditorium of a theatre
cella	the sanctuary of a temple
colonnade	columns set in line supporting a roof
crepidoma	the stepped base on which a temple is set
cuneiform	wedge-shaped symbols, an early form of writing
entablature	the stonework connecting columns, as with the architrave
epistyle	another name for architrave
faience	decorated porcelain
forum	Roman market place
frieze	a decorated section of the epistyle or architrave
gymnasium	a training area for athletes
Hellenistic	denotes the period relating to the rule of the successors of Alexander the Great
heroon	the shrine of a deified hero
hippodrome	the course for chariot racing
iconoclast	a destroyer of images
kathisma	the royal box in the hippodrome
lunette	a semi-circular space where a vault intersects a wall or another vault, used for a window or for a fresco decoration
martyrium	a shrine for a martyr

megaron	a long room or chamber with a central hearth
narthex	a vestibule to a church
nymphaeum	a gymnasium for girls
odeon	a small-sized theatre, mainly for musical recitals
palaestra	a wrestling area of a gymnasium
pantocrator	Ruler of all
paracclesion	funerary chapel
parados	space between the cavea and the stage
pediment	the triangular section above a portico
portico	a roof supported by columns at the entrance to a building
pithos	a large pottery jar for storing oil and grain
pronaos	temple porch
propylon	entrance to a city or sacred complex
prytaneium	a city's administrative building
sarcophagus	a stone coffin
stele	a carved upright stone
stoa	a colonnaded walkway before a building
temenos	a sacred complex of buildings
tetrapylon	four-columned gateway
transept	a cross aisle of a church

TURKISH

aga	village headman
ayazma	a sacred fountain
bedesten	a domed shopping centre
belediye	town hall
Bey	a notable
burc	a strong point or redoubt
cami	a mosque
dervish	member of a religious order
Divan	the Sultan's council chamber
Enderum	the Royal Palace School
firman	a Sultan's edict
Hajj	pilgrimage to Mecca
hajji	one who has made the pilgrimage
han	formerly an inn for travellers, now a complex of shops
hüyük	a hill or ancient mound
imam	a Muslim priest or prayer leader
imaret	a soup kitchen, mainly for the poor

janissary	member of an elite corps
konak	mansion
köşk	a kiosk or summer residence or pavilion
kufic	a style of calligraphy
kumbet	a tomb with a domed or conical roof
medrese	a theological school
mescit	a small mosque
mihrab	the centre or altar shrine of a mosque
minber	the pulpit in a mosque
minare	a minaret
nargile	a hookah or water pipe
paşa	a high-ranking officer
Ramadan	the ninth month of the Muslim year during which a daily fast is held from sunrise to sunset
saray	a palace
sunnet	circumcision
sadirvan	an ablutions fountain
serefe	a balcony on a minaret
seriat	Islamic Canonical Law
tekke	a monastery
türbe	a tomb
yalı	a timber waterfront house or villa

Recommended Reading

ANCIENT SOURCES

Arrian, *Anabasis of Alexander* (in translation) (New York: Loeb, 1929).
Anabasis, a Greek term meaning 'the road upward', describes a military advance first employed by Xenophon, who later became general to Alexander the Great. Arrian, governor of Cappadocia under Hadrian (117–138), wrote in the second century AD, relying on his sources Ptolemy and Aristobulus, who lived closer to the time of the actual event.

Eusebius, *The History of the Church from Christ to Constantine* (in translation) (Penguin, 1990).
Details persecutions under particular emperors, interspersed with stories of saints and martyrs. Born in Palestine, Eusebius (AD 263–339) served as Bishop of Caesavea (Kayseri).

Herodotus, *Histories* (in translation) (London: Penguin, 1954).
The fifth-century BC father of history. Born in Halicarnassus (Bodrum), Herodotus travelled extensively in the Middle East. His history of countries and peoples blends facts, traveller tales and mythology. An easy and enjoyable read in the Penguin translation.

HISTORY: CLASSICS

Bury, J B, *The Eastern Roman Empire* Everyman edition (London: J and M Dent).
An established authority on the history of the Roman Empire after Diocletian (284–305) divided it administratively into East and West.

Cook, J M, *The Greeks in Ionia and the East* (London: Thames and Hudson, 1962).
This details the Greek colonization of coastal areas of Western Asia Minor (the Aegean) circa 1000 BC, when Ionians, Aeolians, Carians were driven out of mainland Greece and its major islands by Dorian invaders from the Balkans. The Greeks established colonies, too, on the Marmara shores and Black Sea Coast.

Czalpluka, M A, *The Turks of Central Asia* (London: Curzon Press, 1973).
A research into ethnological origins of the Central Asian Turks: '...the Osmanli have now more Albanian, Slavonic, Thracian and Circassian blood than they have Turkic; their culture more Persian, Arabic and European than Central Asiatic...' An inquiry undertaken at Oxford University.

Fox, Robin Lane, *Alexander the Great* (London: Allen Lane, 1973).
As erudite an account of Alexander as Peter Green's. Perhaps less critical of the man and his ambition and legacy, but still an excellent read.

Gibbon, H A, *The Foundations of the Ottoman Empire* (London: Frank Cass, 1965).
A detailed history of the first four Osmanli sultans from Osman to Bayezid I. Includes original research made in 1916, which is invaluable for having established the Ottoman Origin.

Green, Peter, *Alexander of Macedon* 356–323 BC (University of California Press, 1992).
A racy, erudite and down-to-earth account of Alexander's upbringing and subsequent conquests. Highly recommended.

Gurney, O R, *The Hittites* (London: Pelican, 1952).
An account of the ancient people who created a civilization in Anatolia, uncovered by the archeological excavation of Hittite sites during the early and middle parts of this century.

Kincaid, C A, *The Successors of Alexander* (Chicago: Argonaut Inc, 1969).
A history of the men who succeeded Alexander and attempted to carry on his achievements, particularly Ptolemy I, Pyrrhus of Epirus, Hiero of Syracuse and Antiochus III.

Nichol, Donald, *The Last Centuries of Byzantium* (London: Rupert Hart-Davis, 1972).
A detailed history of the Byzantine Empire, from the 1204 occupation of Constantinople by Latin princes and soldiers of the Fourth Crusade, until its fall in 1453.

Norwich, John Julius, *Byzantium* (3 volumes) (Penguin, 1990, 1996).
One of the more recent treatments of the Byzantine Empire, from Constantine I to the end. Detailed and highly readable.

Ostragorsky, G, *The History of the Byzantine State* (Oxford: Blackwell, 1956).
A source book for all scholars of Byzantium, including history, foreign policy, economic, ecclesiastical and domestic development over one thousand years. Written in German; translated to English in 1956.

Penzer, N M, *The Harem* (London: Pelican, 1954).
A detailed account of the establishment of the Harem, as well as its state and social significance, recruitment and routines.

Runciman, Steven, *The History of the Crusades* (Cambridge: Cambridge University Press, 1954).
Essential reading for anyone interested in the rivalry between Christianity and Islam, and the struggle for the possession of sites in Jerusalem and the Holy Land.

Rostovtzeff, *The Social and Economic History of the Roman Empire* (Oxford: Oxford University Press, 1926).
Deals with the economic and social aspects of development in the Byzantine State. Essential reading for the student.

Vasiliev, A A, *History of the Byzantine Empire* (Madison: University of Wisconsin, 1952).
Another 'classical' work of Byzantine history, first written and published in Russia. English translation based on French translation of the original.

HISTORY: PERSONAL AND REFLECTIVE

Ascherson, Neal, *Black Sea* (Vintage, 1996).
An absorbing historical and personal account on events and peoples in regions surrounding the Black Sea, corrective of the bad press given to such peoples as the Scythians of the Crimea. As with Herodotus, sometimes turns myth into fact.

Barber, Noel, *Lords of the Golden Horn* (London: Pan Books, 1973).
The Golden Horn is the waterway that runs inland from the Bosphorus (Marmara Sea), dividing Old İstanbul from the New. The Palace of Topkapi stands over it, at Seraglio Point. A colourful history of the Sultans.

Liddell, Robert, *Byzantium and İstanbul* (London: Longman, 1956).
A sober and poetic treatment of this capital city of Greeks and Turks; a personal memorandum.

Luke, Sir Harry, *The Old Turkey and the New* (London: Godfrey Bles, 1953).
A comparative study, personal and interpretive of changes in the country.

Menzies, Sutherland, *Turkey Old and New* (London: W H Allen, 1880).
A late-19th-century personal assessment of Turkey, before the major changes inaugurated by Atatürk.

Rice, David Talbot, *Constantinople: Byzantium–İstanbul* (London: Pelican, 1965).
A scholarly and artistic look at this eternally vibrant capital city.

Stark, Freya, *Alexander's Path* (London: John Murray, 1958).
Indulgent reading. Follow this highly personal itinerary, taken in the present day, along the Anatolian route of Alexander's conquests.

HISTORY: FACTUAL

Bean, George E, *Aegean Turkey* (London: Benn, 1979), *Lycian Turkey* (London: Benn, 1978), *Turkey Beyond the Maeander* (London: Benn, 1980).
Factual, detailed and personal exploration of areas of Turkey, touching on issues of autochthony, colonization, invasion, civilizations: Pagan, Christian, Muslim, contemporary.

Cuddon, J A, *The Owl's Watchsong* (London: Barrie and Rockliffe, 1960).
A present-day young man in the city searches for a future, learning something of its history and monuments, its joy and unhappiness.

Kinross, Lord, *Within the Taurus* (London: John Murray, 1954).
A travel programme, much of it in the lesser known areas of Eastern Anatolia. Personal adventures, discoveries and annoyances, all with historical details.

Maclagan, M, *The City of Constantinople* (London: Collins, 1956).
Detailed memorandum of the city, with historical references, architecture of the palaces, harbours, churches and the great mosques. A solid overview.

Sherrard, Philip, *Constantinople Iconography of a Sacred City* (Oxford: Oxford University Press, 1961).
Reviews the patriarchate, churches and holy icons, plus the Orthodox achievement, significance and legacy.

BIOGRAPHICAL

Kinross, Lord, Atatürk, *The Rebirth of a Nation* (London: Weidenfeld and Nicholson, 1964).
A comprehensive account of Kemal Atatürk from birth to death. A portrait of the man through his military and political triumphs, his reforms and determinations, his personal life and disappointments. Essential reading for an understanding of the development of the contemporary state.

Moorehead, Alan, *Gallipoli* (London: Hamish Hamilton, 1957).
An account of the Gallipoli campaign of World War I, the Allied attempt to put Turkey out of the war at an early stage of it, plus the failure of the Allies and triumph of Atatürk as Turkish forces commander. A great account perhaps marred by a bias in favour of Australian troops who bore the brunt of the fighting there. No self-respecting Australian dares visit Turkey without paying respect to that nation's dead in the cemeteries of Gallipoli.

NOVELS

Horobin, Gilbert, *Kurdish Connection* (Janus, 1996).
An adventure story of international agents, arms smuggling and the search for the last clue to a secret treasure. The action is set mostly in Turkey, from İstanbul across the country to the denouement on the border of Syria between Euphrates and Tigris.

Macaulay, Rose, *The Towers of Trebizond* (London: Collins, 1956).
Trebizond (Trabzon) was the capital of an independent Byzantine Empire that came into existence after the fall of Constantinople to the Latins. It survived as an Empire for some eight years after the Turkish conquest of the city, but then fell to the conqueror. The novel details a contemporary journey to Trebizond, remarkable in its evocation of time and authenticity of place. A good read.

Index

public conveniences 28
Purenli Seki church (Ihlara) 233

R

rafting 50
rail travel, international 17
Red Cross 21
Red Islands (Kızıl Adalar, Princes' Islands) 108
religion 10
    see also specific religion
resorts
    Aegean coast 140
    Anatolia 219
    Black Sea coast 100, 256, 257
    Mediterranean coast 24, 212, 215
Reyhanli Cami (Mardin) 252
Rhodes 179
Rice, David Talbot 261
Rize 268
    tea festival 43
Roxellana, tomb of 85
Rumeli Hısar Castle 96
Rumeli Kavağı 96–7
Rustem Paşa Cami 101

S

sacred springs and wells 156, 172, 205, 216, 232, 249, 254, 258–9
Sadberk Hanim Museum (Büyükdere) 40
Şah Mescit (Niğde) 232
Sahibiye Medrese (Kayseri) 233
sailing 275
    see also boating
St Ann, Church of (Trabzon) 261
St George, Church of (Diyarbakır) 254
St George, Church of (Fener) 90
St Irene (Hagia Eirene) (İstanbul) 60, 68
St John (Apostle), burial site of 146
St John in Studion, Church of (İstanbul) 89, 103–4
St John Prodromos, Church of (Ürgüp) 232
St John Prodromos in Trullo, Church of 103
St John Theologos, Church of (Ephesus) 136
St John Theologos, Church of (Selçuk) 142
St Mary of the Mongols, Church of (İstanbul) 106
St Mary Panachrantos, the All-immaculate, Church of (İstanbul) 106
St Nicholas 8, 187
St Nicholas, Church of (Demre) 200
St Nicholas, Church of (İstanbul) 104
St Paul (Apostle) 8, 138, 145, 179, 213, 220
St Paul and St Dominic, Dominican church of (İstanbul) 104
St Philip, Martyrium of 168
St Philip, Church of (Trabzon) 262
St Saviour in Chora, Church of (Kariye Cami) (İstanbul) 53, 85

St Sergius and Bacchus, Church of (Küçük Ayasofya) (İstanbul) 87–9
St Sophia (Hagia Sophia, Ayasofya) (İstanbul) 11, 23, 60, 72–74
St Theodore in Tiro 105
St Theodosia, Church of (İstanbul) 104
Samandağ 216
Samatya District 105
Samos Island 133, 134
Samsakli 110
Samsun (Amisus) 256, 257, 261
Sancaktir Mescit 105
Şanlıurfa 244, 245, 246, 249, 252, 254, 258–9
    see also Edessa
sarcophagi
    Aphrodisias 169, 171
    Ayaş 212
    Konya 236
    Telmessos 192
    Termessos 204
    Weeping Woman sarcophagus 81
Sardanapulus, tomb of 213
Sardis 8, 163, 164–6, 159
Sarı Han 232
Sarı Saduk Türbe (Diyarbakır) 253
Sarıyer 96
Schliemann 112
schools (ancient) 69
scuba diving 50
sea festival (Çeşme) 43
seafood
    markets 47, 96
    restaurants 96, 97
Seat of Nimrud (Şanlıurfa) 249
Sebaste 212
Sedir Island 192
seers 186
Sehadet Cami (Bursa) 122
Sehidiye Cami (Mardin) 252
Sehir museum 40
Sehzade Cami 101
Selçuk (Ephesus) 49, 133, 142
Seleucia (Silifke) 65, 211
Selimiye Barracks 98
Selimiye mosque (Edirne) 14
Selimiye mosque (Konya) 240
Seljuk see Alanya
Seljuk civilization 179, 189
Seljuk Turks 55, 111
Seljuk Ulu Cami (Nemrut Dağ) 252
Semsi Tebrizi Türbesi (Konya) 241
Seraglio 69
Seraglio Gardens 65
Seraglio Point 72
Serapsu 183
Serpent Column (Hippodrome) 78
Sestos (Eceabat) 111
settlements, earliest 8, 179

shadow theatre 43
shipbuilding industry 187, 256
shopping areas 94
    ancient (Perge) 204
    underground malls 87
shopping receipts, retaining for Customs 19
Side 182, 189, 205, 207
Şile 100, 256
Silifke (Seleucia) 183, 211
Silivri 49
Sillyon 182, 205
silver exhibits 69
Sinan (architect)
    buildings by 14, 69, 93, 216
    mosques by 83, 95, 98, 99, 101–2, 115, 233
    tomb 85
Sinan Paşa Cami 102
Sinasos 232
Sincan 49
Sinop (Sinope) 8, 256, 257
Sırcalı Kumbet (Kayseri) 236
Sis 214
Sivas 47, 63
skiing 47
    see also winter sports
slave trade 189
Smyrna 133, 134–5, 161
Softa 210
Sofular 216
Sogut 55, 108, 111, 116
Sokollu Mehmet Paşa Cami 101
    tomb 93
soup kitchens (ancient) 60, 85
souvenir shops 94
Sovalye Island 194
spas 140
    Çekirge 108, 122
    Pamukkale 168
    see also thermal springs
spelaeology 212
Spice Bazaar (Egyptian Bazaar) 83
sporting equipment, customs regulations for 19
    see also specific sport
stadiums
    Aphrodisias 169
    Ephesus 146
    Perge 204
    Priene 148
statuary 145, 155
    Pamukkale 168
Stavropolis 164
stone carvings 102, 233, 270
Stone and Wood Carvings, Museum of (Konya) 240
Suleimaniye Cami 83–5
Suleiman Paşa Medrese 115
Suleiman the Magnificent 56, 71, 260
    tomb 85
    tugra (monogram) 41

Sultan Ahmet Cami see Blue Mosque
Sultanahmet district 49, 54, 65, 71
Sultan Beyazıt Yildirim (Bursa) 120
Sultan Cami (Manisa) 164
Sultan Isa Medrese (Mardin) 252
Sultan Selim Cami (İstanbul) 102
Sülüklü Plaj 200
Sumela Monastery 268, 270
Süngür Bey Cami (Niğde) 232
sunken cities 108, 197
Sweet Waters of Asia 99
swimming 97
    see also beaches
synagogue (Sardis) 164

T
tailors 83
Taksim square 93–5
Tamerlane (Timur) 220
Tantalus, tomb of 135
Tarabya (Therapeia) 96
Tarsus (Gözlütepe) 8, 183, 190, 213–14
Taşdibi 200
Taşuçu 210
Taurus Mountains 10, 179
taxis
    air-taxis 23
    dolmuş 54, 183
    fares 11, 93, 181
tea
    festival 43
    growing 268
Tekeli (Akkaya) 210
Tekfür Saray 89
telephone numbers
    emergency 21
    use of telephones in chemists 21, 25
telephone system 25
    urgent calls 25
Tellibaba 96
Telmessos of Lycia 186, 192
Temple of Athena (Priene) 152
Temple of Zeus (Euromos) 174
temples
    Aphrodisias 169
    Ephesus 145, 146
    Hattusas 227
    Miletus 155
    Pergamum 126, 130
    Priene 152, 173
    Sardis 166
    Selçuk 145, 146
Tenedos Island (Boscaada) 123
tennis 49
Teos 140
Tepeçik 139
Terme 257, 260
Termessos 181, 182, 204